IRENA'S CHILDREN

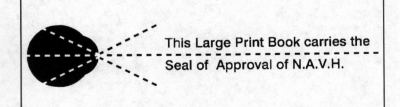

This Large Print Book carries the
Seal of Approval of N.A.V.H.

IRENA'S CHILDREN

THE EXTRAORDINARY STORY OF THE WOMAN WHO SAVED 2,500 CHILDREN FROM THE WARSAW GHETTO

TILAR J. MAZZEO

THORNDIKE PRESS
A part of Gale, Cengage Learning

GALE
CENGAGE Learning

Farmington Hills, Mich • San Francisco • New York • Waterville, Maine
Meriden, Conn • Mason, Ohio • Chicago

GALE
CENGAGE Learning®

LIBRARY OF CONGRESS CATALOGING-IN-PUBLICATION DATA

Names: Mazzeo, Tilar J., author.
Title: Irena's children : the extraordinary story of the woman who saved 2,500
  children from the Warsaw ghetto / by Tilar J. Mazzeo.
Description: Large print edition. | Waterville, Maine : Thorndike Press, 2016. |
  Series: Thorndike press large print popular and narrative nonfiction |Includes
  bibliographical references.
Identifiers: LCCN 2016033454 | ISBN 9781410493101 (hardcover) | ISBN 1410493105
  (hardcover)
Subjects: LCSH: Sendlerowa, Irena, 1910-2008. | Righteous Gentiles in the
  Holocaust—Poland—Biography. | World War,
  1939-1945—Jews—Rescue—Poland. | Holocaust, Jewish (1939-1945)—Poland.
Classification: LCC D804.66.S46 M29 2016b | DDC 940.53/1835092—dc23
LC record available at https://lccn.loc.gov/2016033454

Published in 2016 by arrangement with Gallery Books, an imprint of
Simon & Schuster, Inc.

Printed in Mexico
1 2 3 4 5 6 7 20 19 18 17 16

FOR ROBERT MILES
Ripeness is all

CONTENTS

PREFACE

When I first visited Poland, sometime around 2009, I thought it would be a vacation. My brother and sister-in-law, working with the U.S. State Department, had lived in Kraków for several years already, and had lived for a time in Wrocław before that, and had witnessed the country's integration into the European Union and its rapid second postcommunist transformation. Their two small children — twins and then not yet toddlers — were learning their first words in Polish, and my sister-in-law was the director of an international school located outside the city.

All three of us had grown up nominally Catholic, although none of us have ever had, I think, any particular interest in religion. Because Kraków, unlike Warsaw, escaped being bombed or razed into oblivion at the end of the Second World War, its Catholic heritage is everywhere in the Old Town architecture. It is a beautiful and in some ways still medieval city. But few areas of the city are as atmospheric as the historic Jewish quarter in Kazimierz, where tourists make pilgrimages to see Oskar Schindler's factory and to see the winding streets where parts of *Schindler's List* were filmed for Spielberg's motion picture. On the other hand, if you want to imagine what the Warsaw ghetto looked like in the 1940s, there is no point in going to Warsaw. Only a small percentage of it remains there. The ghetto was razed in the spring of 1943. After the Warsaw uprising a little more than a year later, the rest of the city was leveled, and only ten percent of the buildings were left standing. Warsaw is essentially modern.

The year that I visited, the school was in the final stages of a major capital project, and the campus was being developed and surrounded by fencing. My sister-in-law spent her days, she joked, largely scolding local construction crews, and she had amassed a colorful arsenal of Polish profanity. The site had been rolling farmland for years, and at one edge of the property a wood had been left to grow up in the midst of the fields and, later, scattered suburban houses. Standing together at the edge of the copse, I ventured to ask idly who owned the forest and why it had clearly been left wild for decades. After a moment's pause, she let out a sigh and said to me, "The trains to Auschwitz, you know, used to run not far from here. Not right here, but in the area."

There was nothing in the woods, just parkland, and in the beginning she used to walk there, she said. But the first of November in Poland is All Saints' Eve, and everywhere in the country it is the tradition on that night to light candles on the graves of the dead. It was only on the first holiday at the school, when the roadside that skirted the edge of the woods was burning everywhere with candles, that she understood that something terrible had happened there.

Later, locals told her that it was 1945, at the end of the war, when the Red Army was driving back the retreating Germans. The arrival of the Red Army brought no joy in Poland. Few women — from schoolgirl to most ancient *babcia* — escaped being raped by Soviet soldiers that winter in Kraków. And few Germans who encountered Soviet troops ever made their way back across the border. Across Poland, there were hundreds of nameless massacres like this one. Under communist rule, no one would have dared light a candle in the forest, but things had changed now. There were still old men and especially old women who remembered. "It's everywhere here," my sister-in-law said sadly. "Poland is an unmarked graveyard, and what can you do except leave the past quietly buried?"

We went back to the school, and the bright voices of happy elementary school children came drifting into the corridor from all directions. I thought about the German deaths that happened here and the tracks that lead to Auschwitz and the stories of infants torn from their mothers and smashed against brick walls to murder them. I thought about my small niece and nephew and how I would kill anyone who did that to my children. My brother asked me a few days later if I wanted to see Auschwitz, and I said that I didn't.

A few years later, my sister-in-law was one of the first people to tell me the story of "the female Schindler," Irena Sendler — or, in Polish, where women's last names take on a feminine case ending, Irena Sendlerowa. Unconnected in space and time, those two conversations are, nevertheless, how this book started. I have never been able to separate the threads that connect Irena Sendler's story with that experience of the abandoned Polish earth and the voices of schoolchildren. As a writer, I

12

stopped trying.

In her native Poland, Irena Sendler is a heroine today, although that is also a relatively recent postcommunist development. Her story, like so many stories across Poland, was quietly buried for decades. With her friends and a team of dedicated coworkers, Irena Sendler smuggled infants out of the Warsaw ghetto, past German guards and Jewish police traitors, in suitcases and wooden boxes. She brought out toddlers and schoolchildren through the city's foul and dangerous sewers. She worked with the Jewish teenagers — many of them girls of fourteen or fifteen — who fought bravely and died in the ghetto uprising. And, throughout it all, she was in love with a Jewish man, whom she and her friends spent the war anxiously hiding. She was a feather of a person with an iron spirit: a four-foot-eleven-inch wisp of a young woman, in her late twenties when the war began, who fought with the ferocity and intelligence of an experienced general and organized, across the city of Warsaw and across the divides of religion, dozens of average people into foot soldiers.

Before she was arrested and tortured by the Gestapo, Irena Sendler saved the lives of more than two thousand Jewish children.

At immense risk she kept a list of their names so that after the war their parents could find them. She could not know, of course, that more than ninety percent of their families would perish, most of them in the gas chambers at Treblinka. She also could not have guessed as a left-wing radical and lifelong socialist that after the war her children would be targeted under Soviet communism because of her wartime actions.

But while Irena Sendler was undeniably a heroine — a woman of immense, almost unfathomable moral and physical courage — she was not a saint either. To make her a saint in the telling of her story is, in the end, to do a kind of dishonor to the true complexity and difficulty of her very human choices. Time after time, during my researches and interviews in Israel and especially Poland, those who survived that period in Warsaw said to me the same thing: "I don't like to talk about those years with anyone who didn't live them, because unless you were there you cannot understand why people made their decisions or the kinds of prices they paid for them." Irena's love life was anarchic and unruly, and she struggled with the self-knowledge that she was not a good wife or a good daughter.

She placed her frail and ailing mother in grave danger and kept the knowledge of those risks from her. She was reckless and sometimes myopic, she ranked the abstract before the particular, and, at moments, she was perhaps even selfish in her selflessness. When the time came, she ultimately was a largely absent and distracted mother. She was at once a heroine — although she disdained that word, too — and a flawed and average person. But she was also someone gifted with a sense of purpose and righteousness so powerful that she was able, by her example, to persuade others around her to be better than they otherwise might have been, and to do something together amazingly decent and courageous.

Throughout writing this book, I have been humbled by the courage of those "others" as well: the dozens of men and mostly women who quietly joined her. Irena said that for each child whose rescue she organized, on average ten people in Warsaw risked their own lives in the process. Without the courage and sacrifice of those who joined her, success would never have been possible. For those who aided Irena, the choices were monstrous. Punishment for helping a Jew began with having your family executed in front of you, starting with

15

your children. It is trite and facile to describe to anyone who loves a child what it means to ache in the presence of life's fragility, and the vast majority of those who aided Irena had young children. Yet not once did any of these people — dozens of them — flinch from helping Irena in her mission. No one, Irena once said, ever refused to take in one of the Jewish children.

This is the story of Irena Sendler, the children she saved, and those dozens of courageous "others." It is also the complicated and sometimes dark but courageous story, too, of the Polish people. If there are too many names in the beginning of this book, consider that I tell the stories of some small fraction of those whom we know assisted Irena. And consider that, as the book goes on, the names become sadly fewer. I tell their stories here to do all of them some small honor. Their lives and, sometimes, their deaths speak to what we are capable of as average people in the face of evil and horror.

PROLOGUE

Aleja Szucha. Irena Sendler knew her destination. The door slammed shut up front, and the black prison car lurched into motion. She had been given only minutes to dress, and her fair, bobbed hair was bed tousled.

Janka Grabowska had run down the front path with her shoes and thrust them at her at the last moment, braving the violent caprices of the soldiers. Irena hadn't thought to lace them. She was focusing on just one thing: staying calm and keeping her face blank, placid. No sad faces. That was the wisdom Jewish mothers gave to their children when they left them for the last time in the care of strangers. Irena wasn't Jewish, but it was still true that sad faces were dangerous.

They must not think I have any reason to be frightened. They must not think I am frightened. Irena repeated that thought silently.

17

It would only make what was coming harder if they suspected what she was hiding.

But Irena *was* frightened. Very frightened. In the autumn of 1943 in Nazi-occupied Poland, there were no words more terrifying than "Szucha Avenue." There may have been no words more terrifying anywhere in wartime Europe. It was the address of the Gestapo headquarters in Warsaw. The brutalism of its exterior seemed cruelly suited to the Germans' purpose. From inside the squat complex of buildings, the corridors echoed with the screams of those being questioned. Those who survived remembered afterward the rank scent of fear and urine. Twice a day, just before noon and in the early evening, black vans punctually returned from the holding cells at Pawiak Prison to collect the bruised and broken bodies.

Irena guessed that it was just after six o'clock in the morning now. Maybe six thirty already. Soon the late October sun would be rising over Warsaw. But Irena had been awake for hours. So had everyone in the apartment building. Janka, her trusted liaison and a dear friend, had joined a small family celebration for the feast of Saint Irena that night. After gorging on cold cuts and slices of cake, Irena's frail mother and her visiting aunt retreated to the bedroom. But Janka had already missed the curfew and would have to spend the night. So the younger women camped out in the living room and sat up late, talking and drinking tea and cordials.

After midnight, Irena and Janka dozed at last, and by three a.m. the girls were sleeping soundly on makeshift cots. But in the back room, Irena's mother, Janina, was restless. How Janina had enjoyed hearing the carefree murmur of the girls' voices! She knew from her daughter's taut jawline that Irena was taking chances, and she had a mother's heavy worry. Pain made it hard to sleep, and so Janina let the thoughts carry her. Then, in the darkness, came a sound that she knew was wrong. The heavy thudding of boots echoed from a stairwell somewhere. *Irena! Irena!* Janina hissed in an urgent whisper that penetrated Irena's dreams. Bolting awake, Irena heard only the anxiety in her mother's tone and knew in an instant what it meant. Those few moments to clear her head were the difference between life and death for all of them.

What came next was the racket of eleven Gestapo agents pounding at the apartment door, demanding entry. The fear brought a strange, metallic taste to Irena's mouth, and underneath her rib cage the terror came and went in shocks that felt electric. For hours the Germans spewed threats and abuse, gutted the pillows, and tore apart the corners and cupboards. They pulled up floorboards and broke furniture.

Somehow they still didn't find the lists of the children.

The lists now were all that mattered. They were just thin and flimsy scraps of cigarette paper, little more than rolled bits of tissue, part of Irena's private filing system. But written on them in a code of her own invention were the names and addresses of some of the thousands of Jewish children whom Irena and her friends had saved from the horrors of Nazi persecution — children they were still hiding and supporting in secret locations all across the city and beyond Warsaw. At the last possible instant, before the door flew open, giving way to the bludgeons and pounding, Irena tossed the lists on the kitchen table over to Janka, who with brazen aplomb stuffed them into her generous brassiere, deep under her armpit. If they searched Janka, God knew, it would be all over. It would be even worse if they searched Janka's apartment, where there were Jews hiding. Irena could hardly believe it when the Germans themselves covered up the worst bit of incriminating evidence: she watched, mesmerized, as a small bag with forged identity papers and wads of illegal cash was buried under the debris of smashed furniture. She wanted nothing more than to fall to her knees in that moment. And when she understood that the Gestapo wasn't arresting Janka or her mother but only her, she was positively giddy. But she knew that the laughter rising inside her was tinged dangerously with hysteria. *Dress,* she told herself. *Dress and leave here quickly.* She threw on the well-worn skirt she had folded over the back of the kitchen chair only hours earlier and buttoned her sweater as fast as she could to speed her departure before the agents had a chance to reconsider, and walked out of the apartment into the cold autumn morning barefoot. She hadn't even noticed until Janka came running.

Now, though, she had time to think about her own dilemma as the car swayed at each street corner. Sooner or later there was no question that they would kill her. Irena understood that already. This was how her story ended. People did not return from Aleja Szucha or from the ghetto prison at Pawiak, where arrestees were locked up in between their bone-crushing interrogations.

21

They did not return from the camps like Auschwitz or Ravensbrück, where the innocent "survivors" of the Gestapo were deported. And Irena Sendler was not innocent.

The sedan cranked hard to the right as it headed southeast across the still-sleeping city. The most direct route would take them toward Warsaw's broad prewar avenues, first skirting west and then south of the wasteland that had once been the Jewish ghetto. During the first years of the Nazi occupation, Irena had been in and out of the ghetto three or four times a day sometimes, each time risking arrest or summary execution, trying to help to save some of their old school friends, their Jewish professors . . . and thousands of small children. Now, in late 1943, there was only ruin and rubble. It was a killing ground, an endless graveyard. The ghetto had been leveled after the Jewish uprising that spring, and her friend Ala Gołąb-Grynberg had disappeared inside that inferno. Word in the underground whispered that Ala was still alive, in the forced-labor camp at Poniatowa, one of a group of young militants secretly planning their escape from the prison. Irena hoped that, when this barbaric war was over, Ala would make it back to collect her small daughter, Rami, from the orphanage where Irena had her hidden.

The prison car passed a few blocks north of what had once been the Polish Free University. The institution was another war casualty. Irena had completed her degree in social work across town, at the University of Warsaw, but she had been a frequent presence on the Polish Free University campus in the 1930s, and it was there, thanks to Professor Helena Radlińska, that her resistance cell had been formed. They had been, almost to the last one, Dr. Radlińska's girls in the days before the occupation. Now they were part of a well-organized and daring network, and the professor had been the inspiration for that too. It was a network of urgent interest to her captors. Irena was in her early thirties now, but her girlish, waifish looks were deceiving. The Gestapo had just captured one of the most important figures in the Polish underground. Irena could only hope that the Germans did not know it.

Crammed in beside her, a soldier, in his tall leather boots and with a tangling whip and truncheon, let down his guard. It was the end of their nighttime shift of terror. Irena sat on the lap of another young recruit, and she guessed that the boy wasn't more than eighteen or nineteen. They even seemed, she thought, to be dozing. Irena's face was calm but her mind was racing. There was so much to consider and so little time left to her.

Janka knew exactly how important these lists were — and how dangerous. If the lists were discovered, it would set in motion a chain of executions. The Gestapo would hunt down the Jewish children. They would murder the Polish men and women who had agreed to care for them and hide them. Zofia and Stanisław. Władysława and Izabela. Maria Palester. Maria Kukulska. Jaga. And they would kill Irena's mother, even though the frail, bedridden woman could only guess at the extent of her daughter's shadowy activities. The Germans followed a strict policy of collective punishment. Entire families were shot for the transgressions of a single member. Irena couldn't help but feel that she had once again been a bad daughter. She had always been, she knew, more like her impetuously idealist father.

If the lists were lost or Janka destroyed them as a safety measure, there was another agonizing dilemma. When Irena died, there would be no one to reconstruct them. Irena was the general in this citizens' army and the only one who knew the details recorded on them. She had promised mothers and fathers who went to Treblinka that she would tell their children who had loved them. When she was dead, there would be no one able to keep that promise.

There was one other question, too, that shook her: Who would tell Adam Celnikier? *Adam. Her Adam.* Her husband, Mietek Sendler, was somewhere in a German prisoner-of-war camp, and it would take weeks or perhaps months for word of her execution to reach him. It would eventually if he was still living. But she and Mietek separated before the war, and it was Adam she loved — Adam, whom even now friends were hiding under a false name and new identity. One of Warsaw's few surviving Jews, Adam was among the hunted, and his life was in constant danger.

The engine of the Gestapo sedan reverberated through the silent morning streets of Warsaw. With each turn, the soldiers roused slightly. Irena had to prepare herself now for what came next. She had to prepare herself to give away nothing, no matter what torture was inflicted. Too many lives depended on it. Irena had risked her life to keep the children hidden. Now she was more determined than ever to die with her secrets. What if she was not strong enough to do it? If the pain were great enough,

25

would she even betray Adam in his secret hiding place? She wondered now what she could bear. When they broke her bones with cudgels and pipes in the days to come, that thought would haunt her.

It was a cold morning, and fear was also chilling her. The car rolled now smoothly eastward along the broad avenue, picking up speed on the final stretch of her journey. Soon they would reach Aleja Szucha and her last destination. There they would strip and search and beat and question her. There would be threats and intimidation. There would be lashes and agony and cruel torments that were at that moment still unimaginable. Colder things were coming. Irena slipped her hands into her coat pockets to warm them for a few moments.

Her heart froze the instant her fingers touched something light and thin and crisp. Cigarette paper. Irena suddenly remembered that there was one part of the list that she had forgotten. On it was an address. It would betray the life of someone she had meant to check in on that morning. It was there between her fingers.

CHAPTER 1
BECOMING IRENA SENDLER
OTWOCK, 1910–1932

In Yiddish folk tales, the story of Poland begins at dusk on a still summer night. At the edge of the sky, the forest grows dark. A weary family sets down their belongings in the grassy verge along a long road and wonders: *How long will we wander until we reach a homeland?* They are waiting for a sign, which the ancients tell them will come, but they do not expect it this evening. Their feet are sore, and someone, homesick and forlorn, weeps silently.

Then, from the quiet of the forest, a bird sings out two beautiful notes. They are the very notes for which the family knows they have been waiting. The bird chirps, *Po lin, po lin.* They are the words, in their language, which mean *Live here.* Here, in a place they call forever afterward Poland.

Where is this village at the heart of Poland? No one knows. But it might have been a place very much like the small riverside village of Otwock, set on the edge of a great pine forest fifteen-odd miles southeast of Warsaw. By the nineteenth century, when the words of this Yiddish folk tale were recorded, Otwock was already the site of a long-established Hasidic Jewish community.

And it was not only the Hasidic Jews who were finding a home in Otwock by the end of the nineteenth century. In fact, by the 1890s, Otwock was quickly becoming famous in a quiet way. In 1893, Dr. Józef Marian Geisler established a spa and clinic there for the treatment of tuberculosis. Pleasantly situated on the right bank of the Vistula River, surrounded by tall trees, the fresh air at Otwock was thought to be particularly salubrious. In this pastoral setting, dozens of sprawling wooden villas soon sprang up, built in an alpine style, with large open-air porches and latticework trellises along the eaves of all the nicest houses. The village became a fashionable choice for health treatments. In 1895, just two years later, a certain Józef Przygoda opened the first sanatorium for Jews, because Jews and Poles in those days largely lived by choice in separate worlds, and that clinic also quickly became popular. Indeed, before too long, Otwock, home to a large impoverished Jewish community, became a favorite summer retreat for the upper-middle-class Jews from Warsaw and from other smaller towns across central Poland.

Irena Stanisława Krzyżanowska — for that was her maiden name — was not born in Otwock, although Otwock would be in the years that followed an important part of her story. She had been born on February 15, 1910, at the Holy Spirit Catholic Hospital in Warsaw, where her father, Stanisław Henryk Krzyżanowski, was a physician and researcher in infectious diseases. For Dr. Krzyżanowski and his young wife, Janina, it was a checkered history that had brought them back to his native region. Her mother was a spirited and pretty young woman without a profession. Irena's father was a zealous political activist and proud of being one of the earliest members of the soon-mainstream Polish Socialist Party. He had paid a high price as a younger man for his commitments.

Today, the Polish Socialist Party's "radical" agenda seems modest. Stanisław Krzyżanowski believed in democracy, equal rights for everyone, fair access to health care, an eight-hour workday, and an end to the crippling tradition of child labor. But at the end of the nineteenth century and into the early twentieth century, especially in an area of the world with a feudal and imperial history, this was a deeply unsettling political goal. As a medical student, first at the university in Warsaw and then in Kraków, Stanisław was expelled in quick succession for his part in leading campus strikes and protests agitating for those revolutionary values. You had to stand up for what was wrong in the world, he insisted. "If someone else is drowning, you have to give a hand." It was one of her father's favorite sayings.

It was good luck that things were different at the University of Kharkov, a hotbed of this sort of radicalism some seven hundred miles to the east in the Ukraine, because that was where Dr. Krzyżanowski finally graduated from medical school. The city of Kharkov was also one of the intellectual and cultural centers of Jewish life and activism in Eastern Europe, and her father didn't have any patience for the kind of anti-Semitism that was rife in Poland. People were just people. The Krzyżanowski family had some roots in the Ukraine. So did her mother's family, the Grzybowskis. You didn't have to come from somewhere in particular to be a good Pole; that was how Dr. Krzyżanowski saw it.

After Stanisław Krzyżanowski's gradua-tion and the couple's marriage, Stanisław and his bride returned to Warsaw, and they would have perhaps stayed in the city permanently had the two-year-old Irena not caught a terrible case of whooping cough in 1912. Dr. Krzyżanowski watched his little girl struggle to breathe, her small ribs moving up and down, and knew that children died this way. They had to get Irena out of the congested city. Fresh country air would help her breathe better. Otwock was the obvious solution. Stanisław had been born there, his sister and brother-in-law had some business there, and it was a famously healthy location that should have had plenty of opportunities for an energetic young doctor. That year the family moved to the village. Dr. Krzyżanowski, with the aid of his brother-in-law Jan Karbowski's real estate holdings, opened a private practice as a doctor specializing in the treatment of tuberculosis, and waited for the patients.

The more affluent locals and the fashionable visitors warmed to him slowly. The struggling farmers and the large population of poor Jews were less choosy. Many Polish doctors refused to treat poor Jews at all, and especially not for what they could afford. Dr. Krzyżanowski was different. He cared about making a difference. He welcomed everyone kindly, with a cheerful smile, and didn't worry about money. Since Jews made up nearly fifty percent of the local population, there were plenty of patients to keep him busy. Soon everyone in Otwock said that Dr. Krzyżanowski was a good man and many people in the Jewish community, rich or poor, came to the family villa to see the hardworking doctor.

Although Dr. Krzyżanowski was a physician and many of his patients were poor people — because there were always more poor people who needed the help of a generous man than there were rich ones — he was entirely without pretension. His home was open to everyone, and Janina was a friendly, outgoing woman who enjoyed the company of people. They were delighted when their little girl made friends with children from Jewish families, families who embraced the doctor's daughter. By the time she was six, Irena spoke a fluent backyard Yiddish and knew which gullies behind the sanatorium were the best for hide-and-seek and where the best walls were to bounce a ball. She was accustomed to the sight of Jewish mothers in their colorful headscarves and knew that the scent of bread baked with cumin meant something delicious if the children were lucky. "I grew up with these people," Irena said. "Their culture and traditions were not foreign to me."

It may be that one of the Jewish children Irena met when she was five or six was a boy named Adam Celnikier. No one knows any longer for certain the story of their first meeting. This is the earliest possible beginning, and perhaps even it was wishful thinking. Maybe Adam was a dreamy, bookish boy. He certainly was dreamy and bookish later. He had curly red-brown hair and dark skin, and his long, handsome nose looked just like what some people thought of as Jewish. Perhaps Adam was one of those first playmates, although his family was very rich and, unlike many Jews, spoke perfect Polish. Adam's mother's name was Leokadia, and he had lots of aunts and uncles and cousins with names like Jakob and Józef. And the family didn't live year-round in Otwock. They owned houses and businesses across Warsaw. But Irena may have seen him sometimes in those carefree summers.

Irena's early memories of her childhood in Otwock were magical, and her father doted on his small daughter. Her papa had a handlebar mustache that curled up even higher when he smiled, and he lavished his only child with affection. Her aunts called him "Stasiu," and when he gave her hugs

33

and kisses, the aunts would tell him, "Don't spoil her, Stasiu. What will become of her?" Her father just winked and hugged her harder. He told the aunts, "We don't know what her life will be like. Maybe my hugs will be her best memory." And, indeed, they would be.

Other children, Irena knew, were not so lucky and did not live in a spacious wooden villa owned by their rich uncle. Her family's home was a large, square house at number 21, Kościuszki Street, with twenty rooms and a glass solarium that sparkled in the sunshine. But because many of Dr. Krzyżanowski's patients came from the lowest end of the socioeconomic scale, when her father made his rounds in the village or when patients came to the family clinic, she witnessed poverty and deprivation from a child's intimate perspective. She also slowly understood from others in the village that some Polish people weren't like her father. Jewish culture was familiar to Irena and, in time, so was the Jewish people's hardship.

In 1916, when Irena was six, her father chose to share in that hardship. That year an epidemic of typhoid fever took hold in Otwock, and, as Dr. Krzyżanowski would say, you didn't get to choose not to lend a hand just because it was risky. The rich kept themselves apart from the crowded, unsanitary places where the infection was the strongest. The disease was especially dangerous in homes without clean drinking water and strong soap for washing. The poor had to make do, and so the illness swept off some of her poor Jewish playmates and their families. Stanisław Krzyżanowski carried on treating sick and infected patients, just as always.

Then, in the late autumn or early winter of 1916–17, he started to feel the first shakes and shivers. He knew that it was the beginning of the terrible fever. Soon he was burning hot in the afternoons and whispering in wild delirium. The aunts were always fussing now. The little girl would have to stay far away from the sickroom and couldn't see Papa. Everything would have to be disinfected. She and her mama would have to go stay with relatives. There wouldn't be any hugs and kisses to spoil Irena until he recovered. There was too much risk for the child from the infection.

For weeks the doctor struggled against the disease and waged his lonely, private battle, but he never recovered. On February 10, 1917, Stanisław Krzyżanowski died of the fever. Five days later Irena turned seven.

■ ■ ■ ■

After Irena's papa's funeral, her mother carried herself carefully and tried not to cry too often. But Irena heard her sometimes, and she caught, too, the aunts' worried whispers when they thought she wasn't listening. Would they be poor now like Papa's patients? Irena wondered. That was what happened when you were orphaned. She wondered with her child's imagination if Papa had gone away because she had been naughty, and she tried as hard as she could to be helpful and obedient so Mother wouldn't leave her. Mother was sad, and sadness meant people left. But it was so hard to sit still and be quiet all the time when she wanted to run and jump out in the fields. She carried a little knot of fear in her heart and a weight on her small shoulders.

In truth, with the death of the doctor, his widow *was* impoverished. They lived in a house owned by their family, but Stanisław had not left big savings. Irena's mother was young, but Janina was a housewife and a mother, not a doctor, and it was hard work to run her husband's clinic and take care of her small daughter. The clinic had never been a big financial success. Stanisław had never cared enough about the numbers. He had never been a sensible businessman, just an idealist. It was now a hard, uphill struggle. Without assistance, Janina certainly couldn't pay alone for the fees required to educate Irena. Word of the plight of the doctor's widow spread through Otwock, and it got the Jewish community thinking. Dr. Krzyżanowski had helped their children when they couldn't afford medical treatment. Now they would help his widow and daughter.

When the men came to see her mother, Irena quietly stayed out of the way. The rabbi's long beard wiggled when he talked. He had little wire glasses that made his eyes look enormous. Irena felt more at home with the Jewish mothers, with their long hair braided, their hands that moved like fluttering birds when they chatted and watched over the children. *Pani Krzyżanowska,* they said, *we will pay for the education of your daughter. Pani* was the word in Polish for a lady. Mother dabbed her eyes. *No, no,* she said firmly. *I thank you very much, but I am young. I will support my daughter.* Janina was proud and stubbornly independent, and Irena felt good to have her mama take care of her.

But the result of Janina's independence was a constant struggle with money. It was hard going at the clinic. Irena's uncle Jan owned the clinic buildings and their villa, but in 1920 he said, *No more.* It was time to sell and close the clinic. Uncle Jan and Aunt Maria were rich, but Irena's mother didn't want to live on charity. She hated being a burden and would rather work hard and do embroidery to make some money now. Janina would rather live modestly and skimp a bit than have to ask for a favor. So Janina lifted her chin and just said to her brother-in-law, *Don't worry.* It would be fine in the city. They would go and live in the town where Janina's family was, a place Irena learned was called Piotrków Trybunalski, not too far from Warsaw.

Life in Piotrków was different. Gone were the rustling pine forests and wooden villas of Otwock. Gone were her familiar playmates. Irena was homesick for the country. "I was constantly drawn back to those areas [near Otwock]," Irena said. Otwock was an idyll, part of what it meant to spend the perfect Polish summer. It had been Irena's childhood.

Part of Irena's childhood, though, was already over. When the workmen came to carry on their shoulders trunks carefully filled with her mother's best dishes and the family linens, Irena wondered where they would all fit inside their new city apartment. Piotrków was a busy market town with fifty thousand residents, on the main rail line from Warsaw to Vienna, and gone were the quiet country nights and the sounds of the forest. In Piotrków there were the sounds of streetcars and the calls of street vendors that drifted up to their windows. There were other voices too. Now there were the excited and impassioned conversations of people around Irena talking about politics and Polish freedom.

For centuries Poland had been fighting for its independence from aggressive neighbors in two directions, the Russians to the east and to the west the Germans. The year that Irena and her mother moved to Piotrków, the conflict with Russia was at another turning point, and the city was a hotbed of patriotism and left-wing politics. If there had been a "tea party" in Poland's revolutionary history, Piotrków would have been its Boston. There was a great sense of national pride, and when children in Piotrków like Irena joined the Boy Scouts or the Girl Scouts, they learned more than jamboree camp songs; they learned paramil-

itary tactics for defending their homeland
from the invaders on their borders. After
all, just that summer in Warsaw the Poles
had beaten back the Red Army against what
everyone said were impossible odds. If war
came again, the Scouts were the country's
littlest army. Irena proudly learned by heart
the words of the Scout's oath. She would be
thrifty and generous. She would be as trust-
worthy as the black-haired knight Zawisza
Czarny. The children marveled at the stories
of how in the olden days the brave Zawisza
fought for Poland and never, ever retreated.
But above all, Irena's young heart swelled
with determination when she promised, on
a Scout's honor, to be a friend to everybody
who asked for friendship.

Irena and her mother Janina moved to a
small apartment on Maja Avenue in Piotrków, the site marked with a commemora-
tive plaque today, and she turned ten the
year they arrived in the new city. The little
apartment was cramped and perhaps not
always perfectly tidy, but soon it was filled
with friends and visitors. Janina, after all,
was still a young woman, widowed before
thirty, and a bit of a bohemian in spirit. She
loved fun and the theater. She could be
melodramatic herself, but she was a warm
and caring Polish mother. In Piotrków the

buildings on the square in the Old Town, where Irena and Janina went for the week-end market, were painted cheerful hues of pink and green and yellow, and on warm spring days the Scout troops would head out to the river for practice and picnics. The girls proudly showed off their first-aid drills and learned to march just like the boys in military formation. Irena's crisp uniform, with its fleur-de-lis badge — the insignia of Scouts everywhere — looked very smart. When she moved, in time, to the local Helena Trzcińska Middle School, she also took the Scout's pledge "to be pure in thinking, in speech, and in deeds; not to smoke; not to drink alcohol."

Irena was a fun-loving and high-spirited girl, though, and soon had a steady sweetheart, a high school romance. The boy's name was Mieczysław "Mietek" Sendler. In prewar Catholic Poland, a shy teenage kiss sent pure-thinking youngsters scurrying off to an agonized confession, and by the end of high school their courting was serious. Marriage was the inevitable next step, their families agreed, just as soon as they finished college. When Irena and Mietek both earned places at the University of Warsaw for the autumn of 1927, Janina found a small apartment back in Warsaw for herself and her

41

daughter so Irena could live at home while attending university, and the future was settled.

Soon, however, a little voice inside Irena's head began to wish her future wasn't settled. She tried hard to silence that voice. Being at the university was new and exciting. Mietek decided to study the classics, and Irena said she would study to become a lawyer. Law was a bold choice for a seventeen-year-old girl who was sharp-witted rather than dutiful or quiet, and the old-fashioned faculty in the department did not see the law at all as a woman's profession. At every turn, the professors blocked her ambition. Irena was indignant but, resigned, changed her program to Polish cultural studies and planned instead to be a schoolteacher. Everyone around her agreed that was a far more appropriate livelihood for a well-brought-up young Polish woman.

But it was perhaps in the law department during her first year that she reencountered Adam Celnikier, a fellow student and sensitive young man with dark flowing locks and a penchant for romantic poetry and extravagant gestures. One wonders: Did he perhaps remind her of the chivalrous black-haired knight Zawisza, the legendary Polish

Scout hero? Irena was soon in a study group where she saw Adam often, and the feelings were electric. Soon they spent more and more time together. Sometimes they sat together under the swaying trees that lined the campus avenues and talked about their childhoods. More often, they debated art and politics. They talked about the law and the future of a free Poland. When their hands brushed by accident, Irena felt her cheeks burn; surely it was just the excitement of the ideas they were sharing? Talking with Adam was a heady experience. Irena's politics were already those of her left-leaning patriotic father, but Adam was a radical. Adam was so alive, so of the moment. Mietek was of the past, a student of dead languages and a reminder of that awkward teenage self whose history Irena was busy shedding. Adam wanted to talk about the world around them, wanted to change the shape of the future.

But it was impossible. Even if she sometimes chafed against the constraints of her teenage romance, Mietek was Irena's sweetheart. Their lives and families were already deeply interconnected. Adam was a crush, and a sensible young woman didn't break things off with a nice boy like Mietek just because she was all mixed-up in her feelings. Duty mattered. Besides, Adam was spoken for already, and he could sympathize with Irena's dilemma. Sometime around 1930, bowing to the wishes of his family, Adam was married to a Jewish woman who studied at the university with them, in an Orthodox ceremony arranged by the two families. The girl was one of Irena's friends from her classes.

Other considerations weighed on her during sleepless nights in her small, hard bed in her mother's apartment. Irena could wait, of course, and delay her wedding to Mietek. But to what purpose when Adam was taken? Besides, marriage was freedom. It was freedom for her mother especially. Surely Irena owed her mother that? As long as Janina had to support a daughter, she would have to continue to take money from her family when what she longed for was her own independence. Irena longed to be a good daughter. By marrying Mietek, Irena would liberate her mother. It was too late for other choices. So, at the age of twenty-one, just after graduating from college in 1931, Irena Krzyżanowska did what everyone expected of her and became Mrs. Irena Sendlerowa. In English, the name is routinely shortened to Irena Sendler.

■ ■ ■ ■

The young couple began to build a life together in Warsaw, ultimately settling into a small one-room apartment, where Irena tried to brighten her surroundings and her flagging spirits with bright curtains and dutiful homemaking. But it was no good. Irena and Mietek weren't happy. In the evenings there were more and more quarrels, and Irena started keeping more and more secrets. Mietek was a junior faculty assistant in the classics department by 1932, on his way to a university teaching career, and Irena wanted to keep studying. One day Irena boldly announced her plans for a graduate certificate in social welfare and pedagogy before starting teaching. Mietek might have guessed already that it was futile for him to ask whether his views on this mattered. He already knew his young wife was an intensely willful person. When they had children, there would have to be changes. She would surely stay home then, wouldn't she? But Irena wasn't in any hurry. Irena enrolled in the social welfare program at the University of Warsaw.

Why social welfare? If anyone asked Irena, she would talk about her papa. She never stopped missing him. "My father," she explained, "was a doctor — a humanist — and my mother loved people and helped him in his social work a great deal. I was taught since my earliest years that people are either good or bad. Their race, nationality, and religion do not matter — what matters is the person. This was one truth that was instilled into my young head." Longing to connect with her father, she tried to become his definition of a good person.

But Irena also wanted some adventure. She was just twenty-two, after all, and the 1930s were a thrilling decade in Poland. The Soviets had been beaten back from their borders, and Poland was free for only the second time in its history. But within, the country was torn apart by politics and poised on the brink of explosive social protest. The relatively new field of social welfare was in the thick of the action, and the curriculum was radical and energizing. Students in the program at the University of Warsaw were encouraged to get experience in the field as part of their training. Irena instantly signed up for a community internship across town sponsored by the innovative pedagogy department at the Polish Free University. She had heard marvelous things about the department's director.

The University of Warsaw, with its manicured campus, boasted fine, even palatial architecture and broad open spaces, and was Poland's elite institution. The Polish Free University was another universe. There, professors worked and taught in an ugly six-story building with small, dingy windows and the air of a neglected housing project. As throngs of students rushed from the lecture rooms into the narrow corridors and up and down the stairwells, the scent of warm bodies filled the air. From below, there came the racket of clanging bicycles and the friendly voices of young women. Then the halls were again quiet. On her first visit, Irena held tightly to a piece of paper, craning her neck to read the office numbers. She was looking for a nameplate that read: *Professor H. Radlińska.*

Irena had weighed the internship options carefully, agonizing over her decision. Some students in her program took their field placements as teachers at the groundbreaking orphanage school founded by Dr. Radlińska's colleague, the educational theorist Dr. Janusz Korczak. Other students, especially the girls who were training as nurses, worked on public health research and outreach with some of Dr. Radlińska's affiliated faculty physicians. Dr. Radlińska

47

came from a well-known family of scientists, and one of the most renowned program physicians was her cousin, Dr. Ludwik Hirszfeld. But it was the professor's own grassroots clinics that drew Irena: charitable welfare centers aimed at eradicating poverty. These were places where unemployed locals could come to take free educational courses and the homeless or indigent found legal assistance.

Although it may seem hard to imagine today, in the 1930s this was one of the most exciting intellectual and political left-wing circles anywhere in Europe, and Irena was thrilled to be part of it. Dr. Radlińska, a stout and sturdy Jewish-born woman in her early sixties who had long since converted to Catholicism, was an unlikely heroine. Her thinning white hair and matronly bosom earned her the nickname "Grandma" on campus, and she had the look of a woman who was constantly harassed and worried. But the professor also radiated fierce intelligence and resolve, and the young students who gathered around her — many of whom were also Jewish-born — were at the center of a civil rights movement that was not unlike the ardent student activism that swept across Europe and North America in the 1960s. Along with a handful of eminent

48

psychologists, educators, and doctors, Dr. Radlińska was pioneering the field of social work in Poland. These programs would become, ultimately, the model in most Western democracies for modern social work and state-supported welfare later in the century. There is no way to understand how Irena Sendler and her conspirators came together in the way that they did during the Second World War without appreciating that long before the German occupation began, Dr. Radlińska had already connected them to one another in a tight community network.

Drawn into Dr. Radlińska's orbit, Irena blossomed. She longed for this kind of intellectual excitement and this sense of a vocation. And the professor quickly developed a soft spot for this earnest and passionate young woman. Irena was so clearly suited for social work — so organized, so level-headed, so genuinely outraged by injustice and compassionate about suffering — that Dr. Radlińska quickly offered her newest acolyte not just a student internship but a regular paid job in one of her offices, at the mother-and-child branch of the Citizens' Social Aid Committee, providing support for the city's unwed mothers.

When Irena woke up in the mornings, she

quickly hopped from the narrow bed she and Mietek shared, and her heart felt lighter thinking of the workday ahead of her. Mietek could not have helped but notice that Irena was happier leaving home than she was returning. Home in 1932 was a modern housing complex at number 3, Ludwicka Street, in the Wola district of Warsaw, and sometimes, as Irena rattled down the stairwell, a neighbor would open a door and smile at the young woman from upstairs who was always in such a hurry. The downstairs neighbors were a friendly family called the Jankowskis, who had small children and were often awake early, too, and the building super, Mr. Przeździecki, lovingly tended the shared community gardens and waved Irena off to work each morning. Another neighbor, Basia Dietrich, ran the cooperative kindergarten for the children in the complex, and perhaps Mietek sometimes wondered if their own children would ever get to play in that courtyard. It wouldn't happen unless they found a way to rekindle some marital passion, though, and Irena jumping out of bed was more than half of the problem. The trouble was work was all that seemed to interest her. What she was doing was so *important*. She didn't have time for housekeeping. She was helping struggling families to keep their children. She wished Mietek could see why it mattered so much. Mietek just wished she would focus on *their* family for a change.

The gulf between them was growing deeper, and the fire had already gone out of her youthful marriage. They were left with an awkward kind of old friendship. It wasn't that Irena didn't love Mietek. But he was not her passion. At the mother-and-child center, Irena felt a deep sense of purpose. "Everyone here was dedicated and true to their goals: everything that I had been taught seemed to come to use," Irena tried to explain. She was also making interesting new friends every day among Dr. Radlińska's other students and employees. "The work environment," she said, "was very nice," and so were the people.

She saw a lot of one person in particular: Adam.

CHAPTER 2
DR. RADLIŃSKA'S GIRLS
1935–1940

The lecture was over but still the professor didn't move.

The students on the left side of the lecture hall stood still for a moment longer, too, motionless and breathless. Irena was among them. She was twenty-five years old in the autumn of 1935 and, at less than five feet tall, was shorter than the rest of the crowd. But no one who knew her doubted that Irena had some outsize political opinions.

Those few seconds stretched on slowly. Everyone in the lecture hall waited. A sudden movement from the right and the rush of air as body met body came like a collective exhalation. Irena saw the flash of green ribbon pinned to the young man's jacket. The end of his raised cane shimmered in the light. *Razor blades. The villains had tied razor blades to the ends of the canes they had brought to beat them!* Irena realized. A scream erupted from one of the girls nearby, followed by a surge of motion and the sound of brass knuckles hitting bone. The melee once again had started.

Now the fist and the brass were raised up in front of Irena. To her side stood a Jewish classmate, a young man with dark, curly hair and glasses, and one of the men with green badges raised the cane overhead and barked to him, "Why are you standing?" He answered steadily: "Because I am Jewish."

Turning to Irena, the hooligan demanded, "Why are *you* standing?" Irena was fearless. Friends worried about how fearless she could be. Her more hidebound professors lamented that her youthful idealism was so insistent and so defiant, but Adam loved both parts of her character. Her bold retort now was designed to infuriate the angry young man in front of her. Their eyes connected. "Because," she snapped, "I am Polish." The brass fist smashed into her face in retaliation. She felt warm blood and then the darkness.

What ignited the riots on the University of Warsaw campus in 1935, when Irena and Adam were graduate students, was the informal institution of a "bench ghetto": a seating area in the lecture halls for Jewish students that was set apart from the area for the so-called Aryans. The far right wasn't growing in power only in neighboring Germany. Poland also had its problems. As far as Irena and Adam were concerned, the biggest of those problems was an organization called the ONR — the Obóz Narodowo Radykalny, or National Radical Camp: an ultranationalist and right-wing political group whose violent tactics and racist rhetoric were gaining traction and intensifying ugly feelings of anti-Semitism. The ONR supporters proudly displayed their political affiliation by wearing green ribbons.

The bench ghetto is an outrage! Irena and Adam and all their friends fumed when they said it. Jewish students and their supporters on campus staged angry and impassioned demonstrations, refusing to sit at all during lectures. Some professors ordered the rebellious students to leave the lecture halls. Other professors supported the students and delivered their lectures standing in solidarity. As Irena put it simply: "The years at the University were for me very hard and very sad. A rule was established at the University segregating the Catholics from the Jewish students. The Catholics were to sit on the chairs to the right and Jews on the chairs to the left. I always sat with Jews and, therefore, I was beaten by anti-Semites together with Jewish students." But what mattered was that it was together with Adam. Adam was fascinated by this ferocious wisp of a woman, and, as Irena's family later testified, "their love affair continued even though she [had] married someone else."

At the University of Warsaw, an old-fashioned place at heart, the majority of the campus tacitly supported this discrimination against the Jewish students. Across town, at the Polish Free University, however, things were different. When the ONR thugs came to assault Jewish students there, the entire campus rallied and drove them off with fire hoses and catcall hisses. Dr. Radlińska and the young women in her programs — Irena included — joined the protests and the scuffles. It was exhilarating. At home, Mietek grimaced sourly. He fretted over her safety. But he also worried about whom this new person — this risk-taking activist — was that his wife was becoming.

Irena's new friends from Dr. Radlińska's circle were talented and high-spirited young women, and most of them were Jewish-born — although, as left-wing activists, religion didn't much interest any of them. One of her favorites was Ala Gołąb-Grynberg, a nurse at the Jewish hospital on Dworska Street, who worked closely with Dr. Radlińska's cousin, Dr. Hirszfeld, in studying communicable diseases. Ala's maiden name was Gołąb, but she was six years older than Irena and had been married for years already to a Jewish actor and school principal named Arek. Their friends were exciting people: cabaret singers, actresses, and other performers. Dr. Korczak sometimes invited Ala to speak at his lectures, because everyone knew Ala was a hands-on expert in obstetrics and sanitation. Irena found her friend inspiring and sometimes even a bit intimidating. But Ala was also a funny and fun-loving eccentric, a sharp, angular person, with a sarcastic sense of humor and a terrible fashion sense whose mannish clothes never quite seemed to fit properly and whose wiry black hair always managed to look wild and untidy.

Another new friend, Rachela Rosenthal, on the other hand, was drop-dead gorgeous. Rachela was training in Dr. Radlińska's program to be a teacher, and she was lithe and blond. Men stopped on the streets to talk to her, and often she chatted back because everyone knew Rachela had a bubbly personality. Irena was pretty in a plump and quiet sort of way, but men didn't turn on the street to watch her pass, and her wit was, she had to admit, drier and more abrasive.

The third member of their circle was Ewa Rechtman, a language student working with another professor they all knew well, the jovial Dr. Władysław Witwicki. Ewa was immensely clever, and everyone said she was one of the most talented scholars in the graduate program at the Polish Free University. But Ewa had no hard edges. She had a head of dark, tumbling curls, and her quiet, lilting voice made everything she said sound like a lullaby.

After work or sometimes a lecture, Irena put off going home a bit longer and stopped off with the girls at a café for a coffee or an ice cream and a few laughs. Young women in those days dressed fashionably, in low-slung heels and brightly patterned dresses, and her new friends thought nothing of smoking cigarettes in public. Irena had long since abandoned her youthful scouting pledges. She also no longer felt any need to rush off to confession simply because the thought of Adam made her heart race faster. Irena's hair was cut in a wavy bob that, by then, was no longer scandalous, just practical. She had bright eyes that her friends remembered as startlingly blue and a smile that looked more than a bit like mischief. The other young women were all from Jewish families, and they howled with laughter to hear a Catholic girl like Irena say something in Yiddish.

They would also talk politics, of course. Their work was focused on social justice. The Polish Free University was still a center of radical activism, and Irena's new friends were ardent socialists like her father. Occasionally she would meet someone whose politics went a bit further. "I met a few, illegal members of the Polish Communist Party, right after [their] spending time in prison," Irena confessed. She thought they were "smart, noble people." Adam flirted with communism himself, and perhaps that was part of his allure. When, as the only child of an extraordinarily rich family, he inherited the largest share of his father's fortune in the 1930s, his widowed mother, Leokadia, was aghast at his plans. He planned, he told her boldly, to give it all away to charity. Leokadia wept and pleaded and scolded, but Adam just dug in his heels. *The money has to go,* he told his mother. Adam had struggled his whole life with the curse of wealth, and he didn't believe in inheritances. Neither did new communist friends of theirs, Stanisław Papuziński and his daring, political girlfriend, Zofia Wędrychowska. They lived together and even had a small son already, but they didn't have any plans to get married. Marriage was a bourgeois institution, and they were bohemians.

Irena found it all enchanting. When it came to leftist politics, Irena had an impeccable family pedigree, after all, and her new friends knew it. Her father had played an important role in the creation of the Polish Socialist Party, and there were still party members across Warsaw who remembered Stanisław Krzyżanowski. And no one spoke of Irena's father more fondly or more often than Helena Radlińska, who had known him personally. Helena and her ex-husband, Zygmunt, had been founding activists in the Polish Socialist Party in the early 1900s, and Zygmunt — a doctor at the University of Warsaw hospital — had worked alongside Stanisław Krzyżanowski. For Irena, who never stopped missing her father's presence, it was all a kind of profound homecoming. She joined the Polish Socialist Party herself, and "I fit right in with my political past," Irena said. Unfortunately for Mietek, she had found her true family.

She was moving further and further away

from her shaky marriage and closer to Adam and her new friends in Dr. Radlińska's circles. She was also becoming more politically engaged than ever. That meant *doing,* not *talking. What can be done?* That was always the question Irena asked herself. She looked at her campus identity card, stamped with the word "Aryan," and it made her furious. She scratched out the word and boldly presented it on campus as a silent protest. When the campus administrators learned of her rebellion, however, they decided they had had enough of this petite rabble-rouser and her presence at the University of Warsaw. Irena was slapped with an indefinite university suspension. It would be years before she would be allowed to return to classes.

Mietek might have been forgiven for feeling a bit relieved to learn that his young wife's boisterous and bruising days as a campus agitator had reached an abrupt administrative conclusion. Perhaps he already suspected that her heart was with Adam. Perhaps he was too tired of the quarrels for it to matter. But, in the way of failing young romances everywhere, it's likely he clung for a while to the hope that she would return to him and to her senses. When news came that year that Dr.

Radlińska's mother-and-child center had to be shut because it had run out of community funding and that Irena's job there was ending, too, it seemed like a perfect chance for Irena to settle down at last and have children of her own. After all, Irena was already in her mid-twenties. At any rate, Mietek was soon offered an important career opportunity and a permanent teaching job at the university several hours away in Poznań. He assumed, naturally, that Irena would follow.

But following that path set out when she was a girl was no longer something Irena could imagine. Irena was no longer a dutiful teenager, doing what other people wanted and expected because she could not imagine other options. Duty had caused heartache already for her and for Adam. She knew she had failed as a wife, but she didn't *want* to be married to Mietek. Like her mother and her new friends, she was a bohemian at heart. Like her father, she was born for constant action. She didn't want to leave Warsaw and this new extended family. She was determined somehow to complete her studies and applied over and over to have her suspension lifted. And, whether she said so or not, she wasn't prepared to give up whatever this burgeoning thing was with Adam. She quickly found a new job in the city's municipal welfare services with the help of Dr. Radlińska and broke the news to Mietek. She was staying in Warsaw.

When Mietek went to Poznań, there was no divorce. The Catholic Church forbade divorce, and scandal would not help Mietek. But Irena did not go with him. Suspended from the University of Warsaw and now working full-time as a social worker, Irena lived for the sake of propriety with her mother, but insofar as the rest of her life — and especially about Adam — Irena just kept quiet. That habit of secrecy, later, would prove to be lifesaving.

For three years — years in which Irena's workplace friendships and her romance with Adam deepened — the academic suspension remained in place. Each year Irena petitioned the administration. Each year she met with a stubborn refusal. Those in high offices on campus still remembered her rabble-rousing. It was only in 1938, when a sympathetic philosophy professor at the University of Warsaw stepped in on the sly to process the papers allowing her to reenroll for a year, that Irena had a chance to complete her studies. She made the most of the narrow window of opportunity. In the

late spring of 1939, at the end of the school
year, Irena submitted her final master's
thesis to her advisor, Dr. Wacław Borowy, a
professor of Polish literature and culture,
and was at last allowed to graduate. Adam
had already qualified as an attorney, but the
anti-Jewish feeling in the city, which infuri-
ated him, had dimmed his career prospects.
As far as he was concerned, he was as Polish as anyone. But the senseless laws restrict-
ing what Jews could and could not do of-
fended his pride and patriotism, and Adam
was a moody and sometimes melancholy
young man. He turned inward to books and
poetry and private reflections. Instead of
practicing law, as both he and Irena had
once dreamt of doing, Adam began doctoral
work in political history with Dr. Borowy.

Precisely when Adam's marriage failed,
no one is certain. Even the name of his wife
is only conjecture. Jewish family records in
Warsaw often did not survive the occupation, and Irena's family prefers still to keep
her name a closely guarded secret. All that
is known for certain is that Adam's wife was
one of Irena's friends from the university. A
series of unlikely wartime coincidences and
some old property records in Warsaw sug-
gest that she may have been a college friend
named Regina Mikelberg. If Adam's wife

was not Regina, she was someone like Regina: an educated and assimilated Jewish woman from a wealthy Warsaw family. And, whatever the case, Regina Mikelberg was part of their wartime circle and part of their wartime story. When the war came, Irena and her network would not forget about Regina.

That summer of 1939, Irena and Adam knew, of course, that war with the Germans was coming. They were both politically aware and realistic. They had lived with the specter of European fascism and, indeed, with Polish anti-Semitism for years already. By July, Warsaw buzzed with rumors that the Polish forces were quietly mobilizing. Adam would be deployed himself by the end of August. The young people were naturally apprehensive about how the world was changing around them, but they were also all supremely optimistic and confident. After all, Dr. Radlińska had taught them that the commitment of a small group of well-intentioned people could shape the world according to their vision of it. They were about to test the limits of what was possible.

When the attack on Warsaw started, it still shocked Irena. It didn't matter that she had known that an assault was coming. The wail of air raid sirens across the city awoke Irena and her mother with a start at six o'clock on the morning of September 1, 1939, and her first thought was for Adam. Adam was somewhere out there on a military exercise. This was a declaration of war at last, but since spring there had been armed incursions and scuffles along Poland's western border, and the Polish army had been mobilized for battle two days earlier.

Now Irena joined her rumpled neighbors as they poured out of their apartments and gathered in the empty streets, peering up at the sky and speculating, desperate for some explanation. From the sky came nothing — no bombs, no sounds — but still the siren wailed on, and at last exasperated air raid guards shooed them all back inside. The anxiety and the early hour made people cross, and somewhere in the apartment complex a door slammed loudly. At the kitchen table in their bathrobes and slippers, bleary-eyed and grim, Irena and her mother Janina listened to the news as it came in over the Polish radio. Irena's shoulders tensed as the crackling voice of the announcer spoke the words that everyone feared were coming: Hitler's attack on Poland had already started.

Hovering over the radio, Irena leaned in closer to hear the report. The city leadership now was asking government and municipal workers to stay at their posts around the clock and to resist the German aggressors. Thank heavens. She wanted to be *doing* something. A look from her mother told her to at least sit down and finish her coffee. What could she do at six in the morning anyhow? The next hour passed slowly. *Irena, stop fidgeting,* her mother scolded her with a smile. Irena waited until she couldn't bear it any longer. At seven she flew down the stairs to the open apartment courtyard, past Mr. Przeździecki's gardens. No one was worrying about the flowers that morning, and the yard was empty. Tossing her weathered old bag into the basket of her bicycle, Irena hitched up her skirt just a bit daringly, in case she had to pedal quickly. As her foot pushed down hard and the bicycle glided into motion, she turned east, toward the Old Town, in the direction of her office on Złota Street, with a welcome sense of purpose and determination that morning, powerfully relieved to have something to do besides wait and worry with her mother.

In the office, she went to look first for her boss, Irena Schultz, a thin, birdlike blonde with a big smile. Irena — "Irka" — Schultz was more than just Irena's supervisor, though. She was also one of Dr. Radlińska's girls, and they were a tight-knit sorority. At nine a.m. the aerial attack on Warsaw started at last. The approaching German bombers, one resident of the city remembered, at first sounded like "faraway surf, not a calm surf but when waves crash onto a beach during a storm." Before long the city rattled with the constant "hum of planes, tens, maybe even hundreds" and with powerful, rocking explosions. Girls in the office ran for the cellars and held each other's hands tightly in the musty darkness.

When the squadrons passed, the streets were in chaos. In all her twenty-nine years, Irena had never seen anything like this devastation. But it was only the beginning. What was happening to them? Around her, private cars and hackney cabs, now called into duty as makeshift ambulances, ferried the wounded through littered streets to hospitals. The wheezy car horns blared impatiently around her, but surely the drivers could see it was useless. Where the bombs and artillery had hit buildings, the streets were filled with broken glass and piles of fallen bricks. Irena watched in amazement as flames engulfed the gutted façades of entire apartment buildings. The walls swayed and then toppled in crashes to the cobblestones around her. People pulled their coats tightly around them and hurried across the streets and open squares, seeking the safety of doorways, as the skies grew dimmer. Irena coughed and covered her mouth with her scarf. Clouds of dust stung her eyes and coated the insides of her throat and nostrils. She could see dead horses in the street, killed in their traces, and, sometimes, mangled human bodies. Doctors and nurses helped rush moaning residents to aid points and later delivered supplies to field stations as the fighting edged closer.

Fear gripped Warsaw. Across the city, one anxious thought united residents. What was it like out there, on the front lines, if this was what happened in a city full of civilians? Irena thought about Mietek. She had said a friendly good-bye to him at a depot a few days earlier when he had come to Warsaw for the deployment and had wished him good luck and safety. One of her other friends from the social services office, a pro bono Jewish lawyer named Józef Zysman, had been called up as a reserve officer as well, and Irena worried about him. She would have to check in on his wife, Theodora, and their baby, Piotr, she thought to herself. Then, there was Adam. There were

68

always thoughts of Adam. He was also in a regiment, out there somewhere.

The matter-of-fact question that morning in the office, in a city where a siege was clearly starting, was where to start with services? Irka Schultz was the office boss, and she called everyone together. The trouble was that suddenly everyone was one of the needy. They had never faced this kind of welfare crisis. All morning they scrambled, asking each other what to do first.

Within hours the answer became immediately obvious: someone had to help the displaced and injured refugees already flooding into Warsaw. Someone had to find food and shelter for people bombed out of their homes in the city. The residents of Warsaw would fight to defend the city for nearly a month, and before it was all over there were reports of the cavalry on horseback facing down modern German tanks in a desperate action that told the whole story of just how outgunned the Poles truly were. The numbers of refugees grew daily as people of the countryside and smaller cities sought safety together. They arrived on foot, tired and frightened. Women with haunted eyes told how, along dusty roads, the German planes had swung low and aimed gunfire at families pulling their belongings.

Country folk working in the fields ran for the hedgerows, but on the open roads there was no cover. Irena listened to their stories and tried to keep her hands from shaking. At the time, she was a senior administrator in a branch of the social welfare office responsible for running soup kitchens across the city, and over the next few weeks she and her coworkers set up and manned dozens of makeshift canteens and shelters for the survivors.

On September 24, near the end of the onslaught, more than a thousand German aircraft filled the skies over Warsaw in bombing raids that went on for hours and turned whole districts into rubble. For two more days, the devastation was unrelenting. Some of the worst-hit areas of the city included the quarter just to the north of Irena's office that ran from the Jewish and Polish cemeteries on the west to the great synagogue on the east. All the bombing meant wounded people — people who wouldn't make it to a canteen but were still hungry. Where to start now? Irena knew in an instant. She sped off on her bicycle toward the Czyste Hospital on Dworska Street, determined to find her friend Ala.

The Jewish hospital was a sprawling genteel compound not far from the Vistula

70

River, and before the war it had boasted one of the most modern medical facilities anywhere in Europe. Now the nurses and doctors were already running short of supplies. Ala was working frantically to treat the refugees and the wounded. They were doing thirty or forty serious operations a day, a nurse reported with a quick shake of her head, all without anesthesia. One of those patients was likely to have been Dr. Radlińska. When the bombers flew over the buildings in her district, the floor rocked beneath Helena Radlińska's feet, and she ran for the stairwell and the open courtyard. On the street, the brown dust again filled the air, and then Helena heard the first cries of the wounded trapped inside the rubble. Someone had to help them. The doctor headed back into the building just as another portion crumbled. She felt only pain and then felt nothing. Those who dragged her, moaning and half-conscious, from the ruins could see burns and broken bones that would cripple her for months.

All of Warsaw suffered. There was no water, no electricity, and no food. The "[c]orpses of men and animals are heaped in the streets," one eyewitness remembered. "[M]en of goodwill are burying the dead where they find them; in a garden or a

71

square or the courtyards of houses. Famished people cut off pieces of flesh as soon as a horse falls, leaving only the skeleton." The German planes flew so low overhead that Irena could look up and see the pilots' faces. In the air raid shelters, the injured were piled on stretchers, crying quietly and begging for water. Everyone tried not to think of the men on the front. At home, her mother whispered urgent prayers, and Irena had to admit that she, too, was praying.

On September 27, Warsaw surrendered.

Exhausted, Irena and her boss, Irka, sat together in an office on Złota Street when word came that it was over. Everyone in the office was crying and hugging. The Germans and the Soviet Union had divided Poland between themselves as conquerors. The secret deal had been sealed even before the bombing ever started. In the partition of Poland, the prize of Warsaw went to the Germans, who declared it part of the *Generalgouvernement* and who were even now marching into the city.

Would husbands, fathers, sons, and brothers make it home? And what were they coming home to? Families across the smoldering and hungry city had a hundred anxious questions. Some 40,000 people died in the bombings of Warsaw. The toll on the front lines was even more staggering. Nearly 70,000 men were dead. Another 630,000 were even now en route to Germany and the Soviet Union as prisoners of war. The Germans were never going to let all the young Polish men just go home, where they could harass the occupiers and organize an armed national resistance fighting for a free Poland. Mietek Sendler was among those captured. *We'll pray for your husband,* people reassured each other. Pray for Mietek, yes. But Irena also added a silent, fervent wish for Adam.

Resistance happened quickly in Poland. It was something of a miracle, or so it seemed to Irena, who watched it take shape and flourish. Word spread quietly across Warsaw in the next few weeks. Among the countries occupied by the Germans, Poland was exceptional in several ways. Most exceptional was the fact that, in Poland, an organized and determined partisan movement took shape almost immediately, largely led by older men, by the Jewish community, and by a great number of courageous women of all ages. Some of the most extraordinary were the youngest. But Irena and, miraculously, Adam were also among them. For Adam it was a bittersweet return to a fallen Warsaw. They had failed at the front lines. But the young people across the city were determined to keep on fighting the Germans. The groundswell of resistance was a large part of the reason why Poland was also subject to such brutal tactics of repression.

Already an entire underground state was forming. First, the Polish government-in-exile set up headquarters in Paris. Then it evacuated to London, where it funneled financial and logistical support to "home" branches. As always, the problem with getting it all up and running efficiently was politics and squabbling.

As a result of the squabbling — because Polish politics before the war had been no less divisive — most of the resistance efforts were organized along old party lines. That endless bickering was the result, in large part, of the country's tumultuous history and long struggle for national independence. It was only at the end of the First World War, after more than a century of foreign domination, that the "Polish" state was re-created for the second time in its history. But that treaty did little to settle the matter of its eastern borders, toward the Ukraine, which its watchful Russian neighbors coveted. Its neighbor to the west,

Germany, had other imperial ambitions. Hopelessly caught between a left-wing Bolshevik-controlled Soviet Union — around which swirled any number of wild and ugly theories about the Jewish world conspiracy — and the rise of far-right nationalism and proto-fascism on its western boundary in the 1920s and 1930s, Polish politics was Janus-faced. Which was the lesser of those two evils, the far left or the far right? It was an impossible question. In the absence of answers, people clung to their old political alliances.

The atmosphere at the clandestine meetings of the Polish socialists that Irena and Adam attended that autumn was nervous but defiant. Most of the young men in the city now were Jewish, and Irena had been wild with relief when both Adam and her lawyer friend Józef made their way safely back to Warsaw. Other Polish men — men who were not also Jewish — were sent systematically to prisoner-of-war or labor camps, forced to feed the Nazi war machine. Mietek was captured and incarcerated in Germany. Jews like Adam and Józef, however, were unfit for any use in the eyes of the fascists. Caught up in their tangled logic of anti-Semitism, German functionaries in Berlin asked themselves what to do about

75

this Jewish "problem." If Adam and Józef were not men but something less than human, they could pose no danger as soldiers or combatants. There could be no purpose in sending them off to prisoner-of-war compounds. But the Germans did not wish to live among what they considered to be a species of diseased degenerates, and there would have to be some "solution." Poland was already the planned dumping ground for Jews from across Europe. While the Germans considered how best to arrange a mass forced migration, in Warsaw alone upward of a hundred thousand young Jewish people like Adam were left at loose ends for the time being.

And it wasn't only Adam. Józef, Ewa, and Ala were also determined activists who found themselves suddenly unemployed and idle. They, too, were quickly drawn into the web of these secret political gatherings. At first the clandestine nature of things was exciting as they whispered code words at the thresholds of dim apartments or gathered in the back rooms of shops and basements. The warm camaraderie and optimism buoyed Irena's spirits throughout October 1939, and besides, it just felt good to be sitting next to Adam. *The war will be over soon,* everyone said so confidently. *Per-*

76

haps until then it will not be so bad under the Germans. Irena tried to be hopeful. But evidence to the contrary was mounting quickly.

The Gestapo soon began hunting those it considered troublemakers — and Irena and her friends were unmistakable agitators. A sudden noise from outside the apartment could make an entire room of people jump. The hard wooden chair beneath her creaked as Irena wriggled and tried to get comfortable during speeches that even a war couldn't make less long-winded, and Adam glanced furtively toward the door, longing for the cigarettes resting in his coat pocket. The first order of business, the leaders announced, was to deliver emergency support funds to party members and activists who were forced into hiding. They had all gone underground quickly, and suddenly those most in need included nearly all their former professors. The party needed secret couriers to keep in contact with them and funnel them money. It was a dangerous mission, and they shouldn't underestimate the risks to their own safety. Irena's heart beat faster. Of course she must help! Irena volunteered instantly. She felt a surge of affection for Adam when she saw him smiling.

The professors had wisely gone into hiding when Warsaw fell to the Germans — and it wasn't because they were Jewish. Warsaw in 1939 was one of the world's most dynamic and diverse cities. There were somewhere on the order of a million people living in the city that year, and just over a third of them were Jewish. The remaining residents were largely but not exclusively "ethnic" Poles. The Germans, however, considered the Poles, as part of the Slavic race, to be inferior to Aryans and ominously classified them, right along with their Jewish neighbors, as *Untermenschen,* or "subhumans." Although the citizens of Warsaw hadn't been given a copy of the German memorandum ordering the complete annihilation of Polish culture, it wasn't a mystery to anyone in the socialist party or at the secret meetings Irena attended. To accomplish that cultural annihilation, killing off the country's intellectuals was the first order of business.

But the category of "intellectuals" was a broad one: it included not just professors but also the country's doctors, teachers, lawyers, judges, journalists, writers, wealthy landowners, industrialists, prominent businessmen, hereditary aristocrats, activists, social workers, politicians, priests, nuns, military officers, engineers, communists, and scientists. In short, an "intellectual" was anyone with cultural power. To cripple the professional Polish classes, Hitler gave instructions to kill all people of influence, shutter the schools and universities, and burn their libraries. Another early German memo laid out the plan for the next Polish generation clearly: "The sole goal of [their] schooling is to teach them simple arithmetic, nothing above the number 500; writing one's name; and the doctrine that it is divine law to obey the Germans. I do not think that reading is desirable."

The response of Polish activists, on the left and the right, was to create in Warsaw a mirror world that matched the new German institutions, structure for structure. Patriots erected an entire underground Polish state — the one thing on which Poles from across the political spectrum were united. There would ultimately be secret Polish courts and a secret "Home Army"; the groundwork had already been laid for a secret university.

Adam and Irena's thesis supervisor, Dr. Borowy, immediately joined the underground university and began work on a collaborative publishing project. He and some of the country's most eminent professors wrote, in bold defiance of the Germans, a sociological analysis of the occupiers and their crimes called *Nazi Kultur in Poland,* later smuggled out to publishers in Britain. Dr. Radlińska, hobbled but resolute, quickly joined the underground state and began building from her hideout a curriculum of secret university classes. So did Ala's mentor and medical research partner, Dr. Hirszfeld, and Dr. Witwicki, the Polish psychologist who mentored their friend Ewa Rechtman.

These were the lucky ones — the ones who needed supporting. Helena Radlińska's brother, Dr. Aleksander Rajchman, a prominent mathematics professor at the University of Warsaw, was not so fortunate. Arrested by the Gestapo and interrogated, he was dead in the concentration camp at Sachsenhausen-Oranienburg, north of Berlin, within the first year of the occupation. He was not alone. Some fifty thousand other members of the "intelligentsia" — and more than two-thirds of Helena Radlińska's colleagues — were ultimately executed or sent with Dr. Rajchman to perish in concentration camps. In Kraków, at the Jagiellonian University, the Gestapo arrested nearly two hundred professors — the entire faculty — on the afternoon of November 6, 1939.

Most died in the aftermath. Later, hundreds of Catholic priests were rounded up, in Warsaw especially; few clergymen survived those encounters.

These were the people Irena and her friends knew best. They were their teachers, mentors, political compatriots, and professional contacts in the social services and at the universities. They were the people they looked up to and wanted to become. They sometimes ran the charitable institutions that worked closely with city social workers; sometimes they were Irena's direct colleagues. Then, after the purges, the mass "resettlements" began: another half a million Poles were rounded up on the streets and sent to work as German slave labor.

The Jewish community was not spared a share of the earliest abuses. Germans and their far-right Polish supporters — and they were numerous — in the first months of the occupation smashed Jewish shop windows, attacked on the streets Orthodox men with their distinctive beards, and randomly beat Jews to death for sport and entertainment.

In the emergency room of the Jewish hospital, on the front line of those atrocities, Ala Gołąb-Grynberg struggled to make sense of it. How could this be happening? As a lead nurse in the hospital's ambulance corps, Ala was part of a triage that already seemed endless. She nursed the broken bodies of the old, whose only crime was not being quick enough to follow orders in German accents that they did not understand. For this, they were hauled feetfirst behind horse-drawn cabs along cobblestone streets until their skulls shattered. She saw men whose beards had been torn from their faces or hacked off carelessly with knives, and scrawny street children fighting to survive SS beatings. She kept her face calm and worked quickly. But inside, Ala thought she knew now the furious desperation of a trapped animal. Sometimes throwing open the broad sash of a hospital window, she leaned as far out as she could, sucking in the fresh air. She never thought of jumping. But everyone sometimes thought of falling. At home, Ala wrote poems on bits of scrap paper and tried to make sense of the jumbled images.

And around her, everything was jumbled, no matter how much Ala and her nursing staff struggled to impose order. What had once been gleaming hospital wards now teemed with broken people. Where the artillery fire had blown out the plate glass along some walls, the windows were covered haphazardly with dusty sheets and scrap wood. By late October the wards were already freezing in the mornings. The patched-up room mirrored the patched-up, shattered bodies within them, and at the end of her shift her head ached from clenching her jaw in fury. But, more than anything, Ala was worried and sometimes frightened: worried about these victims of brutality but worried, too, about her own family. Her husband, Arek, had left Warsaw with the mobilization in August. The only news they could get of him was a vague report that he had been seen somewhere on the eastern front in late September in bad condition. Her brother, Samuel, and his wife were already in Russian territory; perhaps somehow Arek would find them? Ala also worried about her small daughter and about money.

Everyone who was Jewish was suddenly worried about money. The Germans slapped crippling economic restrictions on the Jewish community with the goal of making sure that anyone who was Jewish lived in poverty. It began with forced Jewish unemployment. Jews could no longer hold any state or government positions. In the city social services, dozens of Ala and Irena's friends were summarily fired, including their friend Ewa Rechtman and a friendly old doctor they knew named Henryk Palester. Restrictions required Jewish property to be registered, their businesses Aryanized, and their bank accounts frozen. Adam fumed with indignation. In a coffee shop near his apartment on Bałuckiego Street that winter, knee to knee under the table, Adam and Irena had long, urgent conversations about the future. Perhaps they considered flight. Like Ala and Arek, Irena also had family connections in the Ukraine. Maybe they could build a life together there. Hundreds of thousands of Jews — nearly one in ten in Poland — wisely slipped across the Soviet border to the east that year. Those who did were far more likely to be survivors. But both Adam and Irena had widowed mothers. Irena's mother was frail; fleeing with Janina was impossible. So was deserting her. Adam's mother, Leokadia, exasperated him, and now she talked more resentfully than ever of his abandoned inheritance. They quarreled, too, about the collapse of his marriage. But while Adam longed to be free of his mother, he couldn't abandon her either. Leaving was out of the question.

In the first year or two of the occupation, some among the Warsaw Jewry said that there were limits to what could possibly happen. War was hard, of course. People understood this. Terrible things — isolated things — would happen. Others in the Warsaw Jewish community were more wary and cynical. But, at the start, the Germans singled out Poles and not the Jews for systematic purges. In the first year or two of the occupation, ten Poles in Warsaw were murdered for every Jewish resident killed, and it was considered so much safer to be Jewish that there were tales of Christian residents putting on the Star of David armband and adopting Yiddish accents during street roundups. Because the first systematic anti-Semitic edicts were primarily financial, the Jewish population was lulled into a sense of relative safety. That was precisely the intention.

What Warsaw's Jewry could not know — and what Adam and Irena never imagined — was that, in a conference in Berlin on September 21, 1939, before the city's surrender, plans had already been made as well for their future. Reinhard Heydrich, the head of the Gestapo, a man whom even Hitler declared was heartless, sent instructions to commanders in Poland that month: "In reference to today's conference in Berlin," he ordered, "I once again draw your attention to . . . the final solution." The

wheels of the Holocaust were, even now, in
motion.

Chapter 3
Those Walls of Shame
WARSAW, 1941–1942

Behind her, Irena could hear all the sounds of Jewish life in Warsaw. The street criers calling out in Yiddish joked with each other good-naturedly, jockeying for the best corner while they hawked their wares. When one moved along, the stone streets echoed with the scrape and rattle of the iron wheels on the handcarts. She could hear in the distance the streetcar coming down Gęsia Street and the cry of gulls squabbling along the nearby Vistula River. At the doorway marked number one, she hesitated for a moment, taking in the spiced aromas of street food and the cold air of late autumn. Then Irena softly pulled the handbell to the convent of the Ursuline sisters.

The face that greeted Irena from under the starched wimple was unlined by age, and the young nun gravely inquired the reason for her visit. *I'm here to see Pani Rudnicki, please, Sister.* The woman nodded

87

silently and carefully pulled back the bolt on the heavy door. Irena stepped into the shadows of the foyer and heard the bolt drawn smoothly behind her.

The young nun led Irena on, though the courtyard and along the halls to an unremarkable doorway. How strange to be taken to see someone who didn't exist! Mrs. Rudnicki was a fiction. Or, if a person with that name once lived, she did no longer, and in her death had unwittingly lent her identity to a desperate stranger. Rudnicki was the false name under which Helena Radlińska was working from her hiding place inside this walled convent. Already, some in the Jewish community had taken the steps of securing false "Aryan" identity papers.

With a quiet knock, Irena crossed the threshold to where her old professor was waiting, and when Dr. Radlińska warmly grasped her hand, Irena felt a flood of pleasure. For her part, Helena Radlińska admired this young woman's bravery and spirit. But, with the eyes of experience, she could see that Irena did not comprehend the risks or the dangers. Still, Helena was immensely grateful for the assistance. She needed the money if she were to impose upon the kindness of the nuns here in hiding.

Over sweet, milky tea, a Polish staple, the professor told her story. Gesturing to her cane, she talked ruefully of the bombing of her apartment and the loss of all her manuscripts and her library. She talked of finding refuge there in the convent with the Catholic sisters. But, looking at the sturdy walls around her, Helena Radlińska had no illusions. She knew already that the Gestapo was hunting for her. If the time came, the sisters could not save her. Never mind. She was determined to carry on fighting. There was so much to discuss, and the hours ticked by swiftly. Dr. Radlińska, cooped up and still on the mend, wanted to know everything that was happening. What was Irena doing? And what *was* happening?

Irena had to ask herself what she was doing. The political underground was already creating a secret army, a secret government, and publishing resistance newspapers. Dr. Radlińska and the other professors, she learned, were forming a secret Polish university. One of the classrooms would be right there in the convent. But what was anyone doing in the social services? The Jews, Irena could only report, were now banned from receiving any state welfare or working in any state employment, and Irena and the professor both knew firsthand the grim consequences of poverty and unemployment in the most vulnerable segments of that population. Irena's job was doing community interviews, and Dr. Radlińska might have asked her to reflect on what she had discovered. "There were families where one herring was shared amongst six children during Sabbath," Irena said when asked the question later.

Why not build a mirror social welfare system? Dr. Radlińska was toying with the thought. It was something for Irena to consider. That would be a worthy project. That would be true to their work and their values as activists. Precisely when the cooperation between Irena and the professor started is uncertain. So, too, is the exact extent of the professor's guidance. But wartime intelligence files kept by the underground Home Army on Irena's activities document the collaboration. Irena Sendler, the files read, "has large Polish contacts, especially on the left. Works directly with Prof. Radlińska of the Free University." Helena Radlińska was a senior operative in this underground army, and in time she would encourage several of her former students to build networks for the resistance. She would also eventually develop her own independent clandestine Jewish welfare program. And already the leaders of the resistance had a strategy: they would create as many cells as possible, all working for the protection of the movement, in complete isolation from each other. One of those cells would be run by this very capable twentysomething slip of a woman: Irena Sendler.

When precisely Irena and the professor talked may be uncertain, but one fact is clear: it cannot have been very long at all after the fall of Warsaw, because Irena's cell developed quickly. The need in Warsaw was urgent. Whom else to bring into the cell with her was the crucial question. Dr. Radlińska would have warmly counseled Irena to trust Irka Schultz. She was another of the professor's former students — and Irena's boss in the social welfare offices.

Dr. Radlińska could also support readily the decision to bring in another coworker and friend, Jadwiga Deneka, another one of the professor's former students. Jadwiga was a pretty blond woman with a pixie bob, and she had trained originally as a teacher and worked in the innovative orphanage school founded by the professor's colleague, Dr. Korczak, before transitioning into the city welfare service. At twenty-eight, Jadwiga was a year younger than Irena, a bubbly and vivacious woman, and Irena knew her well from their days together at the Polish Free University and the meetings of the Polish Socialist Party.

And there was a third alumna of the Polish Free University in the office: Irena's colleague and friend Jadwiga Piotrowska. Everyone called Jadwiga by her nickname, Jaga, and like Irena she also came from a family with an impeccable pedigree as public servants. Her father, Marian Ponikiewski, was an engineer who worked with the city welfare services designing public housing. Dr. Radlińska knew both Marian and his close collaborator, the social theorist Roman Piotrowski, and, in fact, Jaga had married into the Piotrowski family. She and Janusz Piotrowski had a young daughter and a tumultuous love affair. Jaga was in her mid-thirties, six or seven years older than Irena, a short, sturdy woman with dark eyes, and she was an ardent Catholic. Jaga and Irena had worked together since 1934 in the city offices, and Jaga was one of the support staff working in social services on the placement of orphans. Unlike the others, Jaga was old-fashioned and deeply religious, but Irena trusted her completely.

This trust in Jaga almost certainly stemmed from Irena's friendship with her younger sister, Janka. The two sisters could not have been more different. Like Irena, Janka was a bit of a free spirit. Where her sister Jaga was straitlaced and sincere, Janka was irreverent and ironic. She lived on Karolkowa Street in Warsaw's Żoliborz district with her husband, Józef, who had already joined the underground Home Army. Janka would be there that fateful morning, still four years in the future, when the Gestapo would at last catch up with Irena Sendler. And Janka would also take the lead in saving the life of one of their mutual friends: Regina.

In that first autumn of the occupation, within weeks of the Germans' arrival, Irena turned to each of them. Resisting German rule and keeping alive the spirit of Polish independence was a matter of national pride that had the power to unify even strangers. It certainly had the power to bring together kindred spirits and four of Dr. Radlińska's girls.

The friends and coworkers — Irena Sendler, Jaga Piotrowska, Irka Sendler, and Jadwiga Deneka — gathered together one evening in Irena's second-floor apartment on Ludwiki Street. At the small kitchen table, in between cigarettes, glasses of

93

cordial, and good-natured chatter, the women decided to do something simple — a small but dangerous act of Polish resistance to the new German rulers. They would quietly circumvent the rules, they agreed, and change the paperwork as needed to carry on as usual to help *all* their clients. It was a plan without any grand or overarching vision, just a stubborn response to some practical problems, and it wasn't something they hadn't done before on occasion either. Irena was one of four conspirators, but she was their natural leader, and the decision would bind these friends together in life and death, although they could not know that in the beginning. Not all of them would survive this endeavor.

Great, heroic acts sometimes come from small beginnings, and the four friends could have had no way of guessing either, as the circle expanded, what a vast fraternity of strangers they were creating. In the coming months, that circle of trust and courage would expand quickly — too quickly for the comfort of some — as they were joined surreptitiously in their office fraud by an ever-widening group of friends and colleagues in other social centers and in other municipal divisions spread across the city of Warsaw. At the start, it was nothing more than fiddling with some paperwork to thwart the Germans and help their clients. In time, encouraged by Dr. Radlińska and emboldened by small daily successes, it became a fearsome resistance cell that included at its core more than a dozen people from ten different offices and institutions. At its periphery, it relied on the bravery and decency of hundreds. But the vast majority of those who would become bound together in this network, one way or the other, each had connections that went back to their having worked with Helena Radlińska in the 1930s.

Irena's resistance cell was a wonder of efficiency — and those who knew Irena and were privy to the secret weren't in the least surprised. Irena wasn't a mere organizer. She was a force of nature. Within a year, by the fall of 1940, the small team was providing public welfare support to thousands of Jews in Warsaw. It was based on nothing more than faking files and requisitioning resources, which were then stealthily distributed from Irena's soup kitchens. Her system was brilliantly simple. "The basis of receiving social assistance was collecting data and statistics from the communities," she explained. "So we forged these statistics and interviews — meaning we listed made-up names, and in this way were able to secure money, food items, clothing," which they passed out at the centers. To discourage the Germans from checking up on their fictitious families, they cheerfully added to the dossiers ominous notations about deadly communicable diseases like typhus and cholera. Irena's small office hummed with activity and shared looks. Irena had wanted an adventure and, knowing that they were fighting against their oppressor, even if it was dangerous, made her feel alive.

If the first year of the occupation had been humbling and hard for the people of Poland — Jewish and Christian — in the second year the occupiers turned the screws tighter. By the autumn of 1940, German control of Warsaw was growing more secure. As Polish culture was forced into retreat, attention turned to exploitation and eradication of the Jewish nation-within-a-nation. Faced with a shortage of manual labor, the Germans now plucked Jewish men off the streets for forced-work details. The Jewish population was subject to new punitive restrictions. The synagogues were ordered closed, and the community was forced to endure restrictive curfews. Jews could not send letters overseas, use telephones or trains, walk in the city's parks, or sit on municipal benches. Eventually Jews — forced to wear in Warsaw a blue-and-white badge with the Star of David for identification — were ordered to step off the sidewalk into the gutter when a German approached them.

Adam was not exempt from any of those humiliating regulations. By now Irena and Adam were lovers, and their secret romance was not exempt either. A fair-haired young Polish woman, strolling arm in arm in occupied Warsaw with a Jewish man — even just a friend — was dangerous. They were risking abuse, maybe even an ugly and brutal beating. Anti-Semitic thugs across the city, emboldened by German rules that outlawed "interracial" dating, roamed the streets looking for easy targets — which the armband that Adam was required to wear readily provided.

Something as simple as weekend walks in the park or riding a streetcar across town to a friend's party were suddenly impossible for Adam and Irena. Perhaps it was now that Irena first began wearing the Star of David herself sometimes as she walked with Adam. She wore it in solidarity, she explained later, and in late 1940, before the worst had started, it still provided her and

Adam with some small measure of cover. A Jewish couple risked random street violence, but it would have made their now-forbidden liaisons less conspicuous.

By the beginning of 1941, that was all changing. By January, young Polish ruffians, encouraged and some said paid on the street corners by the German occupiers, prowled the streets of Warsaw in broad daylight, viciously beating anyone with the Star of David. In March the violence descended into an open pogrom. For more than a week, over the Easter and Passover holidays, more than a thousand roving thugs terrorized Jewish neighborhoods, robbing and pummeling anyone brazen enough to try to stroll the street with an armband. The occupiers looked the other way — and so did much of the city's shocked population.

Then, in the first weeks of spring, came the dawning realization that a dangerous typhus epidemic was taking hold in the most impoverished residential districts — districts that, unsurprisingly, were Jewish. Word was trickling across Warsaw that the Germans were making plans to establish a Jewish quarter across the river in the suburbs to isolate the stricken population. In April came quarantine orders of "infected areas." And by summer, just as the epidemic was losing steam at last and unbeknownst yet to the residents of Warsaw, a decision was made to do something even more radical, something that would change everything for Jews in Poland. It would also change everything for Irena and Adam.

In mid-October 1940, posters went up across Warsaw. Anxious residents pulled their coats tighter against the biting autumn wind and huddled around the notices to read them. From the German loudspeakers in the squares, the same awful orders were broadcast in hard tones. The news was stunning, and at first Irena and Adam could not believe it. The residents of Warsaw — Jewish and Polish — were to begin making preparations, the orders said. The Jews would move together into a small, undesirable area of the city that had been heavily damaged during the bombings. This new "quarter" would become the Warsaw ghetto. An area of seventy-three streets in the city — just over four percent of the streets in Warsaw — had been reserved for the Jews, carved out from what had long been one of the poorest and most run-down neighborhoods in the city center. Any "Aryan" residents were to immediately quit the cordoned Jewish area and find other accommodations. Those living on the wrong side of the boundary would have to move, regardless of their religion. The residents of Warsaw had just two weeks to make the relocations.

The city was gripped with panic. The orders affected more than 250,000 residents — nearly one in four in Warsaw, both Jewish and Polish, and there was no organization or system to direct the move. *Let them fight for table scraps among themselves* — that was, more or less, the German position. The German-controlled Jewish council, or *Judenrat,* tried to set up a clearinghouse to match families. Surely if Jewish families and Aryan families could arrange to swap housing based on a simple calculation of the size of an apartment and the size of a family, a good deal of agony for everyone could be avoided. It might have worked had the wealthiest residents on either side of the boundary embraced it. But the rich did not. Affluent families were not prepared to live in small, cramped apartments or to relocate to a street they considered "undesirable" — not when they had pockets deep enough to negotiate fine housing on the open market. The best apartments now disappeared in an instant as families of means snapped them up and signed private leases at increasingly fantastic prices. As middle-class families began the panic, the cost of housing shot up further, and unscrupulous landlords on both sides of the boundary preyed upon the desperate would-be tenants. Families often spent days frantically searching for any place to live, no matter how cramped or dilapidated, only to be outbid at the last moment and to start the search all over again in the morning. The poorest residents were left to scramble for a spot in overcrowded tenement housing. Already, Irena and her colleagues in the city offices were witnessing the catastrophic breakdown of Warsaw's social welfare network.

All around Irena the moment she ventured into the streets in the last two weeks of October, the crowds of unfortunates, pushing their belongings in handcarts and baby carriages, jostled her in their hurry to find a place in compliance with the German order. At the gates to the ghetto, there were long, snaking lines of those waiting for permission to pass; order was maintained by soldiers with guns and rough raised voices. Young mothers struggled to carry overhead unwieldy bundles of rolled linens and bedding, and even small children dragged along overstuffed suitcases. Vans and cars were scarce, and to Jews they were already forbidden. Transportation inside the Jewish quarter was largely by rickshaw, and distraught families were forced to leave behind many of their largest and most treasured family items. All the swapping around was doubly stressful because the Germans kept changing their minds about which streets were to be included in the new district.

The cruel melodrama unfolded everywhere on the streets in public view, and Irena had a front-row seat for the worst of the chaos. What if her apartment had been on the wrong side of the boundary? Irena knew it was all just chance. The ghetto began just to the east of her apartment in Wola. Moving her frail mother was a terrifying thought. Janina's health was a source of constant worry. But if Irena's apartment was not far from the new Jewish quarter, her office on Złota Street was even closer. Złota Street straddled the new ghetto. From the small windows upstairs, she and Irka Schultz could not miss the tragedy playing out in front of them.

But Irena's connection to this heartless diktat was deeply personal. She and her mother had been spared, but Adam and his mother, Leokadia, had not been. They were caught up in the madness, along with the rest of the Celnikier family: his aunts and uncles and cousins. It was only because Adam was her lover and not her husband that Irena was not forced to move to the ghetto with him. Had she been married to a Jew, she would have been treated as one.

In 1940, Adam lived in an apartment at number 18, Bałuckiego Street, in the southern Mokotów district of Warsaw, well outside the ghetto boundaries. Adam was Jewish, and Mokotów was now an "Aryan" district. He would have to move like so many other tens of thousands across the city, and Irena's heart ached for him. Adam struggled with the loss of his home. But it was the loss of his books that gutted Adam and left him stammering with disbelief and fury. A doctoral candidate and an historian, a man who lived inside his books and was already retreating into them more and more resolutely, few possessions mattered more to Adam than his library. And there was no way to take all of it with him into the ghetto. How could they possibly carry them — even if the Germans at the checkpoints did not burn the books of a Jewish man for sport — when Jews like him were forbidden the use of all but the most rudimentary transportation? Irena wanted to tell him they would find a way somehow. Adam brushed off any reassurance and, looking at the stacks of books in his apartment, glowered. He knew perfectly well that there was no way to take it all with him, and that there was no solution to the ghetto.

It wasn't only Adam who faced the pain of being uprooted and dispossessed in their circle. All of Irena's Jewish friends from the Polish Free University and the social welfare offices were forced to make the move: Ewa Rechtman; Ala Gołąb-Grynberg and her small daughter, Rami; Rachela Rosenthal and her little girl; Ala's mentor, Dr. Hirszfeld; Irena's friend, attorney Józef Zysman, his wife Theodora, and their little boy, Piotr. And so, of course, were Adam's Jewish wife and her relatives, including her mother-in-law, Leokadia Celnikier. Irena's part in this bohemian love triangle was suddenly a whole lot more complicated. Adam's mother took a dim view of her son's way of living. Mother and son had never had an easy relationship, and the move to the ghetto did not improve matters. While the name of Adam's wife remains a family secret, wartime property records show that some members of the Celnikier and Mikelberg families now lived in the same accommodations. Regina Mikelberg, though, was not among them. Regina moved, instead, with her parents and her brother and younger sister to an apartment in the north-west sector of the ghetto at number 30, Franciszkańska Street. And then, like everyone in the new Jewish quarter, Regina set about trying to figure out how to keep herself and her family from starving.

On the Aryan side, the practicalities of life were easier, but Irena was focused on this same question: How *would* her Jewish friends survive on the Germans' paltry rations? How would her Jewish welfare clients?

Irena craved the hum of activity and, faced with challenges like this, couldn't imagine herself trapped at home, bored, nursing babies. At work she threw herself into finding solutions and was busier than ever. Her small network of coworkers had started out falsifying internal office records to funnel welfare support to needy Jewish families. Now she was also on the hunt for something else: blank copies of the official documents that sometimes passed through their hands in social welfare services — the paperwork needed to give Jewish friends new Aryan identities.

With new "Polish" papers a Jewish family might, after all, circumvent these orders, if they were just a bit daring. They might, like Dr. Radlińska, disappear somewhere in the sprawling metropolis of Warsaw and pass unnoticed. The trouble was convincing Jewish friends to risk it. Adam simply refused. He would not leave the ghetto. His stubbornness drove Irena wild with worry. It also hurt. Adam was surely free by 1940 as far as Orthodox Jewish law saw it. Or if he wasn't free, he could have been. Divorce in the Orthodox tradition was as simple as him offering his wife a *get* — a written commitment to set her free to marry elsewhere. It was Irena whose Catholic marriage was an impediment. But his refusal to choose bothered her. What did it say about their relationship? The truth was that Adam had plunged into a deep depression and was incapable of any action. And guilt was surely part of this tangled emotional calculus for him. How could he save himself and abandon his extended family?

And anyhow, as repressive as the orders were, most in the Jewish community still believed that they would be safer in the ghetto, living apart from the Germans and from their often anti-Semitic Polish neighbors. Everyone assured each other that the changes would be minor. Most people believed that, like the medieval ghettos across Europe, the gates would only be shut at night, and in the daytime the city would go about its business. *We'll still meet at each other's apartments, just as always,* they told each other. *We'll still live, after all, in the same city.* If the ghetto remained open, what was the danger, really? But already in October work started on a ten-foot-high brick wall that would run through the middle of the block that divided Złota Street from its neighbor to the north, Sienna. A small section of the wall still stands there in Warsaw, a few doors down from the location of Irena's wartime office, one of the few remnants today of the ghetto perimeter.

The new Jewish quarter was an area of the city originally intended for about 80,000 residents, and most parts of the neighborhood had streets with working-class houses that lacked even basic modern amenities. But some parts of the area, especially the grander houses running along Sienna Street, were gracious bourgeois districts. The wealthiest members of the Jewish community quickly snapped up those apartments. Irena's friends were largely among them. Her friends were from assimilated, affluent families, and sometimes they had not actively practiced Judaism for decades. Some, like Dr. Radlińska and her cousin, Dr. Hirszfeld, had Jewish roots but had converted to Catholicism. These facts meant nothing to the Germans. Some, like Adam and Józef, simply thought of themselves as Polish. Others, like Ala and her husband Arek, were proud Zionists whose plans to emigrate to Palestine had been interrupted by world politics. But they were all educated, successful people with graduate degrees and professional careers, and they all spoke Polish fluently. Perhaps most important, they had a wide network of contacts outside of Jewish circles.

Among the Jews of Warsaw, Irena's friends were in a perilously small minority. They were the privileged few. Only a fraction of the city's Jewish community ever blended into the cultural life of Poland, and for the most part the Jews truly were a nation-within-a-nation. By the best estimate, in the words of one wartime survivor, "In Warsaw, there were several thousand Jews who practiced professions in which they inter-mingled with Polish society — lawyers, doctors, engineers, journalists, writers, actors." Irena's friends were all part of that. The rest of the city's Jewish population — more than 350,000 people on the eve of the occupation — lived and worked in shocking isolation from their "Slavic" neighbors.

In the beginning, even in the ghetto,

money could buy considerable protection from want and deprivation. Irena's friends moved to the better parts of the area and mostly tried to be optimistic. In other parts of the new quarter, though, the conditions were far less salubrious, and life was grim from the outset. Those who kept to the old practices and to the old languages mostly found themselves on streets where the apartments were cramped and scruffy. These unassimilated families were typically both much larger and much poorer, and those who had come to Warsaw as refugees were already especially desperate. The majority of these families did not speak Polish, nor could they have known as friends any of their ethnically Polish neighbors in the city. In the apartments above the street-front shops, three, four, even five families lived cramped together in one small apartment, sharing hallway toilets and jockeying for floor space. They were conditions ripe for disease and disaster.

That autumn, one of Irena's friends did steadfastly refuse to move to the ghetto. She was a fellow social worker named Maria, and by 1940 she was already part of Irena's secret welfare fraud network. Maria had not been born Jewish and neither had her husband, another of their friends and colleagues. He was Dr. Henryk Palester, a specialist in infectious diseases in the government's Ministry of Health who worked closely with both Irena's friend Ala and Ala's mentor Dr. Hirszfeld. Maria's May-to-December marriage to a man nearly thirty years her senior had scandalized her old-fashioned family, but it wasn't only the age difference between these two idealistic socialists that rattled her parents. It was the fact that Henryk, a fair-haired, balding gentleman with a long, handsome nose and square black glasses, had also taken the unusual step as a younger man of converting to Judaism. And in 1940 that meant that the Palester family — Maria, Henryk, and their two children, a middle schooler named Małgorzata and a teenager named Kryštof — should have been busy packing for a move to the ghetto.

Maria had other plans, however. Although her husband Henryk had been summarily dismissed from his government job when the Jewish employment restrictions were put in place, they all had Catholic birth certificates and baptism records. Unless the Germans came looking for them, Maria figured there was a better-than-average chance that they could ride out the war under their own name, in their own apartment, by just carrying on as Polish Catholics. They were not disavowing Henryk's Judaism, but this was not the moment to be pointing it out to the occupiers, either. When Maria's Jewish-born friend and neighbor — a professor and the mother of a preteen daughter — let on that she was planning to make the move to the ghetto as ordered, Maria persuaded her to risk it also. Maria Palester was already certain that the ghetto was a trap set for the Jewish community. Something whispered to her that here was terrible danger.

Maria refused to spend the war skulking around and hiding out in her apartment. It was all a game of confidence, she figured. The best bet was to hide in the open. Fear was a gambler's tell, and Maria was a sharp and experienced cardplayer. When her regular bridge game turned out to include some Gestapo informers and even some ethnic German *Volksdeutsche,* she made a point of being charming and vivacious. Maria was a slender woman, with dark, curly hair and high cheekbones, and she knew how to carry it off gracefully. It could never hurt to have a bit of protection if they were discovered, and everyone knew already that bribes could solve all sorts of problems. Maria's Gestapo connections would, before the war was over, be a life-or-death matter for Irena.

Within weeks, there was no doubt that the Palester family had made the right decision. November 16, 1940, was a Saturday. Jewish families, slowly walking to clandestine Shabbat services in cellars and attics, were stunned to learn that overnight the ghetto had been sealed entirely. It came like a thunderbolt, residents said afterward. No one had seen this coming. Jews were forbidden to leave the closed area, ostensibly to stop the recurrence of the communicable diseases for which they were blamed on ugly racist posters that went up around the city.

At first, despite the presence of German, Polish, and Jewish soldiers at the outposts, the barricades were policed lightly. All afternoon and for another week after, the ghetto remained half open. That weekend, as word spread across Warsaw, Polish residents — both friends and strangers — arrived in huge numbers at the walls to bring supplies of bread and gifts of flowers. Others on the Aryan side worked to arrange shipments of fresh produce into hastily organized ghetto markets, and whole families now searched the makeshift market stalls that sprang up out of canvas-covered wagons or on rickety tables for food for their families.

When Adam and Irena walked through the streets of the ghetto together that first week, wet laundry hung from upstairs windows flapped in the autumn wind, and the tide of people carried them along unnoticed. It would be the last time they could walk like this, out in the open, for years to come. Irena loved Adam, but already things were not easy. His fatalism and passivity grated on her, and sometimes now they quarreled. Why would he not leave with her? He could walk out of the ghetto with her today. She would find false identity papers. She would find them for his wife and mother, too, if that were what he wanted. It was not impossible to be together. But Adam wouldn't or couldn't.

Soon the boundaries were guarded with ruthless determination, and, as the food ran out, the prices of everything inside the ghetto rose catastrophically. Market shipments were confiscated, and Irena was aghast when she learned that the official rations allotted to her Jewish friends amounted to a paltry 184 daily calories. Following the law meant certain starvation. Smugglers naturally began to set up cunning operations, using small and nimble street children to climb the perimeter. The

Germans responded by adding loops of barbed wire and broken bottles to the walls, still under furious construction, and by shooting the children. Irena listened to the tap of bricks, one against another. And every day the wall that separated her from Adam grew higher and higher.

When the ghetto lines were drawn, the Jewish hospital on Dworska Street was left on the Aryan side of the boundary. Those unlucky enough to need medical care now had to pass through German checkpoints. So did the hospital staff each morning. As Ala Gołåb-Grynberg lightly kissed her small, sleeping daughter good-bye in the darkness every morning that autumn, it hurt. She knew she might not make it home alive that evening. It had not taken very many crossings at the ghetto boundaries to understand this stark reality. But, as the chief of nursing, Ala had no choice — not ethically. Along with a team of seventy-five other nurses and doctors, twice a day she ran this terrible gauntlet.

The hospital staff huddled together just before seven each morning on Twarda Street throughout November, waiting for the signal. Ala tried not to remember what this street used to be like before the war, when it was a happy bustle of middle-class houses and Jewish shops. Now residents scuttled along the edges of the buildings, as far from the checkpoints as they could press themselves, and farther along the road the Germans had turned the street's grand synagogue into a fodder warehouse and a rank stable for horses. She was glad to see Ludwik — Dr. Hirszfeld — huddling in his overcoat against the bitter morning cold, his tufts of white hair peeking out from beneath a dignified fedora. Leave it to Ludwik to look elegant even in the ghetto, even after what Ala could guess had been another late night in the cabaret café around the corner, where he was a regular. Ludwik Hirszfeld had a passion for sultry jazz and old love songs, and Arek's glamorous cousin, Wiera, was one of the greatest ghetto singers.

As the clock approached seven precisely, the hospital staff gathered together and slowly approached the checkpoint at the corner where Twarda and Złota Streets intersected. Irena's old office wasn't far, and if Ala craned her neck she might have made out the doorway in the distance. But after German review of some office files turned up more questions than answers, Irena had been summarily transferred to a satellite facility well away from the ghetto. Around

Ala, nonchalant police officers with cocked helmets pushed bicycles along the cobblestone streets, guns flung casually over their shoulders. It was just another start of their workday, too, at the ghetto stations.

At the checkpoint, a sign in German and Polish warned, *Typhus Infection Area, Authorized Passage Only,* and beside her Ala heard Dr. Hirszfeld growl softly. Her mentor had said often enough that if you wanted to create a typhus epidemic, this ghetto was an excellent way to do it. Already the hospital staff was on the front lines of that hopeless battle. One in five of her admitting staff would succumb to the disease from treating patients. But long before any of them faced those risks, there was the immediate danger ahead of them. They still had to pass the sentinels, who would frogmarch them under armed guard to the doors of the hospital. That morning, luck was not with them. It had happened before, and it would happen again. But every time they were left shaken and bruised and terrified. As they entered the Aryan zone and began their brisk walk, Ala caught sight of a handful of young SS men sauntering in their direction. Ala dropped her eyes to the pavement instantly. *Don't look at them,* she told herself silently. But looking away made no difference, and she heard herself gasp as the butt of a rifle came down hard on the chest of one of the doctors in the front of their convoy. He fell, and she turned away again from the sounds of thudding boots hitting bone as he lay there moaning. The rest passed in a daze. More rifle butts. More boots, followed by cries of pain and words in German. As Polish residents hurrying to work looked on in astonishment, the doctors were lined up to do jumping jacks, faster and faster, until they toppled over amid howls of laughter and the SS moved on, looking for fresh entertainment.

Soon even these forays outside the ghetto were forbidden. Ala could not say she was sorry. In December the Jewish hospital was closed, and the medical teams were assigned instead to smaller clinics scattered throughout the ghetto, at a greatly reduced capacity. It wasn't enough to meet the overwhelming need, and things inside the Jewish quarter went downhill quickly. By the end of 1940 the district had become notorious as a cemetery for the living. Maria and Henryk Palester lived in constant danger of detection, but it was better by far than the alternative.

It was all part of a final solution that, however dimly conceived, had been inexorably set into motion before the fall of Warsaw. In that same directive, SS leader Reinhard Heydrich reminded his henchmen in Warsaw that "the first prerequisite for the final aim is the concentration of the Jews" in urban areas. Only "cities which are rail junctions should be selected as concentration points," he informed his agents. Warsaw was one of the largest of all those crossroads. As soon as the local Jewish population of Warsaw was rounded up, the refugees shipped in from other cities started arriving. All Jewish communities of less than five hundred were dissolved across the *Generalgouvernment,* and their residents — when they survived — were forced to relocate as well to the cities. Eventually, Jews from Germany would also be deported to the Warsaw ghetto, crowding conditions further. The result was more than a half a million people forced to starve inside a walled and guarded district.

Adam was one of them. Regina was another.

No one was in the least surprised to learn that, within weeks, with her characteristic resourcefulness and determination, Irena had obtained an epidemic control pass that allowed her to be in and out of the ghetto constantly.

Chapter 4
The Youth Circle
WARSAW, 1940–1941

Irena was shivering, but she was trying hard to concentrate. *Rickettsia prowazekii.* Bacterium. *Pediculus humanus humanus.* Louse infection. The room was crowded with young men and women, each scratching cramped notes in the dark on precious paper.

Across the room, Irena exchanged a worried glance with her friend Ala. Ala was rail thin now in the early months of 1941, with sharp black eyes, and her ill-fitting clothes hung from her shoulders. Her daughter, Rami, was five that year, and Irena knew that Ala lived with her parents, Moshe and Rachel; her older brother, Janek; and a two-year-old orphan girl named Dahlia — all crammed into an apartment around the corner at number 4, Smocza Street.

Ala was now the chief nurse in the ghetto, an official appointment by the *Judenrat,* and the position allowed her a rare ghetto pass and the right to make professional visits on the streets of the Jewish quarter after the curfew. She was also in charge of leading the youth circle at number 9, Smocza Street, and she was secretly organizing, along with Dr. Radlińska's cousin, Dr. Ludwik Hirszfeld, community-run sanitation courses and paramilitary medical training like this lecture. Some young Jewish people were already talking about armed resistance. Ala's husband, Arek, who had miraculously survived the eastern front and made his way home to Warsaw, was one of those early activists. Arek, though, had not returned to the Jewish quarter. He lived instead in the forests outside the city and had joined the partisans there. Career prospects in the ghetto, after all, were dim for actors, and already the children were going hungry. Irena could see it all took a toll on her friend.

Now, intoning firmly, the lecturer, Dr. Landau, emphasized his point again by tapping his chalk against the makeshift blackboard. There was one candle in the room, and he taught in the shadows. But he didn't care that they were learning under difficult circumstances or that this was a dangerous, clandestine lesson. Dr. Landau was a strict disciplinarian, unbending. He was firm and gruff, and he had about him something that reminded Irena of a sergeant or maybe even a general.

Sanitation is the key to stemming the epidemic that is gaining on us, he went on, tapping the blackboard from time to time to punctuate another sentence. *Typhus depended on cramped quarters and confined human populations to multiply like this. Death rates have shot up from just under a thousand to several thousand a month, and we will have to work on measures . . .*

He was interrupted in mid-sentence by the stomping of heavy boots outside the door. Someone's pencil dropped to the floor in panic and rattled. These were the feared but familiar sounds of Nazi boots, and the teenage students in the dark room could hear now the horrible bellowing outside the window, the barked orders for the Jews to show themselves. *Raus! Juden raus!* The piercing scream of a child came from somewhere in a nearby building. Gunshots. Weeping.

In an instant, the room turned to Dr. Landau. Where could they hide? What would happen? Dr. Landau tapped the blackboard again, looking at them steadily, forbidding them to move with his gaze, and kept on lecturing. *Infection occurs when the*

121

feces of the Rickettsia prowazekii *bacterium —*

The sounds of the boots echoed farther down the street, and only then did one of the girls in the room start shaking and sobbing. She was gasping for breath in her spasms of hysteria. Others now were starting. Irena watched, awed, as Dr. Landau turned on them fiercely.

"Don't you people understand yet?"

Dozens of wide eyes turned toward the doctor. Only Ala looked calm. Irena marveled at her composure.

"All of us, every day and every night, are on the front lines," the doctor told them sternly. "We are the frontline troops in a war that never stops. We are soldiers, and we must be tough. There is no crying allowed here!"

And then, with the tap of the chalk, he turned back to the blackboard and picked up his chain of thought as though there had been no second interruption. A burst of white dust hung for a moment in the air. No one dared to cough lest the doctor think they were sniffling. There was just scribbling in the dim room and the doctor's firm voice, explaining.

Irena Sendler's presence inside the ghetto

— on the streets or at these secret lectures — didn't surprise any of her old university friends who were incarcerated there. They would not have been surprised to see her colleagues from the welfare offices, Irka Schultz, Jadwiga Deneka, or Jaga Piotrowska, that day either. All four women were in and out of the ghetto sometimes two or three times daily in late 1940 and throughout 1941.

This hadn't started as any planned network or operation. As Irena put it, "I was a frequent visitor to the walled district." She had been since the moment it was created. "My work in the city administration's Department of Health and Social Services made it easy for me to get a pass," she explained. Many of the families she had been supporting were now trapped within the confines of the ghetto, and that was one of her reasons for going. But the real reason was personal: "I knew the suffering of the people rotting away behind the walls, and I wanted to help my old friends." There were matters of the heart, too, she admitted. She wanted to be with one old friend especially: Adam. Adam's depression was now a furious spiral into anger and darkness, and Irena was frightened. One had to *want* to live to survive in the ghetto.

A Polish physician named Dr. Juliusz Majkowski had made the ghetto passes possible.
Irena had known him since her university
days in Dr. Radlińska's circles, and he was
already part of the resistance cell in contact
with the professor. Dr. Majkowski was also,
conveniently, in charge of the Urban Sanitation Works division in the Warsaw munici-
pality, responsible for combating the spread
beyond the ghetto walls of epidemic diseases
and disposing of infectious materials. He
simply added the four office conspirators —
Irena, Irka, Jadwiga, and Jaga — to the list
of his authorized medical corps employees
and provided them with legitimate epidemic
control passes that allowed them to cross
the checkpoints freely. The Germans were
terrified of being infected with the disease
now raging inside the ghetto, so they left
the job of health and sanitation to more
"dispensable" Polish people.

At the gates leading in and out of the
ghetto, squads of SS men with guns resting
on their hips scrutinized Irena's papers,
peppering her with questions and barking
out orders. She steadied her nerves each
time. In theory, none of them were taking
any great risks coming and going in the
afternoons, once they had finished work in
the welfare offices. After all, the papers were

perfectly legitimate, even if the sanitation job was fiction; and, despite the armband with the Star of David that Irena always put on in solidarity with her friends now when she walked the streets of the ghetto, she was not Jewish.

Except, of course, for that little matter of *why* she was moving back and forth across the border to the ghetto several times a day, coming and going from a different checkpoint in a careful rotation.

Irena's friends were starving inside the ghetto. Prices for smuggled food were astronomical. Jewish people, however, weren't permitted to own more than a few thousand złotych. Then there was the increasing cruelty of their guards and captors. Shots rang out at all hours, though mostly at night now, and there were screams that echoed off the buildings when the city was quiet. "Abuses — wild, bestial 'amusements' — are daily events," underground newspapers in Warsaw grimly reported. In the mornings, the dead lined the streets where they were piled, naked and covered with old newsprint and stones, because the rags they wore had too much value for the living.

Above all, Irena's friends were watching hungry small children die each day from typhus, a disease for which a vaccination existed. Friends were often dying. The lead article in the Polish resistance newspaper *Biuletyn Informacyjny* — the *Information Bulletin* — reported that, in 1941, "the population density [inside the Jewish quarter] is unimaginable. An average of six people live in one room; sometimes, however, there are as many as twenty. . . . This increased crowding has resulted in unspeakable hygienic and sanitary conditions. Hunger and unimaginable misery are now prevalent." The German governor of Warsaw boasted that starvation was official policy: "The Jews will die from hunger and destitution and a cemetery will remain of the Jewish question."

Naturally, Irena was smuggling. Each time, she could only take a little. So the only alternative was to go often. Sometimes it was food, sometimes money. Sometimes, more whimsically, she carried across the handmade children's dolls that one of her and Adam's former University of Warsaw professors, Dr. Witwicki, spent his days in hiding sculpting for the littlest ones at Dr. Korczak's ghetto orphanage. Whenever she could, though, it was vials of vaccine that she hand-delivered to Ala Gołąb-Grynberg and Ewa Rechtman. The price for being caught smuggling at the start was arrest and often concentration camp deportation. By that winter, handbills posted across Warsaw announced that the Germans had upped the ante and declared that the price for helping a Jew — and for giving a Jew any food especially — was summary execution.

Irena's friends inside the ghetto had organized themselves just as quickly and as surely as their friends and compatriots in the city municipal offices. They were all social-minded and idealistic young people who had long bonds of friendship and shared experiences, and they were responding to the needs of the people in front of them. The need was appalling. At a refugee center, an eight-year-old Jewish child went mad one morning. Caregivers carried him away as he screamed, "I want to steal, I want to rob, I want to eat, I want to be a German." On her way to see Adam each afternoon, she had to step carefully over the dead bodies of children.

On the Aryan side, the city social services gave Irena and her coworkers access to resources and a cover. Inside the ghetto, the umbrella organization that drew her friends together in a shared project was, increasingly, a Jewish-run charity for orphans called CENTOS (Centralne Towarzystwo

Opieki nad Sierotami), directed by a Jewish psychology professor and attorney named Dr. Adolf Berman. Irena's friend and classmate Ewa Rechtman was an increasingly important figure at CENTOS. She seemed to know everyone in the ghetto. Ewa ran the youth center at number 16, Sienna Street, in one of the richest and most lively parts of the Jewish quarter, where the ghetto children's hospital and, in time, Dr. Korczak's orphanage were both located.

At the refugee centers and in the hospitals, staff fought a daily battle against disease and starvation. But not everyone in the ghetto was struggling, especially not in the wealthy districts. While nearly half a million ghetto residents weakened from hunger, the "ghetto aristocrats" — rich industrialists, many *Judenrat* council leaders, Jewish police officers, profiteering smugglers, nightclub owners, high-end prostitutes, perhaps a total of ten thousand people — were dancing among the corpses. There were sixty-one cafés and nightclubs in the ghetto, and the "orgy of parties," wrote the ghetto's self-appointed historian Emanuel Ringelblum, "is unconfined." The Sienna Street complex where Ewa worked housed one of those cafés, where the bands played on, accompanied to raucous singing.

It was Ala, though, who knew better than most what those wild parties and nightclubs in the ghetto looked like. Like her husband, Arek, her mother and father were also celebrated Jewish actors and theater directors. But the famous relative in their clan was her cousin by marriage, Weronika — Wiera — Grynberg, better known in Warsaw as the sultry cabaret actress with the stage name Vera Gran. Wiera's sexy come-hither crooning made her a prewar starlet, and in the ghetto by 1941 she was already a legendary star attraction. Gestapo officers, *Judenrat* elite, and SS men gathered in the smoky Café Sztuka at number 2, Leszno Street, a few yards inside the ghetto gates, to listen to Wiera belt out sad love songs. Her duets with Władysław Szpilman, the musician immortalized in Roman Polanski's film *The Pianist* (based on Szpilman's memoirs), drew huge, appreciative crowds, including nightly visits from Ala's mentor, Dr. Hirzsfeld, and from Irena's old friend Józef Zysman, both devoted Café Sztuka regulars. Because the café was only a stone's throw from the relocated Czyste Hospital's main ward, now at number 1, Leszno Street, many of the doctors and nurses went there after-hours, and entertainment and social work were not always unrelated. Entertain-

129

ment put on for the ghetto rich was a primary means of charitable fund-raising inside the walled district. Teenagers at Ala's youth center put on plays for the wealthy residents and donated the ticket revenues to buy black-market food and medicine for children. When Dr. Korczak's orphanage needed a fund-raiser, Ala persuaded her husband's celebrity cousin to sing at a benefit, and as always Wiera drew a huge audience with her alluring talent.

Come with me, a grinning Ala urged Irena. *Spend the night in the ghetto and see what happens at Café Sztuka.* How could Irena resist? At least twice Irena took up her friend's daring invitation to join them. And she did go to Café Sztuka. It was forbidden, of course, and she would have been shot had she been discovered. But Irena risked her life several times a day already. Risking it again to spend the evening with friends — and with Adam — hardly seemed now to make a difference. In 1941, acts of impulsive courage still felt energizing and electric. Personal danger still seemed remote and abstract to Irena.

In the smoky darkness of the café, Wiera crooned away. It was good to see even Adam smiling. Adam did not smile often in the ghetto, although since he had started teaching at one of the youth centers much of his private darkness had lifted. From his volunteer offices at number 24, Elektoralna Street, Adam fed starving street children. He had also joined the Jewish resistance and was secretly circulating underground publications from a nearby apartment building. Both Adam and Ewa had caused Irena sleepless nights. They had each battled their way through despair. But Adam no longer said so often that he wasn't sure life in the ghetto was worth living, and she noticed he was more careful. Now that Ewa was working again, she was better too. It was work that saved them both — teaching and work with the children.

As Irena took it all in that night, the scene unfolding before her in the nightclub left her dumbstruck. Here in the café, the laughing waiters sloshed champagne into waiting glasses. Was it possible there was champagne flowing in the ghetto? Only with the first sip did Irena believe it. All around, in a whirl of commotion, giddy women in elegant prewar finery stumbled past small tables, and someone placed in front of her salmon hors d'oeuvres amid the brittle tinkle of drunken laughter. Somewhere in the crowd she thought she caught sight of another of their old friends, the Jewish actor Jonas Turkow, whose talented wife, Diana Blumenfeld, was another of the café's regular star attractions. She craned her neck for a moment but then she gave up and simply listened. As Wiera sang sentimental old songs about love and longing, Irena could only look on in a kind of nightmare-world wonder. *Everyone is crying,* Irena thought to herself. *Everyone.* But they were crying for all the wrong reasons. When they left, warm fur coats on racks lined the foyer. Outside, on the doorstep in front of them, half-frozen children lay starving. When her hand touched Adam's, he squeezed it tightly. Between them, words weren't necessary.

Part of Wiera's attraction was the power of her voice, but it didn't hurt that Wiera was also beautiful. Underneath that silky exterior, though, Irena saw only a hard-bitten and vicious woman. Wiera Grynberg was one of the ghetto's most determined survivors. Already Irena's friends in the resistance were hearing whispers of the starlet's treachery. Wiera didn't sing only in the ghetto. She was also the star attraction at Café Mocha on Marszałkowska Street, in the Aryan quarter, where she entertained enthusiastic Germans. But she was more than just a bit friendly with the Gestapo. Wiera was rumored to be part of a group of

Jewish people actively collaborating with the Germans to bilk her neighbors of dwindling resources, and in time those betrayals would cost the life of one of the friends in Irena's circle.

Careless debauchery might have been the order of the night in the cafés on Sienna or Leszno, but by day Irena breathed a sigh of relief and gratitude for the teenagers at the youth circles, whose spirit of fairness and justice was nothing short of inspirational. One day that winter Irena arrived breathless at Ewa's office. Her cheeks were red from the bitter wind in that famously cold winter. In the ghetto, a big overcoat was a blessing. Greeting Ewa, Irena smiled broadly and shrugged off her jacket. Quickly she showed Ewa her treasure, and Ewa laughed when she saw what Irena was doing. She had smuggled across the checkpoint that afternoon three doses of typhus vaccine. Sometimes she carried them in a bag with a hollowed-out false bottom. Sometimes, like today, she stuffed them in a padded brassiere with small pockets. Most women had one now. It was a joke in wartime Warsaw that women's breasts had grown dramatically everywhere in the city since the arrival of the Germans.

Clapping her hands with pleasure, Ewa called a spontaneous group meeting and held up the three precious doses. But now they faced a serious moral dilemma. *Who should get the vaccinations?* Ewa asked the group of a dozen young people, most of them adolescents and children. It was a life-or-death decision for the youngsters, despite the high spirits and camaraderie at the center, but Ewa let the children make the decision. With great calm, they made their arguments and quickly decided. The doses, the children agreed, should go to two boys whose parents were dead and who were single-handedly supporting younger siblings, and to the girl in the youth circle who worked the hardest. Working hard with CENTOS meant late-night vigils nursing toddlers who were sick with typhus, and it was perilous.

Each day in the ghetto, Irena saw Ewa and Ala and Adam. And there were two more old friends from Dr. Radlińska's circle who were part of this ghetto camaraderie: Rachela Rosenthal and Józef Zysman. These five fellow students and social workers and their old professor Dr. Korczak were the core of Irena's Jewish circle.

Rachela worked on Pawia Street, just a

block south of Ala, and Irena never saw one without stopping in to say hello to the other. Rachela ran another youth circle there, and her group was one of the largest and liveliest in the ghetto. More than twenty-five thousand people lived on Pawia Street; the district had been a traditional Jewish area before the occupation. Rachela worked with several dozen young volunteers providing makeshift social services. Rachela's charismatic charms and irrepressible sense of fun — even in the ghetto — were part of what made her association especially popular. Her family lived in one of the large apartment buildings in the area and surrounded her with love, and she had a bedrock belief in the power of children's laughter. The mother of a little daughter around the same age as Ala's little Rami, Rachela organized playgroups and makeshift entertainment for the small children in the ghetto. But the street she worked on was one of the grimmest. Pawia Street lent its name to the Gestapo prison located at one of its corners, Pawiak, a veritable house of horrors.

Józef headed up the youth association on Ogrodowa Street, the "midtown" ghetto, just a stone's throw from the headquarters of the much-reviled Jewish police forces, and Irena also delivered smuggled supplies to her old comrade-in-arms from their days in the welfare services. Józef had been a prominent city attorney before the German occupation started, and more than once Irena had waited with him in the halls of the courthouse, each of them leaning up against the stair railings and joking. Józef defended people who were illegally evicted from their homes by unscrupulous landlords, and Irena was one of his favorite witnesses in the social services. She reveled in righting an injustice and could be, Józef told the other attorneys with a laugh, very persuasive. In between the audience with the judges, Józef would tell her about the best nightclubs in Warsaw, just as if she were the kind of girl who might be interested.

The ghetto attorneys now filled Józef with disgust. Many members of the ghetto police were former lawyers and even judges who had taken up law enforcement with a zeal born of self-interest and financial opportunity. Elements within the Jewish police service, which reported to the Gestapo, were notoriously corrupt and brutal. Its officers patrolled the ghetto walls, conscripted residents to meet German slave-labor quotas, and often lined their pockets like thugs, extracting from fellow Jewish residents crippling bribes and ransoms.

So Józef did instead what he could to check their growing power. Along with Adam and Arek, he threw his energies into the Jewish resistance movement slowly taking shape. With a small group of like-minded friends, Józef joined an underground socialist press that circulated newspapers and pamphlets urging citizens to action both inside and outside the ghetto.

Józef's secret cell met for weekly organizational meetings in a garden-tool shed on Leszno Street, out behind the old rectory at St. Mary's. The Catholic church grounds straddled the ghetto wall, and secret passageways led from one side to the other. At the end of the long garden, sitting on overturned garden pots and wistfully fingering cigarettes that could not be lit for fear of detection, the conspirators plotted distribution points and debated the finer aspects of how to carry papers undetected by the Germans. Among their company most days was a small and fearless Polish woman — a woman whom those who knew her best suspected had her finger in everything good that happened in the ghetto. It made Józef's heart light to have his old friend Irena Sendler sitting there with them in the shadows.

CHAPTER 5
CALLING DR. KORCZAK
WARSAW, JANUARY 1942

By the winter of 1941–42 — the beginning of the second year in the ghetto — Irena had another, even more daring project brewing quietly.

When the women in the social services offices on the Aryan side met that winter at Irena's apartment and huddled around the kitchen table, they talked in low, quiet voices while her mother dozed in the bedroom, and were not quite so lighthearted as formerly. They had seen enough by now to know what would happen if they were discovered. Already there had been Gestapo purges inside the welfare offices, and one supervisor had been deported to a concentration camp in the east called Auschwitz. Their urgent evening conversations were increasingly about safety measures. Beyond this room they each used code names now as the network expanded. Jadwiga Deneka chose the name "Kasia." Irena chose "Jolanta." The risks of detection grew with every additional person they drew into the circle, and there were now more than a dozen collaborators. There in the innermost sanctum the old friends and conspirators could at least be frank and honest. But that didn't mean there weren't tensions.

The core group on the Aryan side was still the same small circle of Dr. Radlińska's girls too, all of them sometime smugglers now: Irena Sendler, Irka Schultz, Jadwiga Deneka, Jaga Piotrowska, and her sister Janka Grabowska. Forging requisition orders and ferrying food and medicine into the ghetto were dangerous enough, but the women were making plans for a new kind of covert action, too — action in which the stakes were even higher. The trouble was it would take more than six of them to do it. They would need to bring more people into the network. They would once again have to decide whom they could trust. They would have to decide, especially, about Jan Dobraczyński.

On the question of Jan, there was a brewing disagreement.

Jan Dobraczyński was a senior administrator in one of the offices of the Warsaw welfare department, and his family pedigree should have made him a key partner. His father, Walery, was one of the pioneers of the Warsaw social services movement, right along with Dr. Radlińska and other professors at the Polish Free University. In fact, Jan's father had been the director of the city welfare programs until his retirement in 1932, and after forty years on the job Walery still knew everyone in the social services sector.

His son, though, was rumored to be a different kind of character. Jan had followed in his father's footsteps, joining social services the year after his father's retirement, but his real passions were writing and religion. Jan was not part of any left-wing circles, and he certainly didn't go in for socialism. Unlike the conspirators, he wasn't an acolyte of Dr. Radlińska. Jan was a few months younger than Irena, but he acted middle-aged already: an old-fashioned sort, proud of his traditional values and a devout Catholic. What bothered Irena, though, was Jan's repulsive politics. Jan had been an active member of the far-right ultranationalist party for years — the party behind the odious bench ghetto.

That meant Jan was also anti-Semitic. He believed in Poland for the Poles — and in his mind Poles were, by definition, Catholic. When it came to the "Jewish question," Jan liked to think he was fair-minded. But the fact was, Jan didn't mind saying that anyone could see that there *should* be some restrictions on those people. The Jews just had too much power. They controlled some entire sections of the economy, shutting out Poles, and as far as Jan could see, it had been bound to cause conflict sooner or later. What had the Jews expected?

Although Jan was secretly active in resistance movements, too — because resistance alone united the left and the right in wartime Poland — his German supervisors found him cooperative and reliable. After the first office purges, Jan was promoted to director of the Adult and Child Protective Care Unit, with oversight of more than a dozen different institutions and several thousand welfare recipients. And that was the root of the dilemma. Jan was in a position, Jaga insisted, to be helpful to them. Jaga's work brought her into regular contact with Jan, and they had to think of the possibilities. Irena nodded. That was true. Jan's position was an advantage.

His politics, however, told against him. Irena wasn't sure she could trust him further than they already did with their secrets. Jan knew that they were manipulating the paperwork to thwart German regulations. He even helped them cover their tracks — not because he cared about helping Jewish families but because it was resistance. But Irena and her cell needed something more than Jan looking the other way tactfully. And the question remained: Was Jan Dobraczyński seriously going to risk his own neck to help Jewish people? It was hard for Irena to resist making a little moue of distaste every time she thought of Jan Dobraczyński. But she also noticed the sudden blush that crept up Jaga's cheeks when she defended Jan from these aspersions on his character. Irena studied her friend closely. Was Jaga in love with Jan? It occurred to Irena that the chemistry was obvious. Irena, whose own family described her as "an agnostic with an unruly love life," a married woman in love with a married man, took a relaxed view of these things. There was no judgment. But Jan Dobraczyński?

For weeks Irena debated silently about Jan. She didn't trust him. But she did trust Jaga, and her friend's passionate endorsement meant something. She certainly didn't want to quarrel. In January, things came to a point of crisis.

The chief of the German police called Jan one morning with some typically imperious orders. The chief wanted a roundup of street children on the Aryan side of the city. The social services divisions could either get these urchins off the streets permanently, or the police would see the verminous youth exterminated. Typhus was decimating the ghetto, and it was only a matter of time before the epidemic spread farther, beyond the walled quarter. These little lice-covered beggars were likely carriers. The disease was already killing more than a few Germans. Delouse the children and get them off my streets once and for all: those were the chief's instructions. Otherwise, the chief would see to it that the Germans handled it. Jan didn't like to think about how the Nazis handled things.

Jan's job was to oversee the placement of Polish orphans and Polish street children in local institutions. His office completed intake interviews and, most important, reviewed birth certificates and baptismal records to document their family histories. Children with the correct paperwork came and went in a tidy fashion, sent onward to safe places across the city. Jewish children had no business being outside the ghetto and were not eligible for services.

143

The frontline task of locating and caring for Warsaw's children, however, fell to social workers in the field offices — and especially to young women like Jaga Piotrowska and Jadwiga Deneka. Jan, in fact, spent a good part of his day far from the welfare offices, working surreptitiously for the Polish resistance. Officially the Germans insisted that he work long hours. "For an absurdly low salary you had to be stuck in the office ten hours," he complained. But Jan quickly found a way around it. "Of course I was sitting not there for ten hours: I tried to be in the office at the beginning and at the end of the work day." What he did in between, the Germans never seemed to notice.

Jan passed the job along to the field offices, and Jaga swiftly got word back to Irena and the others. Together their team swept the city and rounded up the child beggars. Street urchins were taken in truckloads to one of the city shelters, and the women's plan was to clean them up, get them checked over by the doctors, and send them along — with Jan's stamp of approval as orphan placement director — to one of the care homes where they maintained regular contacts as social workers.

Across Warsaw, the streets were filled with hungry children. Deprivation was not confined to the ghetto. Orphans and starvation were part of the grim reality of wartime. Since the start of the occupation, the number of abandoned or orphaned youngsters they were placing in the city's care institutions had doubled. Whereas they used to send six hundred youngsters a year to the Father Boduen children's home, one of the charitable church institutions Jaga worked with most closely, the number was now more than twelve hundred. Not all of those extra six hundred children, though, were strictly speaking Catholic.

There were, one might say, periodic "irregularities" — times when the paperwork might get a bit inventive. Faking the welfare files to get social benefits for poor Jewish families, the original plan of Irena and her office coworkers, was substantially harder once the Jewish families were trapped inside the ghetto and any aid had to be smuggled across the checkpoints. Increasingly, Irena's team of conspirators was working on new ways to find the elusive documents needed to "complete" those false files and to help the Jewish people who were brave enough to risk living on the Aryan side of the city create a "Polish" identity. That mostly meant locating blank or forged birth certificates, and there were different inventive approaches. One of the simplest methods was also the saddest. When a Christian child died in one of the orphanages, the key thing was to make sure that the death was never reported. The name and registry number were passed along instead, to give a new identity and a place to a Jewish foundling.

Chances to make a ghoulish swap like this required timing and patience. Now, on this winter afternoon, dozens of skinny little children's bodies filled the room, boys and girls caught up in the sweep of street beggars. In wartime, children didn't giggle or scream with laughter, especially not these children. Homeless orphans lived and died wild on the streets of Warsaw's Aryan district, too, and these were the hardy survivors.

Irena moved among them with her calm and quiet voice, reassuring. She was a tiny and trim person, hardly bigger than some of the boys herself. But she was an organizational wonder. The women had a smooth system operating: one by one the girls in the office would cut the children's hair, collect their clothes, and send them off for a good lye-soap washing. The smell of the harsh soap stung painfully, and the room was bitterly cold, but the children were eerily quiet.

Jaga and Irena knew that they would find among these children some boys whose naked, shivering bodies betrayed their dangerous secret. Circumcision was a death sentence. Blackmailers and thugs stopped on the street any men or boys they guessed might be Jewish and ordered them to reveal their penises for inspection, often with sadistic consequences. There would naturally be a handful of Jewish children in a roundup of street waifs. The most desperate ghetto children risked their lives to cross the wall, hoping to beg or smuggle enough to feed themselves and often their families. What the women hadn't been prepared for was the fact that nearly half of the dozens of street children that day were Jewish. Jaga's stricken face told the whole story: this was a disaster.

The children arrived in streams all day, one truckload after another, and when the German police arrived unannounced to "supervise" the baths and delousing of the first arrivals, Irena and Jaga exchanged frantic glances. Jaga gestured toward the back door and smoothed her dress to calmly greet the German arrivals. Irena swiftly nodded. Two little circumcised boys were quickly helped to disappear out through the service entrance. Jaga ran interference with soft smiles and devout protestations. *Take them to my parents' house,* she whispered urgently before turning. *Are you certain?* Jaga shrugged. It was a gesture that said: *What's the other option?*

The two frightened children, without family left to care for them, would pass the night in a house on Lekarska Street where Jaga lived with her parents, Marian and Celina; her sister Wanda; her husband, Janusz; and their small daughter, Hana. It was unthinkably brazen. Jaga's house — just a stone's throw from the German war hospital and the *Volksdeutsche* medical housing — was on a street that swarmed night and day with sentries.

But they couldn't take all these children home. Not any of them could risk that. When the trucks stopped coming that afternoon, the final tally included thirty-two unmistakably Jewish children. What were they going to do with them? They couldn't turn them over to the Germans. Should they tell Jan the truth? *It's come to this,* Irena realized grimly. Jaga seemed so certain that Jan's heart was in the right place. Still Irena hesitated. She knew that her friend didn't understand this suspicion.

In the end, what was the alternative? They would have to find these children safe places to disappear, and that depended on Jan, as section director, helping. Thirty-two youngsters were too many to disappear through a back entrance in an occupied city. Finding dozens of forged *Kennkarte* — the all-important German-issued identity cards — at a moment's notice was impossible. Saving these children would mean doing it without official documents, and that meant they would need Jan's silence and co-operation. There was no way around it. They would have to tell Jan, and they agreed that Jaga would do the talking.

Jan was in torment when he understood what Jaga wanted. There was nothing he wanted more than to please Jaga. He also understood clearly enough what it would mean if the Germans came and picked up the urchins. Jan crossly thought to himself that he didn't need Irena to explain it to him. The penalty for leaving the ghetto was execution, and these children had been found on the Aryan side of the city. Yes, he knew that. But it was also summary execution for any gentile who helped them. And this, in his opinion, was a pretty harebrained operation.

Ultimately, it was up to Jan to make the final decision. He was the one to whom the police chief had given the orders. The chief

149

would ask for a report from him. If there had just been one or two children, it might have been different, Jan told himself. That he might have risked, but this was too many. Surely the women could see that? He implored Jaga to understand. He wasn't willing to authorize thirty-two doomed orphanage transfers, not when the Germans were holding him responsible for this operation. He wasn't willing to ask the orphanage directors — old friends of his father and his family — to take on so many children without Aryan papers.

When he made the telephone call, he told the German supervisor the truth. Yes, there *were* Jewish children. Dozens of them. When he set the receiver down afterward, there was every reason for his hands to be shaking. The German was a bastard. Even as Germans went, he was a bastard. He might still come and shoot them all dead in the street just for the hell of it too. But Jan had done the best he could. In theory, they had come to an arrangement. It had not come cheaply. Jan kept quiet about that part of things. But there were no free passes with the Germans. Jan had twenty-four hours. He would have to pull some strings and he would have to call the old doctor. He already knew that Irena was going to be

150

furious. They had to smuggle the children back *into* the ghetto.

Jan's aging father was a friend of the "old doctor," Dr. Janusz Korczak, the legendary educator and children's rights activist in Poland, who was now the director of the crowded ghetto orphanage set up next door to Ewa Rechtman's youth circle. But Ewa wasn't the only one in their circle with a soft spot for the kindly doctor. All of Dr. Radlińska's girls had admired the doctor since their early days on the campus of the Polish Free University, where Dr. Korczak lectured alongside the professor. Jadwiga Deneka had trained in one of his innovative schools before the war and thought of him as her dearest mentor. Ala Gołąb-Grynberg pulled family strings and even tolerated her cousin Wiera to raise money for the doctor's children. And Irena loved both the doctor and the eager little people who crowded around her excitedly when, on her daily trips in and out of the ghetto, she smuggled across for them small presents of candy or the whimsical Jewish dolls that Dr. Witwicki made for them according to the children's elaborate orders. Dr. Korczak was no stranger to any of them. But for Irena that would never make what happened any better.

In the winter of 1941–42, entering the ghetto wasn't strictly necessary to get a message to the doctor. Telephones in and out of the ghetto still worked in a few places — an astonishing but fortuitous oversight that allowed for more than one daring rescue operation. Jan could only hope the doctor would help him. He needed someplace to send the children. "[At] my request," Jan said, "my father telephoned him." If Jan could get the children back over the wall without the guards shooting them all, would the doctor agree to take the orphans? Dr. Korczak consented. The ghetto was not a place of choices either.

They had just a few hours to plan the perilous operation. There was a breach in the wall that week in the Muranów district, unless the Germans had already closed it. If they had, no matter: there would be another. The ghetto orphans knew exactly where the holes were: the would-be rescuers simply had to ask the children.

Irena could not believe what Jan was telling her. She cursed herself silently. She should have found another solution. He was going to send children back into the ghetto? She was in and out of that hellhole three, four times daily, and she would never agree to this. Only someone who had no idea what happened there would jump at such a cowardly, pathetic nonsolution. There were hard, bitter recriminations. Irena confessed later that it was a terrible quarrel. Jan was reeling. She had not minced words with him in her anger.

But Jan had made his deal with the German inspector.

The predawn hours, under cover of darkness, would have been a better time for this kind of stealth operation. But after curfew the patrols on the streets had shoot-to-kill orders. Jan knew that he would have to help the children crawl back through a breach in the wall that evening, as the last anxious residents rushed for home and cover before the streets went dangerously quiet. On the other side, Dr. Korczak assured Jan, someone from the orphanage would wait to meet them. Jan would go to the wall with the children himself. If he were honest with himself, his conscience was already nagging at him. He knew he could not expect any sympathy from Irena. Beside herself with disgust, she wanted nothing to do with Jan's operation.

On the street, the children edged close to him. Jan listened for every noise. Footsteps now could portend disaster. In the snow, everything seemed louder, and the children's breath in the cold air sent up cloudy wisps of vapor. In his gloves, Jan could feel his fingertips growing cold and tried to rub them in his pockets. His head ached from listening, and when the code word that they had been waiting for came back in a young boy's voice, Jan caught his breath involuntarily. He understood for the first time that it was, on the other side of the wall, a children's operation. There was a little scuffle and rattle, and then a small passageway was cleared in an instant. The children did not wait for his instructions. One by one, without hesitation, the street children smiled their tired good-byes and wriggled past him into that other world. There was the girl with the bright hair ribbon. *Good-bye, Mr. Dobraczyński,* she whispered. There was the small boy who stumbled for an instant in the outsize shoes someone had found for him. And the cheeky pair of brothers whom he did not doubt would be back over the wall before the week was over. He waited to hear their quiet footsteps on the other side. "A few minutes before curfew," Jan said, "I personally escorted the children to the ghetto wall. Each one went through, and thus they disappeared from the official list of young beggars."

The operation succeeded. When Irena checked up on them the next day at the ghetto orphanage, the old doctor assured her that the children had made it to him safely. She should have been relieved, she knew. She tried to understand the logic of Jan's decision. But for Irena this was defeat on the deepest level. Never again would she sit by while children were returned to the ghetto. In the months to come, she would take new, bolder measures. She would smuggle more food and medicine. She would smuggle faster. She and Irka Schultz would manage to get over a thousand doses of vaccine into the walled quarter. Other friends and coworkers in her ever-growing and ever-bolder relief network — Jaga Piotrowska included — would smuggle in another five thousand. She would carry in wads of cash rolled in her undergarments and medicine in her workbag with the false bottom. Already, people throughout the Jewish quarter whispered from ear to ear that Irena — whom most knew only by her secret code name, "Jolanta" — was the woman who could manage anything.

Irena would work now even more fever-

ishly. And she would not tell Jan
Dobraczyński what she was planning.

CHAPTER 6
GHETTO JUGGERNAUT
WARSAW, 1941–1942

Irena's boss Irka Schultz walked slowly away from the ghetto checkpoint. Relief flooded over her. It was always like this. Capricious, cruel things happened there at the gates, and she counted herself lucky any afternoon when she didn't witness something that made her heart ache afterward for hours. Somewhere in the distance a gunshot rang out. A dog barked. A streetcar rattled. All the sounds of life in occupied Warsaw. But when she heard the sound of a manhole cover rattling underfoot, Irka jumped. It wasn't that the sound was unfamiliar; she just knew heartache that afternoon was coming after all.

The noise came again, the tinny sound of quiet scraping and a small child sniffling disconsolately. Looking quickly around her, Irka fell to her knees. She peeled off her gloves to get a better grip and lifted up the cover. The dirty ice from the street spread patches of damp on her skirt.

Irka knew that there was only one reason anyone would be crawling along the city sewers: Jewish street children and ghetto smugglers made their treacherous commute to the Aryan side in search of food through these underground canals.

Irka peered inside. The stench made her eyes water, and she turned away for a moment. When she looked back, a small child's face, etched with fear and hunger, peered back up at her. The little girl had tightly combed blond hair and big blue eyes, but she was more than half-starved and now completely filthy. The child was too frail to climb out of the hole alone, and struggled. Irka tugged her up gently and hissed quietly into the sewer to see if anyone else would follow. *Witaj! Czy jest tu ktoś? Hello! Is anyone there?*

But the girl was alone. Perhaps she had been left behind for moving too slowly. Irka's heart caught when she saw a scrap of paper pinned to the girl's dress with a thin sewing needle. On it, in a shaky hand, was written a single digit — the child's age — a telegraphic mother's plea for someone, some stranger, to help her daughter. That detail would stay with Irka always.

Irka could see that the girl was weak. But

she would have to walk at least a little bit of the way. Anti-Semitic hooligans and petty blackmailers prowled the areas near the ghetto, looking for anyone who looked desperate or famished enough to be Jewish. Jews on the Aryan side were hopelessly vulnerable to extortion. *Stay calm,* Irka urged herself. Walk slowly. Fear was the biggest tell of all. Parents who sent their children out of the ghetto reminded them urgently to wear the best disguise of all: happy faces. She smiled a bright, fake smile at the little girl and drew her fingers up along her cheeks in a silent gesture. Then she put a finger to her lips. *Quiet.* The child's eyes grew wider.

As they moved toward the shadows of a side street, Irka hurriedly considered. The girl needed a doctor. Irena could feel how hot and thin the girl's hand was, and she tried not to hold it too tightly. *Catastrophic.* The word floated to mind and hung there stubbornly. That meant the orphanage on Nowogrodzka Street was the only option. There were physicians on staff.

Irena Sendler had put a system in place already for this kind of situation. It wasn't the first time they had done this. They discovered wasted Jewish foundlings on the wrong side of the wall with depressing regularity, and there was a code. She would clean the little girl up as best she could and get word to Irena. Then Irka would pick up the telephone and ring the Father Boduen children's home. This time, perhaps, she would ask her friend Władysława, *Can I stop by today to drop off that coat I borrowed? Today* meant it was an emergency.

By the time Jan Dobraczyński returned the children to the ghetto, the office conspirators were almost certainly already placing Jewish children living wild on the Aryan side of the city with local Polish foster families and in citywide care institutions as the opportunity and the illegal paperwork presented itself. Sometime early in the winter of 1941–42 they started taking even more daring and organized action. This was what Irena had been planning.

Conditions in the ghetto were deteriorating precipitously that winter. Everyone that year agreed that few winters in recent memory had ever been so cold or unforgiving. And that meant that, by the time the early spring arrived in Warsaw in 1942, Irena Sendler was no longer occasionally helping Jewish families. She and her cell were systematically helping Jews locate the paperwork that they needed to "disappear" into the city. In the autumn of 1941, a lucky break had shown them a new way to do it. The women had made contact with a local priest in the distant city of Lwów whose parish church had burned, along with all its records. The priest offered to give them his remaining cache of blank birth certificates, which now could not be cross-checked by German authorities. Irka had made the dangerous journey to fetch them and carried them back on the train, tucked in an old valise she tried to carry lightly. If the women could find a regular supply of blank documents, they had a solution. Lwów was about to have a birthrate explosion.

That winter the women used a few of the precious blank certificates from Lwów to save an old friend and his family. Dr. Witwicki and his family were still in hiding, and new Polish documents would take him out of constant danger. Irena was still smuggling into the ghetto the professor's handmade dolls for the children, sculpted in a quiet room on Brzozowa Street in the Old Town. Irena had carried a new stash of dolls to Dr. Korczak's ghetto orphanage especially, for the littlest of Jan Dobraczyński's street children. She still fretted about those thirty-two youngsters, and by now she knew all their names and faces.

Irena also badgered her friends in the ghetto — Adam, Ewa, Rachela, Józef, Ala — to flee and go into hiding on the Aryan side. Death stalked the ghetto. She would find them papers; she would find safe houses. She implored them all now. When they shook their heads sadly, Irena couldn't hide her frustration and worry. *It's too risky to hide a Jew, Irena,* Ewa told her over and over. Life was not so different now — not really, Ewa insisted. It was just the same work as on the Aryan side, where there were also hungry, homeless youngsters. "The children all just need a little heart and a lot of bread," said Ewa. Irena doggedly tried to wear her down, to convince her. But Ewa would not risk the lives of her friends. Finally, Ewa was firm with her friend. "Please don't ask me," she pleaded with Irena, squeezing her friend's hand kindly. "I won't stay with you — I can't endanger you like that."

With Adam the conversations were even more maddening. Adam was angry and impassioned. All around him were death and suffering. Crazed SS men used pedestrians for target practice. Bodies lined the ghetto streets like useless litter each morning. Men wept in the streets, begging. All this, and the Poles hated Jews nearly as much as the Germans. Irena wanted him to hide among them? She tried to reason with him, but everything just came out sounding defensive, and Adam retreated from her touch. Could their love survive this? The thought nagged at her. It would break her heart to lose Adam. He drew back into himself and his beloved books. He retreated to the past, trying to find answers somewhere in the dry histories of ancient empires for the nightmare present. When she tried to embrace him, tried to touch his arm or smooth his shirt collar, he turned away brusquely, and there was a small part of her that wondered, too: Was it only the ghetto standing between them? Or did he think in those moments of his Jewish wife and his mother's sense of his failure? Would the fact that he was Jewish and she was "Aryan" divide them from each other, as the occupiers had always intended? Guilt and shame stalked every conscience inside these hellish walls. Children whimpered on the streets for a crumb of bread in front of the shops, and there was no choice if one had bread in one's pocket but to avert one's eyes in horror and walk on. Survival depended on it. But one knew shame in that moment.

Besides, Adam said, he could not leave the youth center. Irena knew it was his trump card, his way of ending their argument. There was nothing she could say. Adam's circle cared for the sickest and littlest of the ghetto orphans, and, like Ala's colleague Dr. Landau, the lecturer at Ala's clinic's secret medical classes, Adam also passionately believed he was fighting on a battlefield in a war against barbarity. His safety, Adam reminded Irena gently, didn't matter. She was risking her life daily for the street children. She was risking her life smuggling vaccines into the ghetto. If he asked her to stay at home to avoid the danger, would she? She knew she would not. So did Adam.

So, instead, Irena and her friends on both sides of the wall threw themselves into a new and even more stunningly courageous mission. Irena would never again let a child be returned to the ghetto. They would find safe homes on the Aryan side for scores of Jewish children. In the spring of 1942, an estimated four thousand children lived alone on the streets of the Aryan side, and two thousand of them were Jewish.

Some of the children on the Aryan side were homeless orphans trying to survive alone by begging and stealing. But desperate families were already sending well-loved but starving children across the wall —

children like the little girl whom Irka Schultz discovered that afternoon in a sewer manhole. Sometimes parents came with them, and for a time families tried to hide together. More often than not, the parents perished, shot in the roundups or at the camps later. Sometimes a quiet sense of duty tore apart families sooner. Some family members were easier to save than others. It was a fact of life in the Jewish quarter. Who could abandon one's aging parents? They could not make the dangerous passage across the walls. Children who could walk were sent out alone by stricken parents or guided out by smugglers into the hands of friends or strangers. Hundreds of children made that frightening passage through the sewers. In 1942, Wanda Ziemska was eight years old when she stepped into the murky waters. "Above the entrance to the sewer, I said good-bye to Father, who stayed behind," she remembered. "The journey through the sewers was quite complicated. At times it looked like a dirty river. . . . I can remember how hard it was for me to climb out of the sewer — I couldn't reach from one rung to another." When Irena heard of children in danger and hiding on the Aryan side, she now had daring solutions.

Soon, Irena would go one step further. What would be the fate of the children who were already orphaned *inside* the ghetto? Toddlers could not flee on their own initiative. There were no parents left to send them. She saw these children every day at Adam's youth circle. And no matter how hard Adam worked to save them, he was failing. There was too much hunger and disease for small bodies.

So Adam and Irena did the obvious. They started taking orphans out of the ghetto sometime that winter. With her epidemic control pass, it wasn't even illegal if the child were desperately ill. Youngsters with a tuberculosis death sentence could be transported by ambulance to one of the remaining Jewish sanatoriums in Otwock. Once again she was walking in her father's footsteps. And sometimes a cough might not be tuberculosis, and a child would disappear into a friend's home in their old village. If she could not save Adam, together at least they could save a few of these children.

If the false cases were discovered, the risks, of course, were colossal. Giving a Jewish child a piece of bread meant death — for both the giver and the receiver. Sending a child out of the ghetto to hide with a Polish family came at the price of a bullet to the head on a street corner. But the draconian consequences also meant, as Irena could not help but observe, that one might as well do more than just smuggle in vaccines. You could die only once, and she and Adam were united at least in action.

In time, there would be myriad routes in and out of the ghetto, and Irena would employ them all to smuggle out Jewish children. On the day Irka discovered the little girl in the Warsaw sewer, the women had already set up one of their first protocols in cooperation with the Father Boduen Catholic children's home. It was a simple extension of their work in the social welfare offices, and Jaga Piotrowska and Irka Schultz were the network's front women in this operation.

There were two indispensable new partners by early 1942. The first was a warm and pretty young woman named Władysława — Władka — Marynowska. Friends marveled at how Władka's upswept tumble of bright blond hair gave her the air of a romantic heroine, and in every photograph of her she is smiling. Władka was also that year the mother of a sturdy little boy, and she worked as a senior housemother and social worker at the Father Boduen chil-

167

dren's home for Polish infants, toddlers, and homeless mothers. Władka's job was to vet prospective foster parents, and that meant that she knew better than anyone how to find caregivers who were willing to take in children for the customary boarding fee the city offered.

Drawing Władka into their conspiracy was an easy decision, born of necessity. One did not draw friends lightly into this network, especially not friends with small children — not if one could help it. And Władka was an old friend already. But that winter the women were faced with a crisis: they had a Jewish child who needed a home, and there was a desperate shortage of false identity papers. In hushed and urgent tones, Irena and Irka considered. Irka fretted. She trusted Władka. More than that, she trusted Irena's judgment. But the Gestapo was already watching the Father Boduen children's home, and Irka worried that the risks were too great. *But will the child be safe there, Irena?* The question hung in the air. Irena lived with that question always. "You can be calm about the child," came Irena's steady reply. "Władka Marynowska is there." Irka nodded and reached for her coat. She would go now and make the invitation.

It was a short walk from the social welfare office on Złota Street to the orphanage. Irka walked briskly. Her path to Nowogrodzka Street took her south only a few blocks. The ghetto checkpoint where Złota and Twarda Streets met had been sealed off with bricks and barbed wire in 1941, when the ghetto boundary was moved northward. The shifting wall was a constant presence. Like Irena and Jaga and Jadwiga, Irka was still in and out of the ghetto several times a day, and this toddler was one of "hers." It was hard not to feel protective. The orphanage was an imposing brick building, and she was still planning what she would say as she climbed the steps, but she was saved from further agonizing when Władka greeted her with a friendly hello. Would Władka take a walk with her? Władka's eyes narrowed intelligently. Anything was better than trying to talk in a building where they all knew Gestapo spies were planted.

Irka knew she could trust Władka. Or she thought she could. But she still hesitated. The war placed all sorts of decent people in impossible positions. Władka waited. Irka took a deep breath. *There's a toddler . . .* She faltered. *There are several children. We need to place them in care . . .* Władka brightened. *Of course, Irka, it is no problem.*

Just take them to the office and —

Irka had taken a deep breath and now interrupted: *Władka, there are no papers.* Then she waited. There. It was done. Only a fool could misunderstand the situation, and nothing about Władka Marynowska was foolish. An undocumented child was almost certainly Jewish. Władka considered. She kicked a bit of melting ice with her boot and then looked up to the sky. She saw the wisps of clouds. Perhaps she thought of her own little boy, Andrzej. She had to think of his safety. The Gestapo was all around her. A spy could be a wet nurse or a desperate mother. Old friends could even be provocateurs in this crazy world of the occupation. The question was not whether she wished to help but whether she could trust Irka. She turned and looked at her friend, and Irka looked back at her. Then Władka took a deep breath. *Yes, I will take the child.* Irka Schultz took a deep breath also. *Thank you.*

"I didn't ask for any details," Władka said later. "She asked me to take those children and to find them a safe home in a foster family. I agreed to help without any questions." Turning toward the orphanage, Władka tilted her head. *I should get back. Come another time, and we can discuss how we make placements.*

170

When Irena returned, she brought with her another contact, a woman whom she explained might sometimes bring the children to Władka. The new contact was a twenty-six-year-old woman, and her name, Irka said, was Sonia. But "Sonia" was the code name of a Polish nurse named Helena Szeszko, one of the newest additions to Irena Sendler's growing network.

Ala Gołąb-Grynberg was the one who had drawn Helena into their conspiracy. Helena Szeszko was a senior operative in a resistance cell in the medical underground. Ala was the chief nurse in the ghetto. They had worked together, hand in glove, for months already. Across the city, there were dozens of small cells, each working in secrecy and isolation. Slowly those circles were finding points of connection.

The need for a medical underground was urgent. After all, neither sick Jews hiding on the Aryan side nor wounded resistance operatives caught in the ghetto could check themselves into local hospitals, and everywhere in the Jewish quarter the need for supplies was desperate. Another old friend was at the heart of this sister network: one of its leaders was Dr. Juliusz Majkowski in the infectious disease offices. Some of his epidemic control passes had gone to Irena,

Irka, Jaga, and Jadwiga. But one of them had gone to Helena. That meant that Helena, too, could come and go from the ghetto. And she could take sick Jewish children and hidden supplies with her in the municipal ambulances.

Władka knew nothing of this. She knew nothing of this until years after. Knowing was dangerous. "It was enough to know that [Irka] had to take the Jewish children out of the ghetto and put them in a safe place," she said. And it was enough to know that "Sonia" — and sometimes also Ala Gołąb-Grynberg — would appear at her door at a moment's notice. Ala's husband, Arek, was still in and out of the ghetto, working with the Jewish resistance, and his underground contacts — along with Ala's senior position at the *Judenrat* — meant that Ala, too, could slip in and out of the ghetto anytime she needed. Sometimes, Ala's daughter remembers today, her mother took the little girl with her on these trips into that other world. "My mother took me out," she says. "I don't remember how. I was out a couple of times coming and going." But mostly Ala went alone.

At the orphanage the women established a code. There was a telephone at the Father Boduen children's home, and when someone rang Władka, the conversations were nothing but frivolous girl talk. They chatted idly about borrowing skirts or scarves. They would make plans to come for tea or check in on ailing mothers. There would be a day and a time. And there would always be something about color. Color and clothing was how the right child could be identified — now and later. Władka kept a careful log of the clothes and the children's appearances, especially the ones who came to her without papers. How else, after the war, would their parents find them? Władka's simple notations would very quickly inspire in Irena something bold and amazing. Władka's modest accounting of the waifs and orphans who passed through her care was almost certainly the reason Irena herself now kept a master list of all the children.

Healthy children who were fair-haired and blue-eyed or those who didn't look stereotypically Jewish could be integrated into the life of the orphanage once the appropriate false documents were located and an official registry number could be given. False documents were one of Helena Szeszko's specialities. Helena and her husband, Leon, got their start in the underground setting up a cell to forge identity papers. "Polish"-looking children weren't the ones who gave

Irena Sendler the nightmares that were already starting to plague her sleep by 1942. Once these children were safely on the Aryan side, saving them was not yet so uncertain. Getting out took courage. And sometimes the children were consummate actors. Ala came from a famous theatrical family. Now she coached children at playing sick in order to save them. More often, though, on their perilous ambulance rides with hidden children, Ala and Helena counted on the German fear of infection and hid the youngster under piles of dirty rags or inside already occupied coffins. That was bad enough, but not what gave Irena night terrors. What jolted her awake at night were dreams about the children with "bad" Semitic features.

Irena's fears were not unfounded. These children couldn't be seen even for an instant on the Aryan side and arrived at the orphanage in burlap sacks slung over a workman's shoulders, delivered to the back door as laundry or potatoes. For these arrivals Władka had to be sure a foster family was ready to take the children instantly and keep them constantly quiet and hidden. These youngsters were rarely at the Father Boduen children's home for more than a few hours. Sometimes they came with Helena, sometimes with Irka or Ala, and sometimes — as the number of children grew in the spring of 1942 — with Jaga Piotrowska and Jadwiga Deneka.

When these children could not be placed instantly, the women had no choice but to take desperate chances and keep them in their own homes until there were arrangements. Irena, Jaga, Jadwiga, and Władka all hid children in their apartments sometimes. At Władka's, her elementary school–age son, Andrzej, had the grave responsibility of helping his mother care for desperately ill younger children. Today, Andrzej is a distinguished elderly gentleman with a warm smile and gracious manner still living in Warsaw. He remembers those days with his mother and how his job as a small boy was taking the young Jewish hideouts to the bathroom down the hall, where someone had to watch them carefully at the toilet. Little bodies coming back from the brink of starvation, he says, with the grim expression of someone who remembers, could suffer from appalling gastric troubles.

The children came and went from the Father Boduen children's home, and with every passing day the Gestapo grew more suspicious. German agents combed Władka's official records, searching for any scrap of evidence. But the real records were never in the file cabinets. Władka would never be so foolish. When the paperwork frustrated them, the Gestapo thugs in their midst held guns to Władka's head in the corridor and bullied all the staff with threats of mass executions. By the spring of 1942, their network grew and so did the surveillance. The children who came and went officially were carefully monitored and their paperwork scrutinized by the occupiers. But it only meant, Irena stubbornly concluded, that more of the children would have to come and go, at ever greater risk, completely off the record.

Although the Gestapo didn't know it yet, it was Irena's network they were hunting. Irena was the tactical commander of this growing citizens' army, which now included nearly two dozen people drawn together from the political underground, the welfare offices, and the Jewish community. The risks with that number of people were enormous — and no one was in more danger than Irena.

When Irena's colleague Irka Schultz discovered the little girl in the sewer, it should have all been easy. But the entire operation nearly crumbled because of another risk they had not weighed carefully enough. The child had "good" looks. Irka passed the emergency code along to Irena and then to Władka. The child needed medical attention quickly, and the orphanage had staff doctors. Because the fair-haired toddler looked so quintessentially Polish, Irena and Irka decided to risk going through legitimate channels at the Father Boduen children's home.

The women quickly agreed on a plan and a story. Irka would take the child to the orphanage and hand her over to the clerk at reception. There would have to be a formal report to the German police, notifying them of a foundling, and Irka would write in her careful hand how she, a social worker, in nothing more than the course of her duties, had chanced upon the little girl in a stairwell somewhere far from the Jewish quarter. When an investigation turned up nothing, the child would be allowed to stay at the orphanage. After all, the world was full of war orphans.

The plan, however, went terribly wrong from the first moment. In the orphanage clinic, a brusque nurse took the little girl away and firmly pointed Irka to a hard chair set far back from the doorway. *Wait here, Pani.* Irka sat. Paperwork, she supposed.

With the Germans, there was always more paperwork. What Irka could not know was that, behind closed doors, her life hung in the balance. The duty physician had taken one good look at this famished child and she was already on the phone with the police, demanding they take action. The doctor never guessed the child was Jewish. She guessed instead that Irka was a child abuser and the little girl's unwed mother. When a Polish policeman arrived to escort her to the station around the corner, Irka was dumbstruck and left reeling.

How do you prove you are not a child's mother? Irka tried asking the policeman. She desperately needed to know the answer. Irka insisted all afternoon that the child was not her own. She explained that she had found her. No one there, the police informed her tartly, believed that story. Irka was flummoxed. And soon she started to be frightened. She could hardly tell the truth. It would be a certain death sentence for her and the toddler. Helping a Jewish child meant execution, and it was obvious to anyone where a child climbing out of a sewer had come from.

They went around and around in circles. At last, the officer snapped shut his folder and stood up, smoothing out his jacket.

There will be a thorough investigation, Pani Schultz, the bored officer warned her. *Until then . . .* He didn't need to explain. He simply slammed the door shut behind him. Irka's head sunk into her hands at the thought of what it all meant. The child would be interviewed. It was almost certain that the little girl would betray her unwittingly by speaking some word or another in Yiddish. She was a child. She couldn't possibly know better. Irka lay awake on the hard cell bed all that night thinking about just one thing. Disaster was coming: How was she going to get a message to Irena?

When a young boy thrust the scribbled message toward her and slipped off quickly, Irena knew it was bad news. Władka had heard about some trouble at the clinic. For days, as the court date loomed, the women in the office network racked their brains to come up with some way to save Irka from a prison sentence that was beginning to look increasingly certain. It wasn't just that prison was a brutal place. Convicted felons were fodder for the concentration camps. At last Irena had to admit defeat. There was only one solution that she could see, and it was one that would endanger all of them. Irena and her contacts at the orphanage would have to take the indignant physician

179

into their confidence as their newest, unwitting conspirator. The orphanage's director was enlisted to explain to the doctor that Irka was not the one who had brutalized this child. It was the ghetto.

The doctor, aghast, immediately agreed to drop the charges, and the courageous director ran interference with the police, blithely offering false testimony. With an apologetic shrug, she explained that, anyhow, the evidence had gone missing. The child's real mother had come to fetch the toddler, and who knew where they had gone? Home somewhere, surely. The ruse worked — because what else could the police do, really? — but Irena knew this was a lose-lose proposition. It all looked very suspicious, and it created a good deal of talk and attention. Talk and attention were dangerous. Now Irena had one more unwitting conspirator to manage and a high-risk operation that was perilously close to being an open secret. They couldn't go on like this. She needed to find a safer means of transferring children to city orphanages. The transfers had to happen higher up the chain.

It also had to happen urgently. A new fear was taking grip inside the ghetto. On her visits to see Ala on Smocza Street, Ala told her now of the terrible rumors reaching her contacts in the underground. Whispered reports were spreading in Warsaw, with news of death in the east. In January, a thirty-year-old Jewish man named Szlama Ber Winer, who had escaped a camp at a place called Chełmno, arrived in the city with terrifying stories. He told of how thousands were murdered in the forest, gassed together in long containers, and his listeners wept to hear him bear witness to the agonized screams of fathers made to piss on the open graves of their families and then made to lie down among them to be executed in a hail of gunfire. But there were whispers, too, whispers that soon the Germans would round up all the children under the age of twelve and take them to a special camp, a city of children. Many in the Jewish quarter could not believe these tales were anything except crazy rumors. Those who did believe them — young men like Adam — began talking about armed Jewish resistance, and families started making immediate plans to get their sons and daughters out of the district. It was no coincidence that, by the spring of 1942, the number of children that Irena and her conspirators were smuggling out of the ghetto was exploding.

Irena knew she would have to bring still more people into the secret. The Father Boduen children's home was just one of the social welfare institutions and orphanages she was using to place children, but the operation at the home needed to be streamlined and expanded. She would also need to find other ways to place children in foster families, through other underground connections. One person had the power to make this happen: the social welfare administrator Jan Dobraczyński, the man whose politics Irena questioned.

Jan Dobraczyński had balked at the danger before and returned dozens of children to the ghetto. And how could she trust a man with politics so different from her own, a man with anti-Semitic feelings? Jaga tried to remind Irena that she was wrong in her judgment of Jan. He was guided by his Catholic faith, and he did not lack a moral compass, even if he and Irena could not agree on which direction true north rested. Jan was as committed as any of them to the underground Polish state that they were all building. Jaga's face said to Irena that she was being narrow-minded and stubborn. *We need his help,* Jaga told her gently. Still, Irena resisted.

Something else was nagging at Irena. What to do about the lists that they were keeping? Jaga understood the problem. She, too, was worried. Only Irena and her closest conspirators ever knew the real names of these children whose identities were disappearing. Only Irena knew everything. What if something happened to her? Would anyone ever again be able to find the children who were already being hidden under false names far across the city?

What if . . .

Irena would have to think up some solution.

CHAPTER 7
ROAD TO TREBLINKA

Since June 1941, some Jewish and Polish prisoners had been working in a labor camp in a small village near the Bug River, less than seventy miles northeast of Warsaw. A few miles away was the railway junction at Małkinia, and in the winter of 1942 the prisoners there worked in the gravel pits, surrounded by forests.

In April 1942, the prisoners had been set to work on a new construction project. There was a branch spur of rail line built from Małkinia junction, just a little zigzag of a track, and long trenches were dug out. Workers from nearby villages were brought in to quickly set up barracks. The guards overseeing the camp were cruel and executed daily a couple of dozen Jewish workers. The field was covered with the dead, left for the dogs in the evening.

On June 15, 1942, the new project was at last completed: a camp for Jews. Its centerpiece was a long brick-and-concrete building surrounded by barbed wire. "The SS men," recalled Jan Sulkowski, a Polish prisoner made to work on the building, "said it was to be a bath. . . . A specialist from Berlin came to put tiles inside and he told me that he had already built such chambers elsewhere." It looked clean and inviting. There were cloakrooms for undressing, with hooks for clothing and storerooms and a cashier's post for storing valuables, and piles of soap and towels. Tickets would be required of everyone entering the baths, and the price would be twenty złotych.

Later, there would be a Red Cross camp infirmary, with a bright white-and-red banner, where those too infirm or troublesome to make the walk to the baths could receive special, faster treatment. The make-believe train depot, with the posted times of imaginary arrivals and departures, would only be built months later, once word of the terrible truth had made its way back to Warsaw. On July 23, 1942, when it received its first Jews from the ghetto, there was simply a railway platform to greet arrivals at the death camp in Treblinka and a flag that waved over the roof when the chambers were running. There was a sign on the platform, in German and Polish:

Jews of Warsaw, for your attention! You are in a transit camp from which you will be sent to a labor camp. As a safeguard against epidemics you must immediately hand over your clothing and parcels for disinfection. Gold, silver, foreign currency and jewelry must be placed with the cashier, in exchange for a receipt. These will be returned to you at a later time upon presentation of the receipt. For bodily washing before continuing with the journey all arrivals must attend the bathhouse.

In time, an orchestra would play Yiddish songs and cheerful camp marches to cover the sound of barking dogs and the screaming.

Henia Koppel was twenty-two in the summer of 1942. She lived in the ghetto with her husband, Josel, who was a rich banker and many years older. Her father, Aron Rochman, a successful businessman, lived not far away with Henia's family, and for a time the combined wealth of the two families offered some protection, even in the ghetto. With considerable foresight, Josel stashed away much of their large fortune in a numbered account in Switzerland, and enough was still hidden in banknotes secreted underneath the floorboards or tucked deep inside a mattress somewhere that there was money that summer to buy Henia one of the coveted German work permits. The permit allowed her to work as slave labor at the Walter Toebbens ghetto factory as a seamstress. Working for the Germans brought a certain measure of safety. Soon mass resettlements to the labor camps were coming. There had been warnings and cryptic announcements. The ghetto had been holding its collective breath since at least April. The Germans didn't so readily ship off to the labor camps outside Warsaw people who were already working in the city, so work papers were precious. By July, permits were selling for upward of 5,000 złotych — something approaching the modern equivalent of $15,000. They cost about the same as another increasingly desirable commodity that summer: cyanide capsules.

There was one terrible flaw in the plan to protect Henia with a work permit. The Toebbens factory didn't let mothers bring children with them during their crushingly long hours. Elżbieta — baby "Bieta" — was six months old and breastfeeding. So the family turned to their friend Ewa Rechtman. Elżbieta's older cousin was already safely in hiding on the Aryan side, thanks to Ewa's intervention and the raw courage of Irena. Irena had smuggled Bieta's cousin across the checkpoints.

When Irena Sendler knocked on the family's door, she knew her proposal was audacious. But she also knew that for the Koppel family and for all the families in the ghetto, the options were disappearing quickly. Would Henia and Josel let her try to save their baby? Saving the infant was also the only lifeline, Josel knew, for Henia. His greatest strength of character was a clearsighted understanding.

Always, families asked Irena the same agonizing question: *What guarantee can you give of our baby's safety?* Josel Koppel asked it now of her earnestly and urgently. Irena could only answer these anxious worries honestly. *I can promise you nothing except that I will risk my life today trying,* she told them. She could not even promise that she and Bieta would make it out alive from the ghetto that day out. Death was waiting for them both if they were discovered at the checkpoint. They might be shot at random on the doorstep while leaving, for that matter. People were shot every day in the ghetto for the most trivial reasons. Josel sighed and nodded. He knew that this was true. It

188

didn't make the family's decision any easier, but the ghetto was already a death sentence for a baby. Henia and Josel agreed to give their daughter to this small, determined stranger.

Irena witnessed scenes like this over and over, and these were the moments that left her sleepless when she woke from dreams of it later. The nightmares came and went, and Adam held her close when she told him afterward and whispered to her that she was just getting worn-out and tired. Now she looked on as Henia held the sleeping baby close to her chest, breathing in the scent of her infant, and Irena saw a face wet with tears that did not stop coming. There was no choice now but to act quickly. Soon the family would not be able to finish what they had started. Some days Irena didn't know if she would be able to either.

Irena reached out and began to take the infant. Henia's green eyes pleaded with Irena. The tears welled up in Irena's eyes, and the two women gazed at each other for a moment. Henia rocked Bieta softly and then just a little bit more firmly. The infant kept on sleeping. It was good. Irena set her hand for a moment on the small chest, just to make sure her breath wasn't too shallow, then nodded. The tranquilizer was working.

Henia Koppel let go of her baby.

Irena promised again. Yes, she would send them word to let them know that they had made it out safely. Yes, she assured Henia, she would make sure, no matter what, that the silver baby spoon engraved with the child's birthdate went everywhere with Elżbieta. But now Irena and the young builder assisting her on this mission, Henryk, the stepson of one of her collaborators, had to act quickly. They were about to risk all their lives to smuggle the six-month-old Elżbieta out of the ghetto.

Irena laid the baby into a wooden toolbox and tucked the blanket around her firmly, making sure they didn't block the little girl's air passages. Irena shut the lid, and the hasp clicked into place. On the street, Henryk deftly tucked the box among the piles of bricks in the back of a flatbed truck and gave Irena a quick, tense smile. His contractor's work pass let him come in and out of the ghetto, and he was yet another new addition to Irena's network. Irena pulled herself up into the passenger's seat, and the truck lurched into motion as Henryk manipulated the old clutch. Irena turned sharply, praying that none of the bricks had shifted or fallen.

They drove in silence toward Nalewki

Street, past the closed bakeries and rusted street signs. Past the narrow apartment buildings, and past the ragged and starving people who littered the street corners of the busy avenue. When they reached the Nalewki Street gate, Irena groaned. *Damn.* She wanted this part to be over, but there was a long line this afternoon. Crossing the checkpoint was the most dangerous part of any day. Minutes ticked by, and the waiting was agony. Irena's hands were cold with sweat and slippery as she fingered the door handle. As if they could escape now anyhow, she reminded herself. There was no turning back from the checkpoint. At last a soldier gestured them forward, and Henryk handed over their ghetto passes with cool self-possession that impressed Irena. The guard looked hard at Irena, then at Henryk. *What's in the back?* His eyes narrowed, and this time Henryk stumbled with the answers. So they wouldn't make it out of the ghetto today alive after all. It was always a possibility. Henryk stepped slowly from the truck and moved as he was ordered. Irena waited.

From the back now, she could hear the sounds of the flaps opening and shutting. The soldier knocked his heavy boots against the bricks and poked under the canvases and in corners. Irena held her breath. And then, a moment later, Henryk was climbing back in beside her, and the guards waved them through the gates to freedom. On the Aryan side, Irena grasped Henryk's arm in relief as the truck slowed at a street corner. *Are you fine the rest of the way alone, Henryk? It will look better.* Henryk nodded. Irena slid from the seat and waved to Henryk as the truck moved on, and then she turned her footsteps in the other direction. All Henryk had to do from there was take the baby home in the toolbox to his stepmother. Irena knew that, if anyone were being watched, she herself was the greatest danger to this mission.

Henryk's stepmother, a middle-aged midwife named Stanisława Bussold, was one of Irena's trusted "emergency room" operatives, one of the liaisons who worked closely in the medical underground with Ala Gołąb-Grynberg and Helena Szeszko. Irena called places like this, somewhat bureaucratically, her "protective readiness distribution points," and they were risky operations. In their first hours and days outside the ghetto, someone had to clean the smuggled children, feed them, and get them medical care, which they often needed urgently after months of starvation. If they had "bad" looks, there would be makeovers to lighten their hair color, and circumcised little Jewish boys were often transformed into little Polish girls for their own protection. If the children were old enough, the "emergency room" guardians would also teach them Catholic prayers and how to speak Polish. Catechism drills were a favorite German "test" to catch out Jews, and knowing one's childhood prayers by heart was the most basic tool of wartime survival. In their first weeks on the Aryan side, the children had to learn how to erase any hint of being Jewish.

Smuggling children out in toolboxes was a high-risk operation, and Irena was searching feverishly in 1942 for better options — options that would let them move not just one child but dozens. "It became necessary to take the children to the Aryan side" that spring, Irena said bluntly, "because it was hell inside the Ghetto. Under Hitler's and Himmler's orders, children were dying on the streets with the consent of the entire world." And Irena did what she always did when she was troubled for answers. She turned to her friends and to Dr. Radlińska.

Helena Radlińska had not left the convent on Gêsia Street since the autumn of 1939, but there was nothing reclusive about the

193

way the old professor was living. Her small rooms were the heart of a daring salon where the underground gathered. When Irena tapped on the small doorway now, she was met with people coming and going. Some were students clutching notebooks, part of the professor's secret classroom. Others had faces her age. A few she recognized from bygone days at the Polish Free University. Sometime in the winter of 1941–42, three of those faces belonged to her old college friends Stanisław Papuziński; his partner Zofia Wędrychowska; and their sister-in-law, Izabela Kuczkowska — Iza. Together, the professor's three former students had formed a daring group running another of the resistance cells that Dr. Radlińska was coordinating from her convent offices. By the spring of 1942, Dr. Radlińska was at the hub of several networks helping to save Jewish children.

For months Iza had been in charge of a smuggling operation, ferrying food and medicine into the ghetto through the basement corridors of the courthouse on Leszno Street. Now, Stanisław, Zofia, and Iza were all about to give Irena one part of the solution that she so desperately needed. Leszno Street straddled the ghetto, and there were doors that opened in both directions if one could just get past the checkpoints on the main floors. If Iza and a helpful janitor in the building could get supplies in, they could surely take children out in the other direction, they reasoned — as long as Irena could find a place to hide them safely. And, for that, Irena had an entire secret social welfare network. Dozens of school-aged children left the ghetto that spring, guided through the courthouse.

But that wasn't the only route that Irena used now. Leon Szeszko, whose wife, Helena, was one of Irena's team nurses and most dedicated collaborators, hit upon another daring idea. Leon worked in the civil transportation office, and every day he knew of a streetcar on the Muranów line that ran in — and out — of the ghetto. Overnight, empty cars were parked in the grubby depot on the northern edge of the ghetto. Who would notice a forgotten package or a weathered old bag tucked under a seat on the first quiet run of the morning? Irena instantly saw the possibilities there too. Sleeping babies fitted snugly inside briefcases. Someone would have to brave the streets of the ghetto in the hours before dawn to make the drop-off in the empty railyard, of course — someone with rare permission to travel after curfew. It was permission given only to a handful of people in the Jewish quarter, but, by great fortune, the chief nurse in the ghetto, Ala Gołąb-Grynberg, had it. And she also had the experience needed to administer just the right dose of sedative to a tiny body.

Soon, when the Muranów streetcar rattled empty down the tracks at daybreak, unnoticed packages rattled southward along with them, waved on unseen by guards at the barbed-wire checkpoints. At the first stop on the Aryan side, Irena climbed aboard swiftly, just another city resident anxious to get on with her morning. Beneath her feet a bag rested, quietly waiting. She rode a long way, quietly looking out the window, until the last passenger who had seen her board alighted. Then Irena would smooth her hair and gather up her packages.

And there were other ways too. There was another small underground cell that had gathered around the All Saints Catholic Church that straddled the boundary of the ghetto. The boundary followed the curves and turns of Twarda Street, and the All Saints Church had doors that faced in both directions. Dr. Radlińska's cousin, Dr. Ludwik Hirszfeld, worked there in secret with Ala's contacts to smuggle medical supplies through tunnels dug out in the church's crypts and basements. And Irena herself still slipped off to the meetings of the underground press that took place in the old rectory potting shed, where her friend, the attorney Józef Zysman, proposed another route that Irena could use to save children. In hushed tones, Józef explained how the junior priest, Father Czarnecki, was with them in the resistance. The senior priest, Father Marceli Godlewski, he said, was willing to provide new birth certificates. Any child with "good" looks who would learn prayers well enough and was a fearless actor could walk out the front door on the Aryan side.

For months Ala had been on the front lines, helping Irena and her coworkers transport children to the Aryan side. As chief nurse of the ghetto hospitals and as a *Judenrat* liaison with the Jewish Society for the Protection of Health, Ala still had a ghetto pass. For months she had been using the pass to guide children out of the Jewish quarter, delivering them to the apartment of another new conspirator in Irena's office network, a fellow social worker named Róża Zawadzka. The orphaned toddler in Ala's charge, Dahlia, was three, and Ala had already spirited Dahlia to safety, passing her into the steady hands of Irena and her network. But Ala's daughter, Rami, was six, and she could not bear to part with her little girl. So she had waited. Ala now made an agonizing decision. She knew she couldn't wait any longer.

What worried Ala in the spring of 1942, as she watched the noose that was the ghetto tighten around them, was how much longer ghetto passes would be permitted. Rumors swirled through the ghetto of coming deportations. Irena begged Ala to act quickly to save both herself and Rami. *I will find a place for you both, Ala.* Ala shook her head sadly. Ala wasn't leaving either. But she agreed at last to part with her daughter. One day in 1942 — Rami does not remember the month or what gate they passed through on their way out of the ghetto — Ala took Rami with her to visit Róża. It wasn't the first time they had gone there together, and so at first, nothing seemed unusual. For a long while Ala and Róża talked in quiet voices, and then when it was time to go her mother kissed her gently and shut the door of the apartment behind her. "One day she left me with Róża," Rami says simply. "She visited me once after. Then I never again saw her."

At first Irena shuttled Ala's little girl from

one orphanage to another, but Rami was one of the difficult children to place. She did not look like what a German thought of a typical Polish child. Róża and Irena finally found a foster family for the little girl, in the home of two Polish aristocrats and underground activists, Jadwiga and Janusz Strzałecka, who had a daughter of their own named Elżbieta. But Rami wanted her mother.

The children numbered in the hundreds, and getting children out of the ghetto was not the hardest part of this operation. Placing them safely on the Aryan side was soon where Irena was running into logistical complications. Irena had run out of other options. She needed Jan Dobraczyński's assistance.

She and Jan were not natural political allies, and she had not forgotten their fierce argument about the fate of those thirty-two street children. But by now the conspirators numbered as many as twenty-five people on the Aryan side of the city and at least as many again inside the ghetto. Ten of her Polish collaborators — all four of the original conspirators included — were actively smuggling children out of the ghetto, along with Ala, Helena, Iza, and some of the teenage Jewish girls in Ala's youth circle. The growing numbers were unmanageable without someone higher up in the orphanage division helping with placements and paperwork. Jaga was sure that Jan would not disappoint them this time. Irena at last took Jan Dobraczyński into her secret.

Irena called together a meeting of women in his division, and a group of a half dozen of them — Irena and Jaga at the lead — marched into Jan's office together. "One day, my staff, namely social workers in the Department, came to me about this matter," Jan explained. "That whole group . . . had for some time, of their own volition, been running operations extracting Jewish children from the ghetto and placing them into one or another of the Section's care centers on the basis of falsified records and interviews, after arranging the entire matter directly with the heads of the different centers. However, possibilities there had now been exhausted."

And Jan did not refuse them. By the spring of 1942, to refuse to help the resistance was its own kind of danger. Those who collaborated with the Germans were already facing justice in secret Polish courts, which brought down its own death sentences. Jan didn't agree for that reason, though. He was already in the Polish resistance on the political right, and no one questioned his patriotism. Jan agreed because his faith and his conscience nagged at him. He remembered the children he had returned to the ghetto, too, and it had troubled him afterward.

Jan freely acknowledged in the years that followed that his involvement in the office network was nothing compared to the risks Irena and her friends were taking. He did what Irena asked of him. "[But] I did not look for these children. I did not transport them. I did not create the false papers," he admitted. What Jan could do, Irena explained, was use his contacts to come to an understanding with the nuns at the Father Boduen children's home and at institutions across Poland about the transfer of Jewish "orphans." And Jan agreed that he would make this happen. "Very quickly," Irena reported, Jan followed through on the promise, reaching out to his contacts in the resistance to find reliable partners. "Jan Dobraczyński came to an understanding with the underground," she explained, "which agreed to guide the Jewish children to centers." With the nuns who ran the homes, Jan made another standing arrangement. Anytime Irena needed to transfer a

Jewish child secretly, he would personally sign the request. "Normally," Jaga explained, "the section manager would not sign these papers. Jan's signature was a code, [a signal] that we were dealing with a child, as we said then, requiring special care and attention." From then on, Ala was in contact with Jan Dobraczyński nearly constantly as Irena's ghetto liaison. It was increasingly Ala who coordinated advance logistics with the Catholic charities when a ghetto child needed to be saved.

Where Bieta Koppel would end up, no one yet knew for certain, but successes like this meant everything to Irena. For the moment, the infant would stay hidden at the home of Stanisława Bussold, who would have to find some story to explain to nosy *Volksdeutsche* neighbors how a woman in her late fifties happened to suddenly have a crying six-month-old baby at home. Soon, in the normal course of things, Bieta would move on from the "emergency room" to permanent shelter. When she did, only Irena would know where she was going and that Henia and Josel Koppel were her parents. It was a chain of knowing as fragile as Irena's life and the flimsy bits of tissue paper on which that truth was written, but it was for

Bieta's safety. Irena added one more name to the list of children. "What we had on those lists," Irena revealed in her typical matter-of-fact fashion, "was the real first and last name of the child . . . based on their birth certificate, as well as their current address. This data was necessary in order to be able to provide them with money, clothing, medicine, and also . . . so that we could find them after the war." On that scrap of paper, next to the entry "Elżbieta Koppel," was penciled in the name of her new identity, "Stefcia Rumkowski."

A few days after baby Bieta was taken across the ghetto walls to safety, a man sat in the darkness of the ghetto thinking about the fate of Warsaw's Jewish children. Dr. Janusz Korczak was awake in a small room at number 16, Sienna Street, writing. He had been gripped all day with a grim sense of foreboding. The doctor was in his early sixties, and the following day, July 22, 1942, was his birthday.

It had been a good life and a long one — although the last few years had been a terrible struggle. He had already been in and out of prison during the occupation for small acts of defiance against the Germans.

His refusal to wear the armband with the Star of David had very nearly been fatal. Dr. Korczak had no illusions about the ghetto or about what his time in prison had cost him. He could tell by looking in the mirror that it had wasted him. He was a skinny old man now, bald and stooped, and he was tired.

In another room, perhaps Stefania was sleeping already. He and Stefania Wilczyńska, one of the other orphanage directors, had been partners, making a life together for each other and hundreds of children in their schools and orphanages for years, and it had been a strange half marriage. Stefania was in love with the doctor. Everyone could see it but Janusz Korczak. All he could see was the children. The doctor couldn't sleep. Turning to his journal, he poured out his thoughts and longings onto the paper. "It is a difficult thing," he wrote, "to be born and to learn to live. What remains for me is a much easier task: to die. . . . I do not know what I would say to the children as a farewell. I would want to say so much. . . . [It is] ten o'clock. Shots: two, several, two, one, several. Perhaps my window is poorly darkened right now. But I will not interrupt my writing. The opposite: my thoughts take flight (a single shot)."

The doctor's sense of doom was sadly merited. In the morning the resettlements that the inhabitants of the ghetto had been awaiting anxiously for months started. There had been no warning. As Janusz Korczak sat awake in the small hours thinking, those outside the ghetto walls might have seen something ominous and fearful: dozens of armed men surrounding the area. In darkness the ghetto was sealed, and soldiers crept to stations on the nearby rooftops and at the checkpoints, prepared to shoot down any residents bent on escaping.

By breakfast, the leader of the *Judenrat,* a man named Adam Czerniaków, had his orders. *Gross-Aktion Warsaw* had started. The removal of Jews from the city, he was informed, was even now beginning. Czerniaków wrote in his diary that day, "We are told that all the Jews . . . will be deported to the East. By four p.m. today a contingent of 6,000 people must be provided and this (at the minimum) will be the daily quota." He was made personally responsible for ensuring that the Jewish police met the quota of fellow Jews boarding the trains that day at the Umschlagplatz, the loading platform for the railcars.

Any ghetto resident who worked for the

Jewish police, who was a member of the *Judenrat,* or who was capable of significant labor in Warsaw was exempt from the resettlement orders. The price that week of German-issued work permits doubled again, and the ghetto was instantly divided into fortunate and unfortunate. Those categorically not able to work — and thus destined for the railcars — included the sick, the half-starved, the elderly, and all the ghetto's children.

Irena rushed to the ghetto the instant the word of the deportations reached her. She needed to see Adam. She needed to know that he was safe; otherwise this panic in her gut would cripple her. Adam knew that she would be frantic, and when she made her way to the youth center, he was waiting to reassure her. He had not been caught up in the first day's roundups — and he wasn't likely to be caught up in the next day's roundups either, he told Irena. The word in the ghetto was that only the old and the very young and those who were not capable of working would be taken. Adam was just the kind of person who might flex an arm jokingly, with a tired smile, in the kind of reassuring silent gesture that said, *See, I'm young and tough.* Adam could always make Irena smile. For now, Adam had a job, and a job meant safety. Rachela, Ewa, Józef, and Ala were safe, too, then. They all had jobs. Irena tried to tell herself that none of them were in immediate danger.

But both Adam and Irena knew already that it wasn't quite so simple. The youth center was in chaos, and there were far fewer young people than normal. Parents were keeping their children close as the word spread throughout the Jewish quarter, and the fear and uncertainty on the streets were palpable. Those who were rounded up most quickly were the orphans and the street children, who had no one to turn to. Adam's work kept him safe. But there was a voice in Irena's head that kept repeating an awful question. When the children were deported, there would be no need for youth centers. *Then what would happen?*

On July 23, the second day of the action, the *Judenrat* leader, faced with delivering a new order for ten thousand bodies and knowing it meant aiding in the murder of infants and toddlers, committed suicide in a long-overdue crisis of conscience by swallowing cyanide in his office. The Germans just made other prominent Jews and the Jewish police responsible for delivering the quotas. At first, naturally, there were few volunteers for these resettlements. The

207

scenes playing out on the streets were vicious, and most residents now preferred to stay out of sight in their apartments. When quota numbers started coming up short, police cordoned off streets, emptied buildings, and marched stricken residents under armed guard to the depot. Soon the goose steps of the Jewish police echoed through the streets of the ghetto each morning starting at eight a.m. for the roundups. To argue or resist meant instant sidewalk execution.

At first, having work papers sometimes mattered. Lucky residents at the house roundups waved them like a magic talisman. They had cost a family's last savings to buy them at astronomical prices. Already, though, there was growing pressure to make up the number of bodies at any cost, and all that really mattered were the German quotas. On the street the "selections" were made. To one side went those selected as fit for work gangs or slave labor in the German munitions factories. To the other stood those destined that day for "resettlement" to Treblinka. One member of the Polish underground who witnessed the roundups that first day — a man who knew Irena — wrote, "Wednesday, July 22, 1942. So this is the end of the ghetto that has been fighting desperately to stay alive for two years. . . .

Jewish police have been hunting humans since noon . . . [C]rowds are led to the connection track in the square of Stawki Street . . . [W]hen a car was full, it was wired shut with barbed wire . . . It is raining and the sight of this agony is . . . unbearable."

Irena, with her epidemic control pass, was still going in and out of the ghetto several times a day, along with Irka, Jaga, Jadwiga, and Helena. The German strategy was to keep up the illusion for as long as possible that this was the resettlement of the unproductive sectors of the ghetto population. Medical care and epidemic control was part of that fiction. Because of their disease-control passes, they were among the relatively few Polish residents of Warsaw who were firsthand witnesses to the coming horror. And they would all risk their lives trying to stop it.

CHAPTER 8
THE GOOD FAIRY OF THE UMSCHLAGPLATZ
WARSAW, JULY–AUGUST 1942

Getting children out of the ghetto now took on a terrible urgency. Irena was desperate in the first hours of the deportations to get in touch with her friend and conspirator Ala Gołąb-Grynberg. All that first afternoon she couldn't find her anywhere. Ala wasn't at her youth center offices. Looking around the quiet room and the tidy circle of chairs, Irena could still remember sitting there with Ala, listening to Dr. Landau's typhus lectures. Irena tried to find Ala at home on Smocza Street, just a few doors down from the youth center. She wasn't there either.

The second morning in the ghetto, Irena was growing frantic with worry. Desperate, Irena tried looking for her at the medical clinics in the ghetto, where Ala was still the chief nurse for the Jewish quarter. Someone told her at last that Ala was at the Umschlagplatz already. Irena's heart sank. She would go to the Umschlagplatz. She had to save Ala.

At the loading area, the barbed wire and misery of the pulsing crowds assaulted Irena's senses and all her sensibilities. Hot tears started to her eyes, and she felt like gagging. Thousands of bodies pressed mercilessly together in the summer heat. The whiff of excrement and sweat and terror was already powerful. There were no facilities, no waiting rooms. There was just this fetid square, baking in the sun, and endless fear and misery. She stared among the crowd, craning her neck. She would never find Ala. But she had to.

There was a sudden commotion somewhere to the right, and a flash of white. Standing on her tiptoes in the crowd, Irena searched again. Somewhere she caught a glimpse of some black frizzy hair that she was sure she recognized. It disappeared among the jostling masses. Then at last she spotted Ala. Just outside the wire boundary, at the edge of the Umschlagplatz, a makeshift medical clinic had appeared from nowhere within hours of the deportations. Around it buzzed nurses and doctors. Ala — soft-spoken, gentle Ala with her poet's soul but fighter's spirit . . . Irena saw instantly that Ala was already emerging that morning as one of the greatest heroines in the ghetto. She was the lead conspirator in a spectacular rescue mission, a ruse played out with riveting bravado right under the noses of the Germans.

It hadn't begun as a ruse, Ala explained to her friend quickly. But in the end one had to fight fire with fire. When the word of the resettlements whipped through the ghetto the day before, Ala told Irena how she had rushed to the hospital. Jewish doctors and nurses — friends and colleagues — milled about anxiously. Perhaps, the hospital staff tried to reassure themselves, these were in fact only resettlements. Ala, with her contacts in the underground, knew better. She had heard the stories about Chełmno and believed the broken man who told them. But the destination hardly mattered now. To send those who were frail or delirious on a hard journey to the east was tantamount to a death sentence, wherever the journey ended. A friend caught her arm as she was rushing past. *Ala, there has to be a medical clinic at the train depot. Think of all those people.* Ala turned to him. Nachum Remba was right. Ala nodded.

Nachum Remba was not a doctor. He was a thirty-two-year-old clerk in the *Judenrat* offices who managed funding and paperwork for her clinics. And, like Ala and Arek,

212

he and his wife, Henia Remba, were activists in the Jewish resistance.

Nachum was a tall, dark-haired man and something of a jokester, always making wry cracks that had people laughing. Ala liked his dry sense of humor and stubborn optimism. But there wasn't much to laugh about in the ghetto that morning. Nachum had a crazy idea. Would Ala join him? What if they rounded up some real doctors and nurses and set up a "medical sanitation" point and dispensary on the outside corner of the Umschlagplatz plaza? It would require, he warned her, some of her brave and brilliant acting. Nachum and Ala both came from famous and tightly knit theatrical families where inside jokes were common. Nachum couldn't help it. Ala rolled her eyes and instantly agreed to help him.

So they did it. Ala and Nachum pretended that they had permission to set up a clinic. They requisitioned an area near the loading docks, a space bordered by barbed wire, and opened for some urgent medical business. They would identify anyone too weak or too young to travel and insist on treatment and sometimes a hospital transfer. They would also find a way to save important members of the Jewish resistance — which included Arek, who was somewhere out in

213

the forests with the partisans.

Very soon a skinny twenty-year-old named Marek Edelman, the coleader of a paramilitary group known as the Jewish Combat Organization (Żydowska Organizacja Bojowa or ŻOB), joined their network at the square at their "official" resistance liaison. Marek had jet-black hair and a boyish air, but inside the ghetto he was already emerging as one of the two or three most important people in the ghetto resistance movement. One day, he would lead the ghetto Jews in a dramatic uprising. But in the summer of 1942 at Ala's Umschlagplatz clinic, Marek was charged with coordinating the transfers between the trackside refuge and the ghetto hospital. Marek Edelman's ties to the underground meant he had no illusions about where these boxcars were headed. It started out as a project to save the weakest and most vulnerable and to liberate the ghetto's most dedicated activists. It quickly became a race to save anyone possible.

What their "rescue brigade" accomplished was astonishing. Nachum Remba played his part to the hilt. He was acting for his life and the lives of others. He convinced the Germans that he was the chief doctor in the ghetto and Ala was the chief nurse. They played along with the German ruse that these were simply resettlements. To keep up the façade, smug Germans humored these duped and deluded Jewish doctors and nurses. Maintaining order during the liquidations was the chief objective for the occupiers, and a few Jews, more or less now, would not matter.

Within days Nachum Remba was the most famous person at the Umschlagplatz, and his authority as the chief doctor of the ghetto — with the aid of some well-placed bribes and a white doctor's coat — went unchallenged even by the Germans. He and Ala insisted that those who were too ill or too young to make a train voyage be released to them and saved from the trains. They commandeered a hospital ambulance and started loading up adults and children. Marek Edelman moved among the milling crowd, his pockets stuffed with documents signed by Ala certifying that the fortunate recipient of those papers was too sick to travel.

The brigade could not save everyone. That much was obvious. Out of the three hundred thousand people deported from the railway square that summer and into the autumn, this small group saved, in the brief, three-week window that it existed, a mere two or three hundred of their neighbors. But those were hundreds of lives that mattered. They were lives that echo still in that exponential way of generations. Among those they saved were all the children from the orphanage at number 27, Twarda Street, whom the Germans had marked for deportation to Treblinka. They saved a resistance fighter named Edwin Weiss. And they saved an old friend, Jonas Turkow, the Jewish actor who knew well both Ala's cousin, Wiera Gran, and Irena Sendler. Ala personally pulled from the crowd as well one of Jonas's younger sisters.

The day that he was saved, Jonas could only remember afterward being astonished by Nachum Remba's raw courage. At the Umschlagplatz, Jonas was caught up in the crush as residents pushed and surged inside the barbed-wire corrals, on the brink of panic. In their midst, Nachum appeared with a placid smile on his face, exuding confidence and calm. Jonas knew that anyone else who approached a German in this manner would have been shot instantly. He and the others had seen it happen. On the loading docks, a bullet was the answer to a Jewish question. But Nachum didn't ask questions so much as he gave orders. *This one is too sick to make the difficult journey east,* he would say, pointing and shrugging good-naturedly, as if it were of no particular interest. Nachum knew the consummate Jewish wisdom of the ghetto: no fear and no sad faces. Those whom Nachum snatched from the masses were trundled off to the infirmary. Jonas was one of them. Life or death: it was cruelly random.

Inside the infirmary, Ala ordered the "sick" patients into beds. All around Jonas the nurses were busy putting on rolls of fresh white bandages. It seemed like a dream to Jonas. Was it possible that he was dead already? A German appeared at the door and the pace grew frenetic. Then Jonas knew that he was indeed still in the ghetto. Jonas lay very still and tried to make himself small until the German disappeared. At last, the all-clear signal came. The doors to the clinic closed. The ambulances were rolling up to move them.

Next, the patients ran a terrible gauntlet. There was no guarantee of safety even — especially — in a clinic in the ghetto. At the door, the cool Germans and their fearsome Ukrainian lackeys made capricious inspections. A man near Jonas did not look sick enough. A rifle butt crashed down on men like this, and Jonas could hear the man's cries of agony as he was dragged to the loading platform. Ala and Nachum looked on in horror. Ala gave her nurses the only orders she could imagine. *We will have to break their legs if they look too healthy. Explain to them the choices.* Anything to convince the Germans someone could not travel. The screams of agony were not acting. Ala could not spare the few remaining sedative doses on the fit. She needed those for the children. Her flowing white coat hung on her thin frame, and more than once Ala did something else bold and reckless. It was for this she saved the drugs in the dispensary. Fussy and frightened children, unable to feign disease, were gently helped to sleep in order to save them, because the guards treated the smallest infants the most harshly. Babies were dashed to the ground and swung by the heels against railway cars until their skulls burst as their hysterical mothers wailed in anguish. So Ala tucked the littlest ones under her coat and marched them out past the sentries, cradled beneath her armpit, and walked them into the waiting ambulances too. She and Remba had diverted an ambulance and Ala trundled patients inside. She only had to get them as far as Irena.

Ala and Nachum's wild ruse continued for

weeks. Irena came to Ala each day, always asking what she and her network could possibly do to help. On the loading platform mothers now thrust their babies at Ala, the woman everyone called "the good fairy." For sixteen hours a day, Ala and Nachum worked alongside the platform. They were a constant presence, in constant motion. And on the afternoon of August 6 that meant that they were among the last unwilling witnesses to one of the ghetto's cruelest tragedies. On that morning, as a prelude to the complete liquidation of the "little ghetto," the SS came for the children at Dr. Korczak's orphanage. Among the doctor's nearly two hundred orphans were the thirty-two Jewish boys and girls whom Jan Dobraczyński had returned through a chink in the wall less than a year earlier. They were the boys and girls whom Irena already thought of as her children.

Rumors that Dr. Korczak's orphanage was being emptied swept through the ghetto just after nine o'clock that morning. Irena usually made her daily visits to the ghetto in the afternoons, when work was over and the loading at the Umschlagplatz was under way. That day she happened to come early, well before noon. Irena was a familiar face at the ghetto orphanage and one of the children's favorite guests at their amateur theatricals. The children shrieked with pleasure at her small gifts and silly antics, and she stopped by to look in on her street children especially. When Irena heard the news that the children were all destined for deportation, she raced toward Sienna Street hoping somehow to get to the old doctor in time to warn or to help him.

But the SS had long since arrived at the orphanage with the orders. "The children were to have been taken away alone," one witness remembered, and the doctor was given fifteen minutes to prepare them. Dr. Korczak steadfastly refused to leave the children. "You do not leave a sick child in the night," Dr. Korczak stated bluntly, his voice barely containing its fury, "and you do not leave children at a time like this." The German SS officer leading the procession laughed and told the professor to come along, then, if he wished, and good-naturedly asked a twelve-year-old boy carrying a violin to play a tune. The children set off from the orphanage singing.

The route to the loading platform was arduous. With children, the march across the ghetto, from south to north, might have taken as long as three or four hours. Irena first saw them coming at the corner of

Żelazna Street, then turning into Leszno Street. It was a swelteringly hot day already — "insanely hot," Irena said — and sometimes the children had to stop and rest, but as they turned the corner they were still marching confidently. Irena understood in an instant that the doctor had kept from them any fear or knowledge of what was coming. Anxious Jewish residents stayed off the blocked streets, and Irena remembered afterward there were only a handful of pedestrians. Those who braved the streets walked quickly, head down, toward their destinations, willing themselves to be invisible. But that day dozens, including Jonas Turkow, watched from windows or street corners in astounded silence as they witnessed the doctor's three-mile walk through the ghetto with the orphans. The doctor's face was a frozen mask of hard-won self-control, and Irena knew that he was already sick and struggling. But that morning his back was straight and he was carrying one of the weary toddlers. *Am I dreaming?* The thought floated through Irena's mind. *Is this possible? What is the possible guilt of these children?* On the empty street corner, her eyes met the doctor's for a moment. He didn't stop to greet her. He did not smile. He said nothing. The doctor just kept walking. The children marched in rows of four, neatly turned out in their best holiday clothes and disciplined. Then Irena saw what the littlest ones were carrying.

In their hands they held the dolls that Dr. Witwicki, her old psychology professor at the University of Warsaw, had carved for them. Irena herself had smuggled the dolls through the ghetto checkpoints. She had given them to children at the centers, and when the boys and girls had only been allowed to take one object on their journey, this was what they had chosen. "Clutching the dolls in their little hands, holding them close to their hearts, they went on their last walk," Irena said. She knew already what they did not. That they were going to the freight yard and to their execution.

At the Umschlagplatz, the guards drove them with whips and rifle butts, a hundred or a hundred and fifty at a time, into the holding grounds. Germans, Ukrainians, and Jewish policemen towered over the children's heads, barking orders. There under the hot sun, after the chaos and bruising gauntlet, the children and the doctor waited until the railcars were loaded in the evening. Did Irena follow them as far as their final destination? If she did, at the outskirts of the corrals, she would have seen Ala and

Nachum.

Nachum and Ala saw the children only at the last moment, when the boarding of the freight trains was about to begin. Nachum, aghast, rushed to the doctor's side, hoping to stop him going. Witnesses say that Nachum was one of the last people to speak with Janusz Korczak and Stefania before the boxcars were loaded. This time Nachum was not his characteristic calm self. He was wild-eyed and desperate. He begged the old doctor to come with him to see the Germans. *We will ask the* Judenrat *for a postponement, Doctor. Please, come with me. We can stop this.* Januscz Korczak shook his head slowly. *I cannot leave the children, not even for a moment.* The doctor knew that if he turned his back, the Germans would herd the children into the waiting railway cars and he would never be allowed to join them.

The children, frightened, turned to Dr. Korczak for guidance. The doctor looked sadly at Nachum for one long final moment. That look would stay with Nachum and haunt him. Then, turning his back on Nachum and the ghetto, Janusz and Stefania calmly ushered the children into the boxcar, and the doctor stepped in behind them. In each arm he held a tired five-year-old. "I will never forget that sight," said Nachum of the doctor's dignity and the even greater dignity of the children who trusted him on this final journey. "It was not a simple boarding of the freight cars — it was an organized silent protest against this barbarism." As Nachum watched the children silently enter the windowless boxcars, whose floors were already spread with the quicklime that would burn them — as the doors pressed shut on too many small bodies and were wired tightly closed behind them — this jovial and resilient actor broke down helplessly on the platform.

Irena was also inconsolable. "Remembering that tragic procession of innocent children marching to their death," Irena said afterward, "I really wonder how the hearts of the eyewitnesses, myself included, did not break in two. . . . No, our hearts did not break." But that evening "I used my last ounce of strength to walk into the house," Irena said later. "Then I had a nervous breakdown . . ." Frightened by the depth of Irena's despair, her mother finally could see no other option but to call a doctor for sedation. "Of all my most dramatic wartime experiences, including my 'residence' and torture in the Pawiak Prison, being tortured by the Gestapo on Szucha Street, watching young people die . . . not one left so great an impression on me as the sight of Korczak and his children marching to their death," Irena said simply.

Still Ala and Nachum carried on, fighting bravely each day at the railway platform. Each morning Ala summoned her reserves and threw herself into the work that had united her and Irena in the beginning: saving the children. But at night, after the freight cars had started their gruesome journey eastward, in the hours before the Jewish police arrived to prepare for the next round of deportations, Ala lay in a dingy attic on Smocza Street thinking. One evening in that first week or two of August, Irena visited her there. The small room looked out over the rooftops of the Warsaw ghetto. The two old friends sat together holding hands, watching the sun setting. Ala was sad and serious. Irena pleaded with her.

Rami was safe on the Aryan side. Arek was with the partisans in the forests outside Warsaw, part of a Jewish fighting group preparing for armed resistance. Ala was in constant communication with the underground and would walk out of the ghetto at any moment. Irena knew a safe place with friends where Ala could go into hiding. She would hide Ala herself if necessary. She begged her friend to let her help her. *Ala, in this envelope there are identity papers. Take them.* Ala let them rest on the table between them. *Irena, look at me.* Irena understood. Ala was a thin, dark-complexioned woman approaching forty in the summer of 1942, with sharp Jewish features and "bad" looks, and Irena could not pretend that it was not dangerous. Papers would not be enough to save Ala if the Germans came looking.

But that wasn't the only reason Ala left the papers untouched. "She was waging a quiet but intense battle with herself," said Irena of those hours they talked that evening. "I understood her. Her child was out there, her husband [Arek] was in the forest, fighting, but this was the place she loved — where her work was, her responsibilities, the sick, the old, the children." Irena understood because, by now, she was also waging a quiet and intense private battle inside herself. She, too, was torn between wanting to save the children and just wanting to save herself and Adam.

Ala needed to wage her battle a bit longer. She needed to consider. Ala could not bring herself to flee yet, not when it meant leaving her people. Others around her were now making a different decision, and Irena tried

226

to persuade her. *There is no shame in living,
Ala.* Ala's friends were already leaving. Dr.
Radlińska's cousin and Ala's longtime collaborator, Dr. Ludwik Hirszfeld, had fled
the ghetto, escaping through the crypts that
ran beneath the All Saints Church and
guided by Jan Żabiński, the zookeeper in
Warsaw and an officer in the clandestine
Home Army. Dozens of refugees were hiding in the empty animal cages and in the
grounds of the zoo, where Irena was a
frequent and welcome visitor.

Ala did not fault the doctor. She was not
a woman prepared to judge the actions of
others when these were the stakes. There
was no right or wrong in Ala's mind; there
were only the dictates of circumstance and
conscience. After Irena left her friend,
promising to come back soon to talk more,
Ala sat awake for a long time considering.
Irena's envelope still rested on the small
table. Finally, Ala made her decision. Picking up a stub of pencil and smoothing out a
small piece of paper, she began to write
what she knew might be a final letter. It was
addressed to Jadwiga Strzałecka, the friend
and orphanage director on the Aryan side
who was caring for Rami. The words were a
mother's farewell to her small and much-
loved daughter. "I give my child in your

care, raise my child as if it was yours," she wrote. And then at last she put her hand out to touch the identity papers. She already knew she would never use them. She carefully tucked them away in her satchel. In the morning she would give them to a Jewish woman on the street — the ultimate gift of survival. As Ludwik Hirszfeld said of Ala later, "She struggled between the instinct of a mother and that of a nurse and a social worker. The latter won — she stayed with the orphans."

As the roundups drew closer, even Adam agreed at last to let Irena and her underground contacts lead him and his remaining family out of the ghetto. Adam had resisted. Like Irena's other Jewish friends, Adam was determined to carry on working and trying to help the children at the youth center. It was work that Irena more than anyone understood and cherished. A shared commitment to helping the abandoned and orphaned children of the ghetto bound them together, and watching Adam across a room, bending over these small children and caring for them, only deepened her love and passion for him. It wasn't only the children either. Adam's family ties, complex and agonizing, fueled his indecision.

All throughout July, that was what Adam's furrowed brow told Irena over and over, and Irena tried to tamp down her worry. And perhaps it was sometimes worry mixed, even, with a tinge of jealousy. At night in her narrow bed, listening to her mother's labored breathing, Irena prayed now. Her lips made the words silently as she asked for the life — and the love — of Adam.

By the end of the month the situation was growing critical. When Adam's aunt Dora was shot dead in Warsaw at the end of July, probably not far from the property that she and his uncle Jakub owned with members of the Mikelberg family, Adam was rattled. When word came that his eighteen-year-old cousin, Józefina, had been gunned down in Otwock after being caught hiding from the Germans, fear gripped the family. How much longer would it be before Adam's mother was another victim of the Germans and their deportations? When Irena pleaded with him to let her find a safe refuge for him and Leokadia now, Adam agreed.

Saving Leokadia was dangerous but not impossible, and that summer Adam's mother was spirited out of the ghetto. It was a perilous undertaking to help any Jewish resident cross the ghetto boundary, of course, but once a Jewish woman was on the other side and had new Aryan papers, her survival depended in large part on how well she could act the part of a Polish woman. However, a circumcised Jewish man, whose religion could be verified in a moment, lived in constant danger, and Adam was a particular challenge for another reason. Despite his new Polish identity papers, which transformed him into the gentile Stefan Zgrembski, his face told a different story. Adam would have to stay hidden at every moment from everyone except his guardians and — if she could arrange it — Irena. Because Irena wanted, desperately, even recklessly, to find him a hiding place where they could be together, and that was, perhaps, the most difficult part of the equation.

Irena turned to another of the old college friends whom she had drawn into her network. Maria Kukulska ran one of the all-important "emergency rooms" for Irena's smuggled children out of the spacious apartment in the Praga district that she shared with her teenage daughter. Climbing the stairs to Maria's apartment, Irena debated with herself: Could she ask this of a friend, even a friend as dear and brave as Maria? She would not pretend. She was asking Maria to risk her life and the life of her daughter to keep Adam. Fear was chilling. Irena cradled the warm cup of tea that Maria poured for her. Maria looked at her friend and then laughed. *You love him, don't you, Irena?* Irena laughed, too, and nodded. In that case, there was no question. Of course Adam would move into Maria's spare bedroom.

Regina Mikelberg, however, was loaded at the Umschlagplatz onto one of the death camp trains that summer. As the door was sealed shut on the dozens trapped inside the fetid cattle cars, Regina grew frantic. When the cars rolled slowly away from Warsaw, the cries of fear and the rising stench were too much for the slender thirty-year-old woman. She still had a sister in the ghetto. She had her family. And, perhaps, if she really was Adam's first Jewish wife, she had a husband she could turn to, however loose the ties that by now bound them. Whatever else was true, Regina knew Adam and Irena, and that would be part of what would save her. If only she could get free, Janka Grabowska and Irena would find somewhere to hide her. In the sweltering heat of the railway car, where body pushed against body, a dim ray of light shone through a small, dirty ventilation window. It was a narrow opening. Regina, though, was slender and determined. She pulled herself up toward the opening, and a man below let her put a foot on his shoulder. His sad, knowing eyes urged her to risk it. With a mighty push, Regina threw herself through the window and onto the hard tracks below. Without looking back, she ran into the darkness as the train rattled onward, bound for Treblinka.

When Irena tried to look for Rachela Rosenthal, another of Dr. Radlińska's girls and also a ghetto youth circle leader with Ewa and Adam, her heart grew heavy. Irena searched everywhere in the ghetto for her friend. Rachela was nowhere. And nowhere, they all knew by now, surely meant those trains destined for the east. Irena's heart whispered the terrible thought that Rachela — bright and boisterous Rachela — might have gone willingly in order to try to find her missing five-year-old daughter. Rachela was living the nightmare of everyone in the ghetto. She had turned her back, and her entire family disappeared to the Umschlagplatz in the interval. There was a powerful incentive to follow them.

Rachela's loss of her child unhinged her. It was a sorrow intensified by another cruel fact of the ghetto. Her child's disappearance was the only thing that gave Rachela any decent chance of survival that summer. During the roundups "hardly anyone bothered about the children," one young Jewish woman remembered. The children "wandered about, neglected among the masses of humanity," during street selections. Anyone over the age of thirty-five and mothers with small children were selected automatically for the railway platform. Children who understood too clearly the stakes ran from their parents now in order to save them. "How wise and understanding they were, those little ones," that young witness recalls, "trying to persuade their mothers to go on without them."

Irena searched and finally abandoned hope. But Rachela was, by astonishing chance, also among the survivors that summer. Pressed into a work gang and marched each morning outside the ghetto for slave labor, she was numb with grief. And Irena was right to worry that Rachela no longer cared one way or the other about survival. She would not have lifted a finger now to save herself, not after she had failed her daughter. Others in her work gang, however, were determined to flee the Germans, and at the end of a shift, as the backs of the guards were turned to them, a young man leaned in to whisper to Rachela, *We are fleeing the ghetto. Get ready.* And then the others scattered in all directions around her. Rachela stood alone in the middle of an unfamiliar street on the Aryan side of the city, and she wanted her daughter. She had no plan, so she started walking. She wandered the streets hopelessly that evening, ready to die, willing someone to shoot her. And when curfew fell, that would be inevitable. She didn't have long to wait now. A girl passing her on the street stopped suddenly in front of her. *Rachela!* Rachela looked up and recognized a Polish woman she had known from before the war at socialist party meetings. The young woman — in the resistance and an activist like Irena — saw in an instant Rachela's danger. *Come with me. There is a safe place where I will take you,* the woman urged her. Rachela let herself be taken into hiding.

Irena searched for her friend for weeks in the ghetto after her disappearance but could not find her. Like Ala, however, Rachela was also destined to become a heroine. In hiding on the Aryan side, she soon joined her Polish friend in the resistance and would become, before the war was over, a ferocious underground fighter.

■ ■ ■ ■

And then there was Ewa Rechtman. Like
Ala, Ewa also could not bring herself to
leave her children at the youth circle — not
while every day the little ones were being
rounded up and deported. Ewa was, Irena
said, "their mother, father, sister, friend. . . .
And they, in turn, became her biggest
consolation." Among the four girlfriends
who before the war had sat at sidewalk coffee tables laughing and talking in Yiddish,
Ala, Rachela, and Irena had all been so far
— crippling personal tragedies aside —
amazingly lucky. Ewa was not lucky that terrible summer.

"It was a beautiful, warm day," Irena
remembered after, "when the hordes of
German troops, armed to the teeth, cordoned off the 'little ghetto,' " where Ewa
was working. Ewa was trapped inside the
blocked-off streets with her orphaned children. Irena rallied friends for a rescue mission the moment she heard, determined to
risk anything and somehow to improvise a
plan to save Ewa and the children from
deportation. Ala's commandeered ambulance, liberated from the Umschlagplatz,
roared into service. Careening south

through the ghetto, Irena's hands shook. They would again use the ruse of the Umschlagplatz, perhaps. Irena would somehow convince the guards that Ewa was too weak to travel. Or they would hide her somewhere. They had done it enough times with children. Irena didn't have a plan; she only had a mission. With her epidemic control badge in hand, she haggled with the guards, trying to convince them that she and her team were there on urgent and authorized business to carry out a district medical mission. If only they could get to Ewa. When one route was cut off, they frantically tried another — anything to gain access to the sealed-off streets.

Across the barrier, dogs barked, and Irena heard gunshots. Someone yelled orders. There was a scream of anguish. Everything else was a frightening silence. One young guard seemed to hesitate as Irena's eyes pleaded with him, and then he thought better of it. At every turn, they were refused permission to enter the cordoned-off neighborhood during the *Aktion*. Late that afternoon, in the heat of an August day in Warsaw, lost among the heaving masses of bodies, Ewa Rechtman was wired into one of the cattle cars at the Umschlagplatz, where doors were fastened shut with wire.

Unlike Regina, she did not wriggle free of death at the last moment. Ewa perished in August at Treblinka in those white-tiled "showers."

Nightmares haunted Irena. The dreams were getting worse, and she would feel tired when she awoke. In those dreams of Ewa, it was always the same horror and futility, always the same terrible imaginings. Irena sometimes heard in her dreams, too, something else, the only mercy in those night-time torments: her friend's voice speaking to her once again, as always, "quiet, soothing, and full of kindness."

Everything else that had come before — all her office networks, all her smuggling and secrets — were nothing, Irena knew, in comparison to the magnitude of these crimes and losses. Worse yet, in mid-August, the deportations were not yet at the halfway mark. They would go on for another month with a breakneck intensity. Irena would match the Germans step for step in her rage and indignation at this barbarity. "Very quickly, we realized that the only way to save the children was to get them out," she said, and she was absolutely, wildly determined.

CHAPTER 9
THE LAST MILE
WARSAW, AUGUST–SEPTEMBER 1942

The ghetto was cleared that summer in orderly sections, and three weeks into the deportations the posters were tacked up ordering all residents in the neighborhood block that included Elektoralna and Leszno Streets to vacate their homes and report for selections on the morning of August 14, 1942.

By August 14, 190,000 people had been transported to their deaths at Treblinka. There were no more open-air street markets in the ghetto, and only a trickle of food made it into the Jewish quarter through underground channels. These were three weeks in which many had not eaten, and not everyone in the ghetto now went unwillingly with the loading platform for one simple reason: the Germans had changed tack and promised large rations of bread and sweet jam to those who "volunteered" for relocation.

So what if death awaits us in the east? families now reasoned. A certain death from starvation awaited them in the ghetto. Often they were also determined to stay together at any price. The twin sisters of the Jewish actor whom Ala and Nachum had saved from the Umschlagplatz, Rachel and Sarah, were among those who decided they would go voluntarily. Jonas and his wife, Diana, pleaded with the women. Ala had already snatched one of the sisters from death on the railway platform. But that had only made them more frightened and more resolute. "They couldn't imagine living without each other," Jonas said later. If they were to perish, they would perish as sisters. At the Umschlagplatz, horrified witnesses in the resistance reported hundreds queuing patiently at the transportation depot. They waited, under armed guard, days before getting a chance to load on the platform. There were so many that witnesses reported: "The trains, already leaving twice a day with 12,000 people each, are unable to hold them all." Nearly all of them were murdered at Treblinka, including Rachel and Sarah.

Those who did not queue for deportation went into hiding in their attics and basements during the street roundups. Even those with work papers or *Judenrat* protection knew better than to risk being seen when a neighborhood was emptied. A Jewish policeman had the sorry task of delivering seven of his fellow ghetto residents to the cattle cars each day — or he would be added to the deportations. "Never before," survivors remembered later, "had anyone been so inflexible in carrying out an action as a Jewish policeman."

Caught up in the roundups on Elektoralna Street that week was a ten-year-old girl. Katarzyna Meloch was already an orphan. Her father, Maksymillian, had perished in 1941 when the Germans occupied Białystok. By then the Germans and the Soviets were at war again, and he and her mother, Wanda, would have fled, because Wanda had Soviet identity papers. But Katarzyna was away at summer camp that June, and they would not leave without their daughter. Maksymillian was sent to the front as a conscript and died there, and Katarzyna and her mother were interned with the other Jews in the city's ghetto. In the middle of the night, over and over, Wanda shook her sleepy daughter awake to ask Katarzyna: *Child, do you remember?* Katarzyna knew that the answer was always: *Twelve, Elektoralna Street.* It was the address of her mother's family in Warsaw. *You must find your way there if anything happens to me. If you are alone, remember your uncle.*

One day, something did happen to her mother. Wanda saw how Białystok was changing and saw danger. The Soviets were the enemy, and the Gestapo searched the crowds for enemies. At last they came for Wanda. "A communist," said the Gestapo man, shaking her passport. And then, reading further, "Of course, a Jew!" Wanda implored him not to arrest her. She had no interest in politics; she only wanted to save her daughter. "I am only a mother," she pleaded with him. But the German ordered her into the sidecar of a motorcycle anyhow, and that was the last anyone ever saw of Wanda. Katarzyna was taken to a ghetto orphanage, and she followed her mother's instructions. She wrote to her uncle, Jacek Goldman, and her mother's family smuggled the girl into the Warsaw ghetto. Katarzyna made the journey from Białystok to Warsaw alone sometime in the winter of 1941–42.

By May 1942, when Katarzyna turned ten, she was living in the Warsaw ghetto, in a crowded apartment shared by the family of her kindly uncle Jacek and her grandmother, Michelina. Katarzyna had no mother or father, so Uncle Jacek threw a children's party for her birthday on the rooftop of the burnt-out shell of the Holy Spirit Hospital, where thirty-two years earlier Irena Sendler had been born and where Stanisław Krzyżanowski had once been a doctor.

But in August the family wasn't living in an apartment any longer. Uncle Jacek found them all a hideout inside a chimney in the ruins of the hospital, where the Germans couldn't find them during deportations. And on the morning of August 14, that was where Katarzyna should have been hiding. But Katarzyna was ten, and instead she was in the courtyard playing in the rubble with several other children. Suddenly some Jewish policemen spied Katarzyna and saw an easy target. One of the men roughly collared the girl, who cried out desperately for her family. But the man held her tightly in his grip and dragged the crying Katarzyna toward the group of women and children destined for selection to the Umschlagplatz.

Among the falling bricks and scattered remnants of the family's last possessions, Michelina heard her granddaughter's frightened cries. What could she do? Michelina carefully and quietly stepped from the shadows. She was an employee of the Jewish hospital and that meant that the family had *Judenrat* protection. *You cannot take the child. There are papers.* The policeman looked at the old woman and shrugged, unmoved and uninterested. Michelina had lost Wanda. She was determined that she would not lose Wanda's daughter. Michelina caught Katarzyna's eye quickly. Somewhere in the distance there was a brief commotion. When the man looked away for an instant, Michelina gestured urgently. *Run,* her hands said. *Run quickly.* And Katarzyna ran. From where she hid among the fallen bricks and twisted metal, the girl watched. The officer laid his rough grip instead on Michelina and pushed her, stumbling, toward the group destined for the railway platform.

At the Umschlagplatz, Michelina was thrust toward the crowds, hot and frightened, and for long hours in the sun she waited. Then, unexpectedly, she saw a white coat and a familiar face walking along the barbed wire. It might have been Nachum Remba, but it was far more likely her colleague, Ala. She felt herself being drawn quickly toward a makeshift clinic, and afterward she was never quite sure how it had all happened, but when the transports crept that night toward Treblinka, Michelina was not on one of them. She made her way back to the chimney hideout by morning.

Despairing of Michelina that night, however, the family huddled in their hideout making urgent plans. Uncle Jacek said they would flee the ghetto and join the partisans in the forest fighting for an end to all this madness. One of Katarzyna's aunts said she would carry on hiding with the children. Uncle Jacek never returned from the forest, and parts of Katarzyna's family managed to survive on the run for several months before being murdered together. But Katarzyna was not with them. Her salvation came from an unexpected direction, and it was thanks to an old friend of her mother's.

Before the war, Wanda Goldman had been a Latin teacher, and one of her students was a working-class girl from the town of Łódź named Jadwiga Salek. Wanda and Jadwiga, teacher and student, later became friends, and then life took them in different directions. Jadwiga moved to Warsaw, where she became a teacher in the 1930s at Dr. Janusz Korczak's orphanage school in the Żoliborz neighborhood, on the northern end of the city. She joined the Polish socialist movement and eventually became a city social worker in the division that found foster families for orphans. In 1942 she was thirty-one years old and her married name was Jadwiga Deneka; she was one of Irena Sendler's earliest partners. Jadwiga, Ala, and Irena were about to save Katarzyna.

All throughout August, Irena and Ala were smuggling children out of the ghetto at a ferocious pace. It was in the period from August 1942 until January 1943 — the next six months — that the vast majority of the children they saved were rescued. "We witnessed terrible scenes," Irena said of those days. "Father agreed, but Mother didn't. We sometimes had to leave those unfortunate families without taking their children from them. I'd go back there the next day and often found that everyone had been taken to the Umschlagsplatz railway station for transport to the death camps." These scenes played out now, too, in Irena's recurrent nightmares. Never again would she be free from the dreams that came to her unbidden. Survivors of Warsaw in those years — and especially survivors of the ghetto — speak of this universal haunting. The only grace in all this was that, with the attention of the Germans focused on deporting thousands of Jews each day to Treblinka, there was a chance in the other direction. The friends took advantage of that monomaniacal focus to smuggle out of the ghetto as many of the district's children as possible.

One of those children was Katarzyna. Katarzyna, today a retired journalist living in Warsaw, doesn't know whether Jadwiga Deneka happened to recognize her friend's daughter or whether Jadwiga came to the ghetto looking for her particularly. Like Irena, Jadwiga had a ghetto pass and was in and out of the Jewish quarter daily, smuggling out children. Perhaps Ala and Nachum learned of the child at the Umschlagplatz from Michelina and contacted Jadwiga and Irena. What Katarzyna remembers today is only that, one day, in the period from August 20 to August 25, when the Jews in Otwock were being liquidated and when there was consequently a brief lull in the deportations inside the ghetto, Ala led her through the gates to the Aryan side in a rescue brigade ambulance. Beyond the gates Jadwiga waited. Katarzyna walked with her mother's friend up the stairs to a small apartment at number 76, Obozowå Street, in the Koło district, where Jadwiga and her brother Tadeusz ran an "emergency room" for Irena's children. "I walked out of the ghetto," Katarzyna says, "in a very hot summer (1942). From the apartment in Koło district I can remember huge tomatoes in the window, ripening in the sun. They caught my eye when I walked out of a district where you didn't think about whether it was summer or winter."

These "emergency rooms" — Irena's "protective readiness centers" — were linchpins in the network's system for saving Jewish children, and there were at least ten of these houses, maybe more, scattered across the city. In Jadwiga's apartment, two Jewish families and their small children lived there in hiding at times during the war, and children came and went constantly. Irena had one in her apartment. Jaga Piotrowska and her husband hid more than fifty Jewish people in their apartment during the occupation. Children were hiding with Irena's old friends Stanisław Papuziński and Zofia Wędrychowska, with Maria Palester and Maria Kukulska. They stayed with activist Izabela Kuczkowska, orphanage housemother Władysława Marynowska, and midwife Stanisława Bussold. And there were perhaps a half dozen others. They all took Jewish children smuggled out of the ghetto into their homes in the first hours and days that they were brought out to safety and prepared the children for their new lives and their next destinations. Some hid Jewish children for years and acted as foster parents for decades afterward.

Now, in 1942, thanks to Jan Dobraczyński and his coded signature on transfer papers, the children were usually sent on to convent refuges as soon as new "Polish" identity papers could be found. Dozens of children were hidden at the Father Boduen children's home; dozens more passed through the orphanage and on to destinations with the aid of Władysława Marynowska and Jaga Piotrowska. Some were placed in a religious home in Otwock, and more than thirty Jewish children were ultimately hidden at the Sisters of Service convent in the eastern town of Turkowice. The inspector there knew there were Jewish children there, and he agreed to look the other way on the condition that all the children had convincing if fake Aryan papers.

When Katarzyna's false papers came, her new Aryan name was Irena Dåbrowska, the daughter of an unknown Polish woman named Anna Gåska, and her birth certificate made her one year older. Those were facts that fate demanded she memorize completely. The smallest slip — anything that might give her away as Jewish — would be fatal in her new life. Fortunately, Katarzyna had grown up speaking Polish. Had she not, saving her would have been far more difficult. Almost all the children Irena and her network managed to save that summer and into the autumn came from assimilated Jewish families, from professional backgrounds, and, if they were not babies, they already spoke Polish.

From the emergency shelter, Katarzyna followed the familiar route for children in Irena's network. She went to the Father Boduen children's home, as one of their coded "special care" children, and then the nuns transferred her to the sisters at the rural convent in isolated Turkowice. First in the "emergency room" at Jadwiga's apartment and again at the church-run orphanage, fairhaired women gently drilled her in all rites and rituals of a young Catholic girl. At the convent, to brighten her dark coloring, each morning the nuns braided her hair tightly with white ribbons and asked her again to repeat her catechism. But for a Jewish child, it wasn't remembering that was hard; it was forgetting. Forgetting what one had seen in the ghetto; forgetting one's family, words, experiences, and language. It was imperative for a Jewish child not to reveal his or her true identity, and there were blackmailers waiting. But the greatest threat often came from other innocent but dangerous tattletale children.

■ ■ ■

Often the children rescued from the ghetto were baptized and "became" Catholic. With that rite came a new set of authentic church records and documents that did not have to be faked or manufactured. Sometimes, however, Jewish parents shook their heads when Irena told them that baptism was part of how their children would be hidden. Baptism in another faith for these families was an insurmountable obstacle. Jewish religious law is clear, Orthodox fathers told her. *We cannot exile our children from the Jewish nation simply to save them now.* Among themselves, Jewish families across the ghetto debated the points and called upon the rabbis to guide them. *We must not acquiesce in the spiritual destruction of our children,* Jews said to each other now. *If more than 300,000 Jews are to be annihilated in Warsaw, what is the use of saving several hundred children? Let them perish or survive together with the entire community.* Other parents threw aside questions of religion. *Save my child,* these parents told her. *Do what you must to save my daughter.* A fracture was growing inside the Jewish community, and Irena and her network were at the heart of the controversy. Much depended on personal trust in the people doing the "saving." It was another part of the reason why those whom Irena and her network smuggled out and helped to hide were disproportionately orphans, the children of old friends, or the children of culturally assimilated families.

A fissure was also growing inside Irena's network. Irena was not a devout young woman. She embraced secular values and above all politics and action. She had also grown up surrounded by Adam's Jewish culture and did not dismiss its beauty or its power. Jan Dobraczyński and Jaga Piotrowska, though, were growing closer than ever, and both were ardent Catholics. Jan's faith gave him great influence with the convent nuns and religious home directors. His influence saved lives, and Irena was grateful for his signature on those documents. For Jan and Jaga, however, baptism of these children for its own sake mattered deeply. And the Jewish community was already starting to place Jan Dobraczyński and Irena Sendler in different categories.

One day in 1942 a Jewish man in hiding on the Aryan side of Warsaw took the risk of making an unannounced visit to Jan Dobraczyński's office. The man was a community leader. He explained to the astonished welfare office boss that he was a doctor. Although the name of this mysterious visitor was never recorded, the Jewish envoy was almost certainly Dr. Adolf Berman, the wartime director of CENTOS, the orphan care organization in charge of the ghetto's youth circles. Dr. Berman knew Irena well and admired her work. About Jan Dobraczyński he had a different perspective.

I have come to speak to you about the issue of baptizing Jewish children, Dr. Berman said bluntly. He had thrown aside concerns about denunciations and blackmailers. He was risking arrest in coming. But the doctor demanded, on behalf of the Jewish community, a frank conversation and some kind of explanation. Everyone in underground circles knew that there were anonymous social workers scrambling to hide Jewish children in church orphanages. But now the word had spread that those children were being baptized as Catholics. Why, the doctor wanted to know, were these children being initiated into another faith? What was Jan's agenda? All the children needed were the documents and a safe place to stay until their families could reclaim them from this terror.

For their safety, came Jan's blasé answer. *Surely that's obvious.* Jan shrugged his shoulders and gave the doctor a thin smile. Jan had no interest in debating philosophy. Baptism was the price of his assistance, and the Jewish community could take it or leave it. The doctor was indignant. Paperwork was one thing, of course. Yes, the children needed papers. Give the children baptism papers, by all means. But did the children have to be alienated spiritually from their families by ritual? Did they have to speak the words of conversion? Jan was firm — rigid, even — on this point. *If children and their parents want them to return to the Jewish faith when the war is over,* Jan said coolly, *this will be the child's decision.* Until then, the children in the convent homes, he insisted, would be raised as Catholics. They would be raised — for such were Jan's blinders — as what he understood to be Polish. "Those are tough terms," the doctor snapped. Jan shrugged. Jewish parents were not in a position to argue.

Irena was caught in the middle. She accepted that there were certain practical realities of wartime. But she was also the one who stood in broken-down, ruined apartments in the ghetto and begged Jewish

253

families to trust her with the lives of their children. She was the one who had to tell Bieta Koppel's family that the infant would be baptized. Henia Koppel never stopped longing for her missing baby. The young mother was still alive in the ghetto at the end of the summer, thanks to the Toebbens factory work papers, and Henia would sometimes find some way from inside the ghetto to telephone Stanisława Bussold, at whose home Bieta was still in hiding. Henia asked nothing of Stanisława in those moments except that she might hold the telephone close so she could listen for a few moments to Bieta coo and babble. On the distant end of the line Henia wept quietly. Once or twice Henia was driven to wild risks and slipped out of the ghetto for a few hours to see her baby. There was no part of Henia that did not ache for her daughter. Bieta's father, Józef, was dead already. He was shot on the platform of the Umschlagplatz when, with his characteristic clear understanding, he refused to board the cattle cars to Treblinka.

Aron Rochman, baby Bieta's grandfather and Henia's father, somehow survived the summer, and Irena knew that he left the ghetto working as German slave labor sometimes in the early mornings. When

Irena learned that autumn that Bieta would be baptized, she knew she would have to be the one to tell him. How could she live with herself if she dodged that responsibility now? Irena knew that Aron and Henia would feel this loss deeply. One crisp morning that fall, Irena stood outside the ghetto checkpoints and waited until Aron's gang passed the street corner, eyes down, marching. There on the street, despite orders that Poles and Jews not communicate even, she spoke to him for a moment and the words came rushing out too quickly. *I had to tell you.* Aron looked away. There on the street, amid the footsteps of strangers and the ruin of war, Irena watched, thinking her own heart would break as the older man broke down and cried for his family's spiritual loss of his infant granddaughter. Irena stood helplessly. She longed to reach out for Aron's hand, but anything more and it would be Aron who was in danger. She turned and walked away slowly.

A few days later, Irena was the one crying. A package had come for little Bieta. Inside, carefully wrapped, was an exquisite lace christening gown and a bright golden crucifix for the baby, wrapped carefully in tissue paper. There was no note. There didn't need to be, because the message was clear: it was a family's good-bye to a desperately loved child, and it had come, Irena knew, at the cost of everything they must have saved inside the ghetto.

And this was the difference between Jan and Irena, finally. Irena saw the agony of these Jewish parents who were compelled to consent to the erasure of their children's identity. Jan did not take children out of the ghetto. Irena was a witness to it, sometimes more than once daily. She called the scenes she saw that summer "hellish." There, in cramped apartments, families would splinter and fracture in their despair. Fathers would say yes. Grandparents would say no. Mothers wept disconsolately. The choices were too appalling. Irena made her peace with it in the only way she knew how. She made a solemn promise to those parents who would trust her with their children. Despite the dangers it created, her list of the children's real names and families kept growing.

Irena's "list," however, was never the stuff of Hollywood movies, and in the beginning she did not even bury them. Irena called them her card files, and they were just a cryptic collection of names and addresses, scrawled in code in a stubby hand on bits of tissue-thin cigarette paper and rolled up tightly for safekeeping. All the women in her network kept these lists, Jaga and Władysława especially; each saw dozens of children come and go. Irena gathered them together to reduce the security risks to the children and their guardians, and at home each night she had a plan for what to do if the Gestapo made a nighttime visit. She carefully laid the lists nightly on the kitchen table by the window and practiced quickly tossing the tiny scroll into the lower garden. The real card file — the complete one — was lodged firmly in Irena's mind anyhow. Although dozens of friends could fill in pieces, Irena was the only one who knew either the big picture or the small details. Through the summer of 1942, keeping track of the children in this haphazard fashion wasn't impossible. At that point, despite heroic efforts and almost unthinkable risks, Irena and the women in the welfare office network had hidden only a couple of hundred Jewish children.

Keeping the lists was, in part, just good accounting. Money was always part of the equation, and money — or the lack of it — increasingly preoccupied Irena. Finding ways to requisition welfare supplies and funds in the city offices had been how all this started. Sometimes, if Irena could finesse the paperwork, municipal resources paid for the cost of taking care of these children. But that was becoming harder and harder as the city coffers dwindled and the need grew enormous. More and more often now, wealthy Jewish ghetto parents paid for the support of their children a year in advance and trusted Irena with the money. Irena felt morally obliged to keep a record for the family to show she had been honest.

That summer, just as the need was greatest, when Irena was still racing against time and against the timetable of those railcars rumbling away from the Umschlagplatz, crisis struck in that quarter. The Germans grew suspicious of irregularities in the welfare office files. Irena and Irka survived undetected, but a friend, the director of welfare services in their division, was shipped off to Auschwitz in the crackdown. Irena was under more and more careful scrutiny daily — and in even greater danger. With thousands — sometimes tens of thousands — being sent to the Umschlagplatz every morning and with thousands of others hiding, suddenly the network was collapsing beneath her, and she ran out of money. Time was running out, and Irena had no solution. She knew that soon, no matter how brave any of them were, saving more children would be impossible.

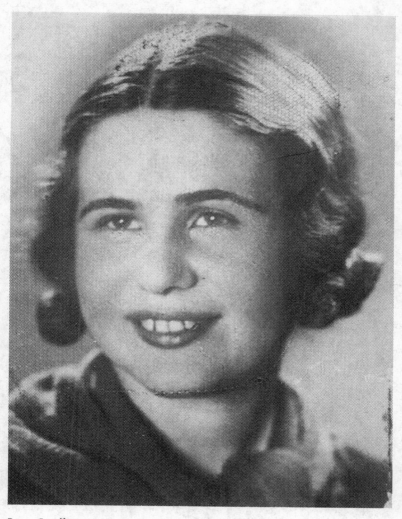

Irena Sendler as a young woman. *Yad Vashem*

1940–1943, ghetto market. *Yad Vashem*

1941, street children
in the Warsaw ghetto.
*United States
Holocaust Memorial
Museum, courtesy of
Günther Schwarberg*

Dr. Helena Radlińska
Mateusz Opasiński, CC ASA 3.0

Dr. Ludwik Hirszfeld
Yad Vashem

1941, a Jewish policeman speaks with a woman on the street in the Warsaw ghetto. *United States Holocaust Memorial Museum, courtesy of Günther Schwarberg*

Irena in her office at the welfare department. *East News Poland*

1940, the children of the Korczak orphanage in the ghetto.
Ghetto Fighters' House Museum

Dr. Janusz Korczak with several orphans in his institution.
Yad Vashem

1942, Jews from the Warsaw ghetto boarding trains at the Umschlagplatz during the deportations. *United States Holocaust Memorial Museum, courtesy of Jerzy Tomaszewski*

Irena's parents, Stanisław and Janina Krzyżanowski. *East News Poland*

Irena's friend and collaborator, Ala Gołąb-Grynberg, chief nurse of the Warsaw ghetto. *Courtesy of the Gołąb-Grynberg family*

Adam Celnikier
East News Poland

Spring 1943, Jews marched to the Umschlagplatz at the end of the Jewish ghetto uprising. *National Archives and Records Administration*

Spring 1943, Jews led by the SS to the deportation trains at the end of the Jewish ghetto uprising. *National Archives and Records Administration*

Spring 1943, Jews marched to the Umschlagplatz for deportation at the end of the Jewish ghetto uprising. *National Archives and Records Administration*

SS soldiers dragging a Jew in the street during an *Aktion* in the ghetto. *Yad Vashem*

Ala's daughter, Rami Gołąb-Grynberg (right), and Elżbieta Strzałecka (left), whose family hid Rami. *Courtesy of the Gołąb-Grynberg family*

1943, Jewish child in hiding poses outside in a garden wearing her First Communion dress. *United States Holocaust Memorial Museum, courtesy of Alicia Fajnsztejn Weinsberg*

Julian Grobelny, Irena's friend and collaborator in Żegota.
Yad Vashem

Pawiak Prison, where Irena and many of her friends were incarcerated by the Gestapo. *Yad Vashem*

Krzyštof Palester (right), the teenaged son of Irena's friends Maria and Henryk Palester, with two female medics during the Warsaw uprising. *Photograph by Joachim Joachimczyk*

1944, Home Army fighters among rubble during the Warsaw uprising. *Yad Vashem*

Summer 1944, members of the Polish underground on a tank they have stolen during the uprising. *Yad Vashem*

May 1, 1945, view of the ruins of the Warsaw ghetto. Pictured in the middle are the walls of Pawiak Prison. *United States Holocaust Memorial Museum, courtesy of Juliusz Bogdan Deczkowski*

July 1, 1945, survivors of the Jewish underground pose after the war atop the ruins of the bunker at number 18, Miła Street, in the former ghetto. *United States Holocaust Memorial Museum, courtesy of Leah Hammerstein Silverstein*

1945: Jadwiga Strzałecka with her daughter, Elżbieta (second from right), and three Jewish girls, including Rami Gołąb-Grynberg (second from left). *Courtesy of the Gołąb-Grynberg family*

Adam and Irena, with their first child, after the war. *East News Poland*

Irena Sendler as an elderly woman, when the world was rediscovering her story. *East News Poland*

Chapter 10
Agents of the Resistance
WARSAW, AUGUST–SEPTEMBER 1942

The four-year-old boy and his aunt stood in the shadows waiting for the signal. His aunt held his hand firmly, but all her attention was focused on the empty street in front of them and on the German soldiers in the distance. Their guns swung when they walked, and they were the only ones in the ghetto who were not frightened. In her other arm, his aunt held his baby cousin. The soldiers turned in the other direction at the end of the street, and Piotr felt a hand on his shoulder. His father? The boy couldn't remember afterward. But his father was not coming with them, and neither was his mother. The boy had never been away from his parents before, and even now he didn't understand what was happening. Someone hissed, *Run!* Piotr ran as fast as his little legs could take him, toward the trees where the hole was waiting.

A man he had never seen before helped

Piotr and his aunt and his cousin Elżbieta down into the cavern. His aunt coughed at the smell of the place. It was dark and terrible. "Be quiet," the strange man said to them. "And you must not cry," he told Piotr. In the tunnel, the noises came from a long way away, and there was a small, greasy trickle of water that filled their shoes. The water ran for miles underneath the city, but Piotr was too small to have any idea of distance. But this was not a place to get left behind. He watched the man's back carefully as they trudged for a long time through the underground river.

Sometimes the man stopped suddenly to listen. From above sometimes came the sounds of rattles and distant voices, but they kept walking. At last the man stopped and waited carefully before he drew aside the grate and urged Piotr quickly up the ladder. When they looked back, the man was gone, and ahead of them was another stranger, a small woman with a friendly smile. *Come,* she said. And they followed.

Was that woman Irena Sendler?

Piotr was the four-year-old Piotrus Zysman, the only child of Irena's friend Józef and his wife, Theodora. The parents were heartbroken. Józef understood the stakes clearly in the summer of 1942 and was among the hundreds of Jewish parents who trusted Irena to save their children. "To this day, I can see the look in his kind and wise eyes, when he gave me his son," Irena said of that moment. Józef did not think he would live to see his little boy again. It was hard to reassure him. At the height of the deportations, they no longer had any expectation of survival. It would take a miracle to save his parents.

When he speaks of that escape in newspaper interviews and lectures to schoolchildren studying the Holocaust, what Piotr remembers today is only that passage out of the ghetto. And perhaps it was Irena who met him in his first dangerous moments on the Aryan side. Of all the moments in an escape, the first minutes on either side of the checkpoints were the most perilous. And if it was not Irena that day, it was one of her collaborators. It was Irena's network that saved Piotr.

A plan was already in place for the boy's safety, a relief for both Irena and Józef. A Polish couple named Wacław and Irena Szyszkowski — friends of Józef and Theodora — agreed to care for the boy in their apartment. Wacław had been a law student at the University of Warsaw in the 1930s along with Adam and Józef, and in 1942 Wacław and his wife had three small children.

Would Wacław take their son? It was an immense thing to ask. Wacław was a big-boned and jolly-looking man with a shock of blond hair, and he was already a senior member of the Polish resistance. It mattered hugely that little Piotr had "good" looks — the looks of a child who might not be Jewish, who might belong in a blond-haired family. Wacław worried about the danger to his own children, but he could not refuse his friend Józef this life-or-death favor.

The protocol was to take children instantly to an emergency shelter. It's not known who fetched the little boy in those first minutes outside the ghetto, but Piotr went home to Irena's apartment that night. For as long as it took to prepare the toddler, he would stay with Irena and her mother. Piotr learned his Catholic prayers and his new Polish name. *Never talk about your mama or papa,* Irena told the little boy earnestly. *You must always say, Piotr, that your house was bombed. Remember, never say you are Jewish.* It was a wretched thing to teach a child to recite, but Irena knew there was no other option. Then, when the time came, there was a rendezvous with a liaison, and Piotr was passed to the kind care of Wacław and Irena Szyszkowski. "They treated me," Piotr says, "like their own child," with love and affection.

That might have been the end of Piotr's story of friendship and survival. But in 1942 in Warsaw, nothing was ever so easy. Wacław quickly realized that adding another child to their family was not as easy to keep a secret as they had imagined. The neighbors suddenly grew nosy and suspicious. With strange looks and whispers they hinted to Wacław's wife over cake and coffee that the child they were hiding was Jewish. Wacław got word to Irena. At any moment the Gestapo might come search the apartment. Piotr had to be moved instantly, but Irena didn't have a foster home prepared for him. He was moved from one safe house to another for several weeks. Moves like this were common and took an immense toll on small children. One little boy, in despair, begged Irena to tell him that year: *Please, how many mothers can you have? I am on my third already.* Irena could not keep the boy. She suspected that her apartment was already under surveillance. There was no other option. Piotr disappeared into one of the Catholic orphanages in her network, along with the rest of "her" children.

■ ■ ■ ■

The risks to them all were growing daily.
Sooner or later it could only end in disaster.
Irena knew it. So did the women in her
network. Jaga Piotrowska, though, was fearless. Jaga and her husband lived on Lekarska Street, and their home was one of Irena's most important "emergency rooms,"
where people came and went at all hours.
That was dangerous enough. But Jaga,
perhaps because of her devout Catholic
faith, was one of the network's most daring
liaisons, responsible for guiding children out
of the ghetto and across "Aryan" Warsaw.
Caring for youngsters who were three or
four years old — too young to censor
themselves — was like handling explosives,
and Jaga was taking a young Jewish boy to a
safe house on the city streetcar on a mission
one day when the long-feared "explosion"
finally happened.

The boy was a small and skinny child, and
he looked around nervously. As the streetcar
clanked to each stop, he grew more skittish,
and Jaga was starting to get seriously worried. The streetcar was busy, and people
swayed together as it rolled along its tracks
along the city streets, creaking and hum-

ming. They were sitting close to the front of the car, and Jaga hoped that the view would distract him. But suddenly the little boy gasped. Something had frightened him. Perhaps it was a glimpse of the ghetto wall with barbed wire. Perhaps it was a mother walking, hand in hand with her children. Jaga never knew for sure. But the small boy began to cry and — catastrophically — call in heartbroken Yiddish for his mother. Jaga's heart froze too. The other passengers on the streetcar fell instantly silent. Jaga registered the startled looks in her direction and then the dawning horror of those jammed in the streetcar with her. *Yiddish. That child is Jewish.* She could see from the faces around her the thought registering. And that meant that everyone in the streetcar was in danger. Jaga could see from the driver's quick look over his shoulder that he understood what was happening, and she could see the growing fury of the woman sitting next to her.

Jaga's mind raced. With the rush of fear, the world narrowed to one question: Would someone betray them at the next stop to the police? It was too likely. Anti-Semitic feeling still ran strong in Warsaw. The streets were filled with blackmailers looking for just this kind of opportunity for life-or-death extortion. Jaga felt panic rise. She had to be

265

brave, she told herself. And she had to act quickly. "I hid my fear," she said, "in my pocket." She turned to the streetcar driver. She needed to get off the streetcar this instant. *Please, help me,* she implored him in a hissed whisper. When he turned away without a word, back to the track rolling in front of him, Jaga's heart sank. It was futile. As she held the crying child, she felt her own tears well up. She had a daughter. As the streetcar lurched a few times and came to a jolting stop, Jaga reached to stop herself from falling. Shopping bags clattered to the floor, and a piece of bruised fruit rolled under the benches. Someone swore quietly and turned to help an older lady.

In the midst of the chaos, the driver bellowed: "Okay, everyone out! The tram is broken, we're returning to the depot." He opened the doors and waved the passengers out brusquely. People scattered. Jaga gathered up her things and the child, preparing to step down into the street and take their chances. The odds were not with them, she knew. The driver shook his head. "Not you. You stay." He gestured to her to get down, and she obeyed wordlessly. Then he calmly put the empty train into slow forward motion. "Where do you want me to drive to?" They rolled along until they reached a quiet

266

area surrounded by houses with small gardens, where the streets were quiet, and the nameless driver stopped the streetcar. *You'll have to get off here. Good luck.* Jaga turned to the man. *Thank you.* The man just shook his head and gave her a sad smile as she and the little boy descended.

Irena would later say of that summer of 1942 in the ghetto, "What was happening was as horrible as could be. The tragic summer of that year was quite simply hell. There were constant roundups in the street of ordinary passersby, famine and typhus were producing piles of corpses every day, and in addition entirely innocent people were being randomly shot all the time." But, to the world beyond the walls, it was all largely and conveniently invisible. The Jews of Warsaw and the people of Poland who were helping them knew that their only hope now would come from abroad, and they were desperate to persuade the British and the Americans to assist them.

That week, an agent with the code name "Witold" arrived in Warsaw on a mission from a sympathetic Polish underground organization. He was coming to meet with Ala and Nachum's friend from the Umschlagplatz, the ghetto resistance activist

267

Marek Edelman, and with one of Marek's conspirators in the underground, a prominent Jewish attorney named Dr. Leon Feiner. Along with Marek Edelman, Leon Feiner was one of the leaders of the ZOB, the Jewish Combat Organization, which had grown in the summer of 1942 out of the youth circles in the ghetto where Irena's friends had all been center leaders. Another of the ZOB leaders was someone else whom both Irena and Jan Dobraczyński knew well already: Dr. Adolf Berman.

Witold's mission was to tour the ghetto. From there, the underground agent would smuggle himself into the death camp at Bełżec and then travel covertly across occupied Europe to deliver to the Polish prime-minister-in-exile and to the Allies in London a firsthand account of the atrocities against the Jewish people. When that was not enough, he would travel to the United States to tell the American president in person about the horrors he witnessed. The agent's name was Jan Karski. And Jan Karski was about to meet a courageous young Polish woman whose name he would never know, Irena Sendler.

The last weeks of August in 1942 were agonizingly hot, and for a month Irena had been working feverishly against the tide of the ghetto deportations. At home that evening, even her lightest dress felt sticky with the weather, and her mother said she looked tired. Irena knew that the strain on her face was showing. From the kitchen, she heard the knock on the door. It was a light tap, meant to be reassuring. Irena lived in terror of the unannounced arrival of the Gestapo. But the Gestapo did not tap lightly.

Knocks on Irena's door were not unusual. Her apartment was a refugee point, and there were often liaisons and friends coming and going. But the fair-haired gentleman standing at her door now was not one of her teenage runners. He introduced himself gravely as "Mikołaj." But his real name was Leon Feiner. Her own code name, "Jolanta," was a word known throughout the ghetto, and Irena did not yet understand sufficiently that she had been under intense surveillance for months already — not by the Germans but by the resistance. They knew that she was working specifically with Dr. Radlińska.

Irena stepped back and gestured to the stranger to come in. As Mikołaj stepped inside, Irena closed the door quietly and raised an expectant eyebrow. After all, he was on her doorstep. It wasn't up to her to open the conversation. And the conversation was a delicate and roundabout one. Talk was a risk for both of them. Ultimately, Mikołaj came to the point of this curious visit. Would Irena agree to act as a signpost for Jan Karski on his trip into the ghetto? Would she help show the outside world what was happening in Warsaw? They needed a guide who knew all the twists and turns, every nook and cranny, of the ghetto streets. Irena didn't ask the details of the mission. She certainly did not know that day the name of the secret agent. But turn down a request from the resistance? Never. By Irena's standards, the operation was no special risk anyhow. She braved death every day in and outside the ghetto. Underneath the foundations of the building at number 6, Muranowska Street, on the northern edge of the ghetto, Jewish children had dug out a tunnel forty yards long and four feet high to smuggle what they needed for survival. Jan Karski and Leon Feiner slipped through that tunnel into the ghetto. On the other side, their living street sign guiding their way was Irena. Within weeks that small act of helping the Jewish resistance would have unimaginable consequences for Irena and for the children she was hiding. Soon the resistance would return the favor and help Irena.

And Irena needed help. By early September, the "Great Action" in the ghetto was in its final stages. The children who remained on the Umschlagplatz platform now were sick and weak, decimated by the stress and hardships of hiding, and there was no one there left to save them. By the third week of August, the Germans had ordered Ala and Nachum's railway medical clinic closed, and Ala was banned from the Umschlagplatz by special order. So Ala carried on in her position as the head nurse at the hospital on Leszno Street, where the sick and the starving were multiplying. Her husband, Arek, was part of the inner circle of the Jewish resistance, and in her own way Ala was another of their frontline fighters. When ambulances filled with supplies and dirty linens trundled through the checkpoints, Ala made sure that there were small stowaways aboard. Often these children were sent on to Irena. But Ala had contacts in the underground with other people who were, by now, running other rescue operations.

At the hospital, the skeleton staff called an urgent meeting early on the morning of September 6, 1942. Ala was tired. She leaned against the wall and listened. There was panic in the doctors' voices. The day before, posters had gone up across Warsaw offering amnesty to any Poles who turned in Jews they were hiding. That day everyone in the hospital, even the sick and bedridden patients who crowded the wards, was under strict German orders to report for a final registration. No one had any illusions any longer, and Ala knew that many on the staff had deeply personal reasons for their worry. Doctors and nurses had tried to save their own elderly parents and small children by falsely registering them there as patients. They were charged with deporting their families. Ala watched as one of the nurses realized this and broke down crying.

Ala had the beginnings of an idea that morning. *What if . . .* But the thought was interrupted by the clatter of heavy boots and the barking of orders in German. The hallway was suddenly in commotion, and a doctor rushed past her. Ala stood frozen. She turned to a young nurse with big, fearful eyes but could not reassure her. *Oh, God, I know what is happening,* thought Ala. Ala couldn't bring herself to say the next bit aloud. It was going to be Dr. Korczak's walk to the Umschlagplatz all over again.

The thought energized her, and Ala swung

into motion. She had witnessed the horrors of the Umschlagplatz and had not thought anything could surprise her now. But even Ala was shocked to see SS men walking calmly down the rows of beds, shooting in the head anyone who was delirious or immobile. Frightened patients in their flimsy hospital gowns were pushed at gunpoint toward the doorways, and at the front of the building the damned were herded into open trucks for transport. Nurses and doctors ran into a ward ahead of the SS men, desperate to save their children, at least, this final terror. Hands shaking, they poured precious doses of cyanide into the mouths of their family members. Ala watched in horror as a weeping doctor could not go on and turned to a nurse. He asked her to administer the fatal dose to his father. Ala knew better than anyone that it was the greatest mercy. As her friend Marek Edelman put it bluntly: "To offer one's cyanide to somebody else is a really heroic sacrifice . . . for cyanide is now the most precious, the most irreplaceable thing." It was the gift of dying quietly.

Ala couldn't bear to watch. But that kernel of an idea was growing. She raced to the children's ward, where the bright room was already in chaos, and turned to a duty nurse and gave swift instructions: *Run, tell the kitchen staff we are coming.* Ala needed the kitchen workers to fill a truck with food supplies and empty vegetable boxes. Ala clapped her hands. *Children! We must line up now very quickly.* Daisy chains of toddlers and small children held each other's hands, and teenage trainee nurses carried two or three infants at a time in bundles. Thirty children followed Ala swiftly down the back staircases and into the kitchens, where they were tucked in and among the wooden potato boxes. Ala ordered the cook to drive, and moments later Ala watched as the truck pulled away and disappeared around the street corner.

Ala saved thirty children that morning. Hundreds in the hospital perished. After September 6, the ghetto hospital was empty. By mid-September the state of the hospital hardly mattered. The quarter had been decimated. Eighty-five percent of the original total ghetto population of 450,979 had been deported, and those who remained lived in constant fear and hunger. Some 30,000 Jews had been pulled out of the final selections after being deemed fit for slave labor in the ghetto factories. Another 30,000 — many of them families with small children — escaped the roundups and were living "wild" in burnt-out ghetto ruins, basements, and attics. They were ruthlessly hunted. At the ghetto factory owned by Walter Toebbens, the workers in the fall of 1942 included Henia and Nachum Remba; baby Bieta's mother, Henia Koppel; and Ala.

Soon tuberculosis and starvation would have filled Ala's empty wards again, but by now the hospital was in ruins. There was only one good thing that came of illness. As long as disease continued in the ghetto — and how could it not under such conditions? — Irena's epidemic control pass remained valid. And that meant that Irena and Ala could continue to work together to smuggle out children.

Irena was not the only person in Warsaw running a covert operation to save Jewish children and their families. She wasn't even the only underground network that Ala worked with directly. When Ala smuggled children out of the ghetto, she sometimes passed those youngsters along to another cell that had sprung up in the resistance and to a woman named Aleksandra Dargielowa. By the late fall of 1942, Aleksandra had saved the lives of more children than even Irena — more than five hundred — and the system that she used was remarkably similar. Not surprisingly, Aleksandra was also in contact with the indomitable Helena Radlińska.

Aleksandra's organization was called the RGO — for Rada Główna Opiekuńcza, or the Central Welfare Council — and, like Irena, Aleksandra was a social worker. Since 1940 the RGO had operated as the official German-sanctioned relief organization, charged with managing refugees, prisoners of war, and impoverished residents. But by 1941 the underground had infiltrated the RGO and under the noses of the Germans its staff worked secretly with Jewish charities and the Polish government-in-exile to funnel aid to families in the ghetto. By early 1942, Aleksandra ran a division within the RGO that went a step further. She was hiding Jewish children in city orphanages under false papers. Some of those children were the youngsters whom Ala and Nachum whisked away from the Umschlagplatz. Some of them were children whom Ala smuggled out of the ghetto in ambulances and under boxes.

Ala could see that Aleksandra was on the brink of exhaustion that fall, although she did not know all the reasons. Ala was on the brink of exhaustion herself. But Aleksandra wasn't only running a rescue operation for Jewish children through the RGO. She had also just become the head of the children's welfare division in a new secret resistance organization code-named "Żegota." At first the founders of this underground action group called their network the "Aid Committee for Jews." As the RGO resistance was folded into the group, it became the "Jewish Relief Council." Soon, the organizers decided that the word "Jew" was too dangerous to use in any communication, even in coded messages. So, instead, members pretended they were talking about an imaginary person named Konrad Żegota — a "man" who very soon shot to the top of the Gestapo's list of Poland's most wanted.

Żegota was a latecomer to the Polish underground. Established as a working group only on September 27, 1942, its founders were two women who came from different sides of the political spectrum. Zofia Kossak-Szczucka was, like Jan Dobraczyński, a conservative author and far-right Catholic nationalist; like Jan, her outrage at the crimes against the Jewish people came not from liking Jews but from her conviction that genocide was unchristian. "Our feelings toward Jews have not changed," she wrote in a political pamphlet to the Polish people, published in Warsaw in the summer of 1942. "We do not stop thinking of them as political, economic and ideological enemies of Poland." But, she went on, "we are required by God to protest . . . We are required by our Christian consciousness." Zofia Kossak-Szczucka's cofounder in Żegota, on the other hand, was Wanda Krahelska-Filipowiczowa. Wanda was also a Catholic and the wife of Poland's former ambassador to the United States, but she was a liberal-leaning socialist like Ala and Irena. The two women imagined a collaboration that would bring together the Catholic left and the Catholic right in charitable aid of the Jewish people.

Within weeks, Żegota outgrew the mission of its founders. On December 4, 1942, the "committee" was reorganized again, and group activists argued passionately for the inclusion of representatives from a far broader range of political perspectives. In particular, some of the members wanted to include on the committee representatives from the Jewish political community. That didn't sit well with everyone. And although Irena didn't know it yet, she knew many of Żegota's earliest members. A man named Julian Grobelny, whom Irena knew from meetings of the Polish Socialist Party, was nominated to be the new general chairman. Dr. Adolf Berman, the wartime director of the Jewish charity CENTOS and one of the youth circle activists who had worked with Ala and Adam, represented the Zionist party on the leadership council. Dr. Leon Feiner — the man who, during the secret visit of Jan Karski, had asked Irena to act as their ghetto signpost — was the Jewish Bund representative.

But Żegota's chief link to the Polish underground was a man named Aleksander Kamiński, a renowned educational theorist and the editor of the Home Army's underground newspaper, the *Biuletyn Informacyjny* — the *Information Bulletin*. Kamiński was a major player in the Home Army, the largest branch of the resistance. The Home Army — an offshoot of that underground state that had existed in Warsaw since the first days of the occupation and that Dr. Radlińska had helped to fashion — would eventually absorb most of the smaller military resistance units forming. In late 1942 the Home Army was already one hundred thousand strong in Poland. By 1944 there would be at least three hundred thousand Home Army members. And Żegota's chief link to Irena Sendler was her old school

279

friend and another of Dr. Radlińska's "girls," Izabela Kuczkowska.

Iza was a dark horse, and even Irena wasn't privy to all her friend's secrets. Sharing secrets was too dangerous. In the Home Army, no one knew the name of his or her superior. Many in Irena's network knew each other by code names only. According to secret wartime intelligence files in the Home Army records, Aleksander Kamiński and Izabela were close wartime collaborators. And, like Irena, Iza was working directly with Dr. Radlińska.

But Irena was linked to the founders of Żegota in at least half a dozen different directions and at the closest levels. After all, she had been part of the underground state since the beginning, and Irena was passionately political. Many of these men already knew her personally, and, despite her guarded secrecy and her careful cryptograms, word was out in the underground that Irena was running an astonishing operation to save children. They knew because for months she had been under constant surveillance.

They would soon reach out to Irena. She had earned their trust when she helped guide the secret agent Jan Karski through the ghetto so he could carry word to the world of the atrocities being perpetrated by the Germans. Now it was Żegota's turn to help Irena. What none of them knew was that it would quickly place Irena in the sights of another organization dedicated to surveillance: the Gestapo.

CHAPTER 11
ŻEGOTA
WARSAW, SEPTEMBER 1942–JANUARY 1943

Irena's old metal desk was scattered with notes and bits of paper, and there was hardly room to move her chair around in the small office where she spent her days jammed in among the file cabinets. In the corridor of the welfare office, the *tap-tap-tap* of someone's sturdy heels came and went, and Irena thought that whoever it was hesitated outside her doorway for a moment. She realized she was biting on her pencil again. She was stressed. It had been three or four days since she had seen Adam, who was still in hiding at Maria Kukulska's apartment, and she missed him. The wind outside was rattling the window, and Irena pulled her sweater closer around her and closed her eyes for a moment. Where she wanted to be that afternoon wasn't there in her cramped office, slogging through paperwork. She wanted to be curled up somewhere quiet and warm next to Adam.

But when she opened her eyes, she was still in her office. And the same hard lump was sitting in her stomach. What she was looking at, on the papers in front of her, was a disaster.

Irena kept her lists — those flimsy bits of cigarette paper with the names and addresses of hundreds of hidden children — buried in her satchel. There were no hidden bottles yet, for the simple reason that Irena did not yet comprehend the scale of her danger. But she would never work on those lists of the children in the office. Not in the open. But she couldn't help trying to work out some troubling sums on a piece of scrap paper.

When Irena looked down at the figures she had scratched out, there was no way to make it all add up. She could see everything they had worked so hard to accomplish unraveling. The Germans had cut off the funds to the social welfare office. It was the beginning of December in 1942, and Irena was out of money, pure and simple.

Irena heard the *tap-tap-tap* coming down the hallway again, and this time the shoes definitely stopped outside her door. She slid the scrap of paper into a budget file and waited. When a moment later her friend and colleague Stefania Wichlińska popped her head around the corner, Irena was relieved. Stefania looked sympathetically at the scattered paperwork on Irena's desk. *Do you have a moment?* she asked. Irena raised her hands in mock despair at the files in front of her and smiled, and Stefania threw herself into the rickety little chair across from her. *Ireeeennna,* Stefania began slowly. Irena raised an eyebrow. A friend beating around the bush was never a great start to a conversation. Irena steadied herself for what she knew must be coming: she thought grimly that she didn't need any more bad news this morning. The figures were depressing enough. Stefania plunged ahead, and Irena was mildly surprised when her topic was welfare and money. Stefania, of course, was in on the office secret. Everyone in the office knew about the scheme to funnel cash to Jewish families, but the German crackdown had ended that program. Now Irena was startled when Stefania starting talking about hiding Jewish children and someone who perhaps could help her. Stefania was a friend, but some secrets were too dangerous. Irena started to protest, but Stefania stopped her quickly. *Irena. Will you go to 24, Żurawia Street, apartment 4, on the third floor? Ask for "Trojan."*

Irena debated with herself all afternoon.

She debated much of the next morning too. The risks were obvious. It wasn't that she didn't trust Stefania, but what if she and Stefania were both being led into a trap by Gestapo provocateurs? On the other hand, Irena reasoned, what were her options? Stefania said that "Trojan" could help her, and Irena desperately needed assistance. At last, she decided. She made sure her lists were well hidden, and the next day she took her coat off the rack by the door and left the office early. Her path led her to the east of the ghetto and a nondescript apartment building. The name on the bell read *Eugenia Wasowska,* and when she knocked on the door a woman's voice asked to know who it was. Irena responded with the password, "Trojan."

A gray-haired woman with a flushed face opened the door. The apartment was spacious but dim, and the shades were drawn tightly. A man beckoned Irena to enter. Irena could see that the woman was nervous; oddly, that made her feel better. Irena later learned that her name was Halina Grobelny. Halina ushered her through a series of doorways until she came to a small room at the end of the apartment. There, Halina introduced "Jolanta" to her husband, "Trojan" — the code name of Julian Grobelny, the leader of Żegota.

Irena kept her face stony, determined to reveal nothing. But her mind was racing. Julian Grobelny was a stocky man with a thick neck and a dark beard, and his eyes darted with an unmistakable intelligence under a pair of wild and bushy black eyebrows. She guessed that he was in his fifties, though he moved with the careful, considered step of an older man. Was this a Gestapo trap? Were they informers? It was always a gamble. Irena had no way of knowing that her office friend Stefania was a courier for the Home Army and had a second underground life in the resistance herself. Julian understood Irena's hesitation, and he took the first risk by telling her the secret of Żegota. They were already partners with the RGO, Julian explained to Irena. Aleksandra Dargielowa was chair of their new child welfare division. They were working under the auspices of the Home Army. They were already in contact with Irena's friend inside the ghetto: Ala. Would Irena and her cell join their network? he wanted to know. *We will not interfere with your current operations.* Those words to Irena were magic. Żegota received funds dropped into Warsaw by parachute from agents in London, and they knew that Irena's cell was broke. They wanted to fund her operations.

To hell with the risks. This was a godsend. "In the course of this unusual meeting, when I had the honor of representing the employees of the Department of Social Services of Warsaw, it was decided to form our relationship with the leaders of Żegota," Irena explained later. But, standing there in the apartment that afternoon, Irena looked Julian Grobelny squarely in the eye and stuck her hand out to shake on it. Julian laughed. "Well, Jolanta," he said, "we're striking a good deal together. You have a team of trusted people, and we will have the necessary funds to help a larger number." Money meant that Irena and her team could expand their operations. But most of all, money meant that Irena could continue to support the children in hiding with the monthly food stipends on which so many of the host families depended. An extra pound of black-market butter, or double that amount of sugar, cost nearly 500 złotych now — twice the average monthly salary in 1942 of a Polish laborer. Julian explained that there were secret "postboxes" scattered across Warsaw where she could pick up bundles of cash and messages, and of course "Jolanta" was always welcome at the Żegota safe house.

When Aleksandra Dargielowa discovered that Irena was on board, within weeks she asked to be relieved of duty as Żegota's child welfare division director. It wasn't because she didn't support Irena; Aleksandra's nerves were shattered. She and Irena were fighting a daily war against inhumanity and depravity, and Aleksandra had reached the point of battle exhaustion. Irena understood all too well the soul-crushing pressures and the effects of living with fear as a companion. Irena was treading ever closer to that breaking point herself. Adam could see it, but Irena would not or could not listen. And for Aleksandra there was another constant worry: she was the mother of a small child. With every step that broadened the network, the risk of arrest and interrogation increased exponentially. The chances of any of them surviving this were slim, and one had to be prepared for the worst. If she were honest with herself, Aleksandra knew that, faced with the torture of her child, she would crumble. Irena had to ask herself the same question: Would she be able to risk so much if she had to consider Adam's baby?

But Irena was not a mother, and there were times when even the idea of being with

Adam — really being with Adam — seemed like a fantasy. Aleksandra asked Irena to take over, and within weeks she did. "In the fall of 1942, I took control of the Child Welfare Division of the Polish government-in-exile's Jewish Aid Council (Żegota)," Irena said, "and this strengthened my ties to the walled district even more. It all gave me more opportunities to help." Anything that brought her closer to the ghetto and the plight of the families trapped inside felt like a way of being loyal to Adam. It ultimately made her one of the Second World War's great heroines as well. Some sixty thousand Jewish people were hiding on the Aryan side of the city, constantly at risk from the Gestapo and blackmailers. Another sixty thousand Jewish families were still trapped inside the ghetto, and the noose around their necks was tightening. Many of the families living "wild" inside the ghetto had refused to go to the Umschlagplatz precisely because they had children. In the next ten months — from December 1942 to October 1943 — Irena's Żegota cell, into which her own network was quickly integrated, would take out of the ghetto and save from the streets thousands of those children. Irena would make sure that each month some money to support the children made its way covertly to their courageous guardians. And Irena would note down the sums and all their identifying information on her paper card files — an astonishing wartime archive and testament to the courage of dozens upon dozens of average men and women across Poland.

Żegota solved the resource problem that had been holding Irena and her friends back in their rescue operations. Now it was possible to think on a larger scale. It was possible to imagine. In the late autumn of 1942, Irena went from being the leader of a relatively closed network of old college friends, prewar political comrades, and coworkers to being a major figure in the Polish underground. It was like being promoted from army captain to general. No one who knew her doubted that this was her destiny. She was brilliant.

Irena relied throughout on her girlfriends, who now took on larger roles in her network — although without knowing themselves in many cases that such a thing as Żegota ever existed. Irena was the only point of contact on the Aryan side with Julian Grobelny. And on the ghetto side, Irena's comrade-in-arms was Ala. Nurse Helena Szeszko took charge of setting up a system of medical hideouts with a number of doctors, including Dr. Majkowski, the man who had given Irena her ghetto pass in the beginning. These were places where Jewish people could get aid and where sick children could be hospitalized. More than a thousand children would be placed in orphanages and care institutions across Poland, many of them thanks to Jan Dobraczyński's signature. One of Irena's team members personally arranged those transports, often to rural areas hundreds of miles away. More than two hundred children would go to the Father Boduen children's home, where other team members were now the primary operatives. Collaborator Jadwiga Deneka was the hidden children's guardian angel, and she crisscrossed Warsaw and much of central Poland in order to check on their welfare and deliver the financial support that Irena was now able to provide, thanks to Żegota. Irena's old friends Zofia Wędrychowska and Stanisław Papuziński opened their home as an emergency shelter, at immense risk to their large family of children. Irena's apartment was always a last resort for the network.

And, as always, there was Adam. Adam was restless and resentful. He had fled the ghetto at Irena's urging in the summer of

1942 only to find himself, months later, still cooped up in Maria Kukulska's apartment and going more than a little stir-crazy. Maria's teenage daughter, Anna, had more freedom than he did, and Adam was brooding. By nature, he was a man of dark and melancholy moods. Right now he needed a job that had some meaning. It was hard for a man when his girlfriend was risking her life in an underground cell while he had to skulk around uselessly in an apartment full of women. Irena confessed later that she was always looking for ways to keep Adam busy.

Now there was work that needed doing. Adam took charge of paperwork and finances — her bookkeeping — and it was another reason to be grateful to Julian Grobelny and Żegota. Irena was running a large, dangerous, and remarkably well-funded operation. That meant record keeping. And record keeping would be fatal if the files were discovered. But for Irena there was no other option. "Vast sums passed through my hands," she remembered, "and it was a great relief to me when I could prove that the money reached the right place. . . . It was in my own interest to keep these receipts . . . [T]hrough my hands passed very important sums, and I wanted to be able to prove that they had been received by those for whom they were destined." Her budget amounted to a fortune each month; sometimes she saw 250,000 złotych — approximately three-quarters of a million dollars today — come and go. The money came from sources in the Polish government-in-exile and from the Jewish-American community. Conscious of the sacred trust placed in them, she and Adam kept careful records of every złoty.

But the money wasn't what was exhilarating. It was the fact that, by January 1943, the names of more than a thousand children were on the lists. Every single child Irena had placed in the Warsaw convents was still alive. They had not yet lost a single precious one of them. It was nothing short of a miracle. By the end of the war, ninety percent of Poland's Jews would perish — some three million people — but not Irena's children.

But Irena was not saving children only: she was hiding anyone who needed to escape from the Germans. For Jewish teenagers — boys and girls — hiding in homes or orphanages was often impossible, and some of those teenagers joined Irena's network as trusted couriers. As German control over the ghetto tightened, the old secret routes no longer worked, and escaping the ghetto usually meant a dangerous and frightening journey through the city's miles of sewers. Irena's teenage couriers acted as guides through those underground waterways, leading families out of the ghetto and delivering messages and money. In fact, resistance was heating up now on the Aryan side of Warsaw, and many of the young people were joining the partisans. Maria and Dr. Henryk Palester, whose conversion to Judaism placed them in danger, were still hiding on the Aryan side. Maria was part of Irena's office network. Now the couple's teenage son Kryštof also joined an elite resistance scouting squad known as the "Parasol" battalion, in which the young people carried out, among other things, assassination missions. The "special courts" of the Polish underground were taking aim at local Nazi functionaries and Gestapo collaborators, and every day brought news of three or four lethal attacks on the streets. Some of the most fearsome assassins were young women, who used their girlish charms to distract the Germans. An innocent face allowed them to get close enough to pull off point-blank executions.

Other teenagers were helped to flee to the

forests outside Warsaw, to join partisans like Ala's husband, Arek. In addition to assisting the hidden children, Irena's cell was soon supporting nearly a hundred teenagers and a group of resistance fighters being hunted in the woods by the Gestapo. What Irena didn't know yet was that her lost friend Rachela Rosenthal was already living out there and fighting for survival among them. Now part of the resistance, she had new Aryan identity papers. Rachela embraced her new life completely. Anything else was unbearable. She had erased her past and lived in the woods as a Polish girl under the name "Karolina." She had taken a new Polish lover, a handsome engineer and a fellow resistance member named Stanisław. Stanisław knew nothing of her past, and Rachela, who was still beautiful, vowed to herself that he never would. And when she fought, it was with a raw and reckless courage. She had nothing left to lose there in the forest. She had turned her back in the ghetto for a moment, and lost all her family.

With access to new resources, Irena rented two rambling old buildings, one in her former hometown of Otwock and the second in a small hamlet just a few miles away called Świder. Jewish men and resistance organizers were terribly vulnerable, and Irena soon had a plan to help partisans like Arek and Rachela. Along with Otwock, Świder had long been a summer holiday retreat, and the countryside was dotted with drafty villas set amid forests that followed the contours of the river. Some of those forests were home to the resistance fighters and adult Jewish refugees whom Irena was supporting. In one of those small villas Irena now registered a tuberculosis "rest clinic" for a motley assortment of new "patients."

An elderly Jewish woman with particularly "Aryan" looks and good identity papers named Mrs. Zusman ran the day-to-day operations at the refuge in Świder. A streetcar line connected downtown Warsaw with the village and, using her cover as a city social worker, Irena visited the clinic often, bringing Mrs. Zusman money, underground doctors, or forged identity papers.

The station at Świder was nothing more than a platform in the woods, and when Irena stepped off the train one day she wrapped her coat tightly around herself and set off for the villa on foot over the frozen winter ground. When she arrived, "Auntie" Zusman quickly shooed her, tut-tutting, into the back kitchen to sit by the fire, and over a cup of tea the women settled down to business quickly. Irena never stayed long, and soon dusk would be coming. She needed to get back to Warsaw shortly. But first Irena insisted that Mrs. Zusman tell her how each of the men was faring. There were five Jewish men with her that day, Mrs. Zusman explained. Some of them were frail from a winter in the forests, and all of them were tired of always running. From one of the rooms nearby came the sound of someone coughing. Irena raised her eyebrow. *One of the residents is a doctor; we are managing,* Mrs. Zusman assured her. Irena smiled her relief. *Dr. Bazechesa?*

Roman Bazechesa was a sad story, and Irena worried about the Jewish doctor. He had come to Warsaw from the east, from the town of Lviv, and for months Dr. Bazechesa scrambled to hide alone on the Aryan side from the German pursuers. But the doctor had such strongly Semitic looks that it was impossible. He lived in constant terror, and only his sleepless vigilance saved him. More than once he fled a retreat in the small hours of the morning, steps ahead of Polish blackmailers and the Gestapo. At last he was broken by the strain. Better to die quietly than to live this animal existence. Just as Roman Bazechesa hoisted himself over the balustrade to throw himself into the icy river, where he would perish, Maria Palester passed him on the street and put out her hand to stop him. Maria understood all too well the doctor's desperation. More than twenty Jewish people passed through her apartment "emergency room" during the war, and more than half of them were killed as a result of blackmail and betrayal by *szmalcownik.* Maria, nevertheless, led Roman home, and within hours, Irena's network had swung into motion to help him. Irena herself had introduced him to the hideout in Świder.

Mrs. Zusman was reassuring, and Irena could feel the warm tea relaxing her nerves for a few moments. A moment later everything was electric.

Fists pounded furiously on the front door of the villa. Irena's chair clattered to the floor as she reached for the identity papers. *Jesus. The Gestapo?* The identity papers were a death sentence. The women exchanged a horrified look, and from behind her Irena could hear the muffled sounds of feet in quiet motion. Irena lifted a finger to Mrs. Zusman and pointed her toward the front doorway. That silent gesture spoke volumes. *One minute,* it said. *Give me one minute.* Mrs. Zusman nodded and walked slowly and loudly toward the sound of the pounding. *Coming, dearies, coming.* Minutes were everything now. The men crouched low, waiting, and Irena smiled quickly at the doctor, trying to stay calm. As Mrs. Zusman fiddled with the lock on the front door, to the howls of the impatient men outside, Irena and the five refugees slipped out the back door. The sharp, cold air bit at her lungs as she ran with all her might toward the waiting forest.

They scattered in all directions, and in a quiet copse Irena stopped at last, heart pounding. The men were now far into the woods. No one would return to the house until Mrs. Zusman's fate was settled, and Irena knew that the chances of the Jewish matron's survival were slim. But Irena could not leave the old auntie without knowing. She hid the papers carefully among the forest leaves, then crept quietly back toward the villa.

The scene unfolding on the front doorstep astonished her. Hands on her hips and eyes blazing with fury, Mrs. Zusman was yelling at her unwelcome visitors. Irena took in instantly that they were Polish blackmailers and not Germans. *We know you are a Jewish den. Give us money.* Mrs. Zusman knew perfectly well that to give the blackmailers anything was to be forever in their power.

Once there was no more money, they would still call the Gestapo, and she was fighting for her life in that moment. So she drew herself up and went on a wonderfully dramatic counterattack. *How dare you disturb the peace of a Polish Christian,* she berated them. *You foul bandits! I will have the Germans come arrest you for coming to abuse an old lady!*

Shocked, the blackmailers stood for a moment on the doorstep, hesitating. Mrs. Zusman carried on screaming out her outrage and indignation. Confused and rattled, the *szmalcownik*s looked at each other. Then they turned on their heels and ran away down the driveway. Behind them echoed the shrill voice of Mrs. Zusman ordering them to come back that very instant. When Irena stepped from the shadows afterward, she and Mrs. Zusman laughed tearfully at the old woman's brazen courage and good acting. But there was nothing funny about the situation. The hideout was "burned," as people said in those days. As the dusk settled over Świder, Irena had to figure out now where, at a moment's notice, she was going to relocate six Jewish people.

For an immediate answer, Irena turned to those closest to her that December: Maria

Kukulska and Adam. Irena knew that, if necessary, Maria would find room for Roman Bazechesa too.

Maria Kukulska was another of Dr. Radlińska's girls, at least after a fashion. Before the war, she had been a favorite student of the celebrated educational theorist and social welfare professor Dr. Władysław Spasowski, a colleague and friend of Helena Radlińska's, but she and Irena had known each other for years from local meetings of the Polish Socialist Party. A teacher by training, Maria led courses in the underground wartime university, but perhaps most important Maria Kukulska had an adolescent daughter named Anna, a "comely" girl with soft brown hair and a trusting and apparently unthinking disposition. Teenage impulsiveness might easily have killed both Adam and Irena that winter.

It started so simply. Warsaw had been known before the war as the "Paris of the East," and the small, brightly colored squares that still dotted the city in late 1942 were pretty and romantic. Anna walked arm in arm with a girlfriend, showing off their figures. As they strolled, Anna caught the eye of two handsome Polish boys named Jurek and Jerzy hanging out in the square. Jurek decided to set his cap on Anna instantly. With all the subtle charm of youth, Jurek began to stare at her until she noticed him. Soon their eyes met. Before long, the four teenagers were talking and flirting. Anna was smitten. Hoping to continue this pleasant interlude, Anna, with the unthinking confidence of an adolescent, invited both boys home with her to meet her mother and their lodgers, an attorney named Adam and a doctor named Roman. As Anna came bouncing into the apartment at number 15, Markowska Street, with the two young strangers, Jerzy saw in an instant that her mother's look was one of raw horror. Maria hurried into the back bedroom, and now there were murmurs of a heated argument in hushed voices.

When the door opened at last, a tiny blond woman with blazing blue eyes stepped out to meet them. Maria's worried eyes scolded Anna, who obediently followed her angry mother down the hallway. Jurek could see that Anna was in trouble. But Jerzy's focus was all on this small woman standing in front of them on the carpet. He could see her making an instant assessment. Perhaps, he says, more than seventy years later, Irena Sendler could tell by looking at them for a long moment that they were two Jewish boys on the run from the ghetto. They had been loitering in the square because they had nowhere else to go to. Jurek and Jerzy had narrowly escaped a Gestapo roundup at a safe house on Idzikowskiego Street; they had survived the raid only by crawling out a rooftop window and running. Perhaps Irena believed the wild story they told her now, when they hinted knowingly that they were brave young Polish resistance fighters. The boys at any rate were brazen actors. Jurek had taken to heart the advice of a wise old man who had told him that the key to survival outside the ghetto was forgetting: "Forget that you have something in common with the Jewish tribe. Act as if you are not concerned." But if you ask Jerzy — whose name today is Yoram Gross and who lives in Australia — he will tell you that not much got past Irena Sendler. Irena listened, and then she nodded. And that was it. The boys were not only allowed to stay, but they soon became part of Irena and Adam's extended wartime family.

And when Adam and Roman stepped from the back bedroom to meet them, too, Jerzy understood in an instant why their arrival had caused Maria Kukulska such a panic. Jerzy could see plainly that Adam Celnikier was Jewish. So was Roman

Bazechesa.

Jerzy and Jurek came and went often from Adam's hideout as Jurek's romance with Anna deepened, and there was always a risk in any new foot traffic. But the person who posed the greatest danger to Adam was Irena. Irena was a major player in the underground now, in charge of eight or nine different safe houses across the city, still moving Jewish families across the ghetto walls, and hiding hundreds upon hundreds of children. The Gestapo was already hunting for "Jolanta." They simply did not know yet that Jolanta was Irena.

Irena watched carefully everywhere she went, to be sure she was not being tailed, but it was impossible to be sure that no one was watching. If she misjudged, she knew that any day she might lead the Germans right to Adam. It would have been wiser to stay away from anywhere Adam was hiding — wiser to keep her love affair and her underground "business" separate. But Irena was in love. She could not bear the idea of living with this kind of grinding uncertainty and not being with Adam. And Adam could not bear to be idle.

So Maria Kukulska's apartment also became a regular meeting place for the

Żegota cell. Maria was involved in many aspects of Irena's secret network and was doing more than just hiding Adam and Roman. That meant they were both anxious to take every precaution. To hedge their bets the women set in place a complex system of codes and signals. On her approach to the Praga district, Irena scanned the faces of loitering strangers and watched carefully in the reflections of shop windows to see if she was being followed. The area was dangerous. In the old state mint at number 18, Markowska Street, the underground was busy forging fake German stamps and identity papers. Not far away were German barracks. Sometimes, paranoid with worry, she would change her destination at the last minute and duck into a shop or a laundry. More often, when she thought she was being followed, she would turn her steps a few blocks north and stop in to see her friends at the Warsaw zoo, Dr. Jan Żabiński and his wife, Antonia, Irena's coworkers in the resistance. The doors to the couple's white stucco bungalow were always open to Irena, a favorite visitor, and Irena would often see old Jewish friends passing through in hiding, or other members of Żegota. But on those days Irena would not be able to see Adam.

On days when Irena felt certain she was alone on the streets, she watched carefully for Maria's sign in the front window. A sign meant it was all clear on Maria's side: that the hallways were not filled with nosy neighbors and that there had been no visits from the Gestapo or blackmailers.

Irena tried to come by the Kukulska apartment each day, or at least that is how Jerzy remembers it. At any rate, he and Jurek visited nearly every day — by now Anna and Jurek spent a good deal of time on the couch kissing — and each time he saw Irena there with Adam. Jerzy's memories are a window into the private love affair between Adam and Irena that flourished that winter. Despite all the dangers of Irena's work — despite Adam's perilous position in hiding on the Aryan side of Warsaw and the sense that they were snatching this time together in the midst of terror and chaos and uncertainty — it was the first time as a couple that they had ever had this complete freedom to simply revel in each other's company while shielded from the eyes of family. Their love had the space to deepen that winter in part because their lives were hidden.

Looking back on those afternoons in Maria Kukulska's apartment, Jerzy remembers how Adam adored Irena, how his eyes followed her everywhere. Adam had his own small room to which they could retreat in private, and it wasn't all work and Żegota. The two stole precious hours together behind closed doors. All anyone could hear were low murmurs and sometimes quiet laughter. But Jerzy also saw how nervous and tense Irena was becoming. Part of what made her anxious was Adam. Adam was an energetic man who couldn't sit still, and unlike Roman Bazechesa he never doubted that he was going to survive the Germans. He was bored and sometimes defiant. Adam was angry and reckless, even. But his strong Jewish features made it dangerous for him to so much as stand near a window. A glimpse from the street might be enough to betray them all to the blackmailers and the Gestapo. Freedom — what it meant to leave this cage — was sometimes grasped simply by walking close to a pulled curtain, and Adam could not resist the temptation to break free just for a moment. When he did, Irena panicked. Irena spent a fair bit of time behind closed doors trying to manage Adam and especially trying to prevent him from leaving the apartment. The idea of a short walk in the fresh air was his idea of heaven. The empty, open park at the Warsaw zoo seemed to beckon. Adam promised, but

Irena could not trust him completely. When she was away, she worried endlessly. She began to show signs of the pressure.

Maria, Anna, and the two teenage boys treated Irena now with kid gloves, showing her careful respect and great deference. Even the young people, who were told nothing of Żegota, knew that Irena was in charge of something important and dangerous. In private, Anna and the boys sometimes wondered aloud what it was, and Anna hinted that it had something to do, she thought, with Jewish children. Sometimes at Maria's apartment, small boys came for their cross-dressing "makeovers," and Maria and Irena huddled together quietly with the children in the small bathroom while the biting chemical aroma of hair dye filled the air. The "blonding" of dark-haired children told its own story.

Jerzy observed it all, too, and for several weeks he considered. Surely he understood what he was seeing; if so, then he didn't like to lie to Adam and Irena. Maybe they didn't know that he, too, was Jewish? Jerzy and Adam were friends, and Adam listened sympathetically while the boys talked of their teenage angst and girl problems. At last Jerzy decided to confide in the older man: *Adam, I'm Jewish,* he said. Adam nodded to indicate that he understood what the boy was saying. Then Jerzy added, *I know you're Jewish too.* Adam frowned, gesturing toward his dark hair and strong features, and shook his head firmly. *No,* he told the boy. *I'm not Jewish. My mother is just Hungarian.* Jerzy knew it wasn't true but said nothing.

The boys needed a safe house themselves, and Irena and Adam arranged it. Irena sent Jurek and Jerzy to the safe house in the villa at Otwock. But Adam also set them to work. He needed helpers. Adam and Irena were working together in Żegota, and Adam's role had to be behind the scenes. He could not leave the apartment. But his job now was to allocate the grant money that Irena received from the leader of Żegota, Julian Grobelny, each month, and from his bedroom office Adam kept all her documents in careful order. In coded messages sent by courier, he arranged scholarships for the older children whom Irena was now placing in secret schools run by the resistance where they could continue their Polish education. He matched false identity papers and stolen birth certificates with the appearance of children. Adam needed runners with "good" looks and fair complexions. Jurek and Jerzy were at hand, so the boys took messages across the city for him, and sometimes they delivered dangerous packets with papers.

Danger surrounded them constantly. Irena, above all, they knew lived on the razor's edge of disaster. But there was love in Maria Kukulska's apartment, and sometimes there were rollicking good times with the young people. In wartime one grasped hard at small pleasures. On December 31, 1942, the streets of the Aryan side were filled with people celebrating the New Year — in Poland, the Eve of Saint Sylvester — with music and raucous laughter. Teenagers in costumes took turns playing pranks, and good-natured snowball fights left the groups of young people hollering with pleasure. Inside the ghetto, all was dark and silent. December 31 was the last day any Jew was allowed to remain free in German territory, by order from Berlin, the official end to that summer's mass deportations, and festivities in the sealed quarter were forbidden.

Adam and Irena, in hiding, could never have joined the throngs on the streets, but inside the Kukulska apartment half a dozen friends gathered for their own party. At the table there was warm bread in the traditional shapes of fanciful animals and sweet *paczki* donuts that Maria had brought home

310

from a nearby bakery, where the windows were filled with rolls and bright candles. Someone tried his or her hand at fortune-telling, a New Year's Eve tradition, and Irena and Adam collapsed in laughter and leaned toward each other in the way of old lovers. Jurek kissed Anna when he thought no one was watching, and Jerzy sat contentedly on the sofa.

Before the stroke of midnight, this group, more like family than friends, posed together for a boisterous portrait, piled up alongside each other on Maria's small living room sofa. There was no champagne in the winter of 1942, but no one needed champagne to toast the New Year. It was enough to be together and happy. As the church bells rang out at last across Warsaw in wild peals of music, Adam turned to kiss Irena and said the words of the traditional midnight toast in Polish: *Do siego roku! Good wishes for the New Year!* Irena leaned and for a moment rested her head on Adam's shoulder before she replied. Perhaps she allowed herself to think for a moment about what lay ahead. It was an all-too-human weakness and cast a shadow on her pleasure. No one believed any longer that the war was going to end tomorrow. From her contacts in the resistance, Irena knew that dark

311

things were coming. It took strength to live only in the present. It was the only way that Irena — one of the strongest of them all — kept going. She turned to Adam and whispered, *Do siego roku.* Irena had to believe in a different future. Together.

Chapter 12
Toward the Precipice
WARSAW, 1943

A knock at three a.m. never meant anything but disaster, so the quiet tapping that startled Irena from her sleep one night in the spring of 1943 set her heart racing.

They could be betrayed at any moment to the Gestapo. As German fears grew about the strength of the Polish resistance movement taking hold in Warsaw, the efforts to ferret out the dissidents had become ferocious. When the Gestapo came, however, they would not knock discreetly. One had to remind oneself of that. Those visits came with the pounding of boots, and shouts, and the splintering of wood for the maximum terror effect. There was a precise etiquette to wartime knocks, and this was the reluctant predawn signal of a conspirator.

That could only mean one thing: something terrible had happened on that night's rescue operation. Pulling her robe tightly around her, Irena hesitated. She did not turn on the light. A silhouette could betray her. But even in the darkness she knew where the most recent additions to the lists and the week's account books were. They rested on the kitchen table, under the window, as always. It was her private protocol. In one swift motion Irena silently dropped them from the window, and watched the cigarette papers on which the lists were written flutter to the ground and settle among the garbage cans and stacked refuse. There, no one would notice a scrap with a few light pencil marks. "For safety's sake, I was the only person who kept and managed the files," Irena said later, adding, "I practiced many times to [hide them] swiftly in the eventuality of unwelcome visitors."

Looking around the room quickly, Irena reassured herself that all was in order. She could hear her mother's quiet breathing in the back bedroom and was glad that the knock had not awakened her. Irena worked carefully to keep her mother in the dark about her dangerous activities. It was the best way, when the worst came, to protect her.

Irena slid back the lock and opened the door as quietly as the battered wood and old hinges would allow. Her heart froze with

314

terror. She thought she could just catch a glimpse across the hall of her neighbor's door quietly closing. Had the old woman beaten her to the knock? At Irena's door stood a teenager with four small children. All of them were drenched in sewage.

The teenager was a steely sixteen-year-old girl with dark eyes and a tangle of curls pulled back severely under a cap. Irena didn't know her real name; all the Jewish couriers in her network had code names. So did Irena, of course, although the true identity of "Jolanta" had long been an open secret in the resistance. But one could only tell under torture what one knew, and so it was better not to ask any questions, and Irena never asked the girls where they came from.

Jolanta, the young woman whispered. Irena opened the door wider and urged the soggy group inside the darkened kitchen. *I didn't know where else to go.* Irena nodded reassuringly. She understood without any explanation: they had been running an operation that night, moving a group of Jewish children through a secret passageway in the city's underground sewers. The guide was meant to deliver the children to one of the guardians, and from there Irena's network would help the children disappear into private families or one of the convents where the sisters hid hundreds of Jewish children. Irena would add each of their names secretly to the lists that she carefully guarded. She would make sure that each month some money to support the children made its way covertly to their courageous caretakers. And Irena would note down the sums and the addresses in her tissue-thin records.

Tonight, with the *Aktion,* they had lost track of some of the children. The Germans had run a patrol and arrested the sewer guide and the other couriers. The couriers would face a brutal interrogation. These were the moments that gave Irena night-mares. The safe houses were compromised. There would almost certainly be executions. There was no guessing what people might tell under torture, and there was no point in blaming anyone who cracked. Everyone in Warsaw knew that the things that hap-pened at the Gestapo centers were unspeak-able.

Irena glanced now at the children stand-ing in her entryway, wet with filth. Her chest tightened. Someone had dressed them care-fully, in their best and warmest clothing, a parent's last loving gesture. Details like this haunted Irena. One of the children was six

316

or maybe seven. He had "good" looks — the looks of a child who might not be Jewish. But the children all had one thing in common: the sad, frightened eyes of ghetto children.

Irena's mind swung quickly into action. Solving problems was her strength, and doing something was the only way not to go crazy. She had other safe houses. If she needed to, she could take the children to Jaga for the time being. But they would have to scrub the children clean, somehow wash and dry their clothes, and sneak them back out of the apartment building unseen before the halls were filled with curious neighbors. There was another time pressure. In the morning, at seven a.m., one of her mother's friends would come as always. Irena trusted her mother's friend — the Nazis had killed her husband and she had no affection for the Germans — but not enough to share a secret like this. It was an immense risk, and Irena did not gamble with the lives of children.

At best, they had a few hours until dawn. They would have less time if her neighbor betrayed them. Irena had no idea how her neighbor felt about the Jews, but this wasn't the way she would have wished to discover it. Already the Gestapo might be coming for them, and, if they were caught helping these Jewish children, death for all of them was certain. But there was no help for it. The children couldn't travel until they were clean. Neither could her courier. The muck in which they were covered was a telltale sign. And no one could travel until the nighttime curfew was lifted anyhow.

Irena began heating water. It would have to be hot. Her father had died from typhoid helping Jewish children as a doctor almost three decades earlier, and Irena had watched the disease devastate the ghetto even before the liquidations. The sewage through which the children had traveled could be a death sentence for all of them unless she was careful. Hot water and plenty of soap were critical. As the girl and the children began undressing, Irena searched the wardrobe for old towels to wrap them in, rinsed the garments in the sink with a tiny sliver of precious soap, and then scrubbed her hands and beneath her nails carefully.

The children huddled together, and soon the little trousers and shifts were wrung out and left to dry near the heater. They would still be damp come morning, but there was no other solution. The children were hurried off silently to the bath, Irena whispering to them to step lightly. The neighbors downstairs were friends. But others in the building would be suspicious of the sounds of footsteps at this hour. Suspicion could be lethal.

Irena's heart sank when she saw her mother standing feebly in the doorway, watching her. Janina, made unsteady on her legs by illness, took in the scene silently. The four little naked children and the dark-haired teenager required no explanation. In her mother's eyes, Irena was grateful to see only acceptance and worry. The children climbed gingerly into the tub, and the first three were scrubbed quickly. As she warmed the water for the last child, Irena reached for fresh soap. Only then did she realize they had used the last of it.

Soap was a precious wartime commodity. Made from animal fats and ashes, it was easy to come by in times of plenty. But in the winter of 1942–43 the hungriest citizens of Warsaw resorted to cooking old shoe leather for soup stock and protein. Lard and bacon drippings were gourmet treasures. Better to be dirty than hungry, if those were the only choices. Irena and her mother were lucky to be able to get small supplies of lye soap to do their laundry.

Soap? Her mother shook her head. There was nothing left but the small half sliver in the kitchen, now a thin and flabby wafer, not enough to wash the last of the children. Lack of soap was such a little thing, but it might cost them everything.

Irena thought for a long moment. Alternative plans, alternative scenarios? She could see none. What else could she do? There was no other option. So, going to the doorway, she slipped into the hallway. She would have to ask her neighbor. Irena drew a breath and knocked quietly.

She knew it was an act of wild faith. She would have to gamble that her neighbor would not betray her. The door opened cautiously, and the woman's eyes were wide with terror. Irena realized in an instant that she, too, was worried that a knock could only mean the Gestapo. Irena quickly tried to reassure her. *Soap? I am doing my laundry. I can't sleep.* It was four a.m. and the old woman had not been sleeping either.

The woman turned wordlessly, but she did not close the door behind her. Irena stood, waiting. What did it mean? Was it an offer of help or a sign of betrayal? Was she summoning the Gestapo even now? Was it an invitation? The harsh light in the hallway showed the nicks and scratches in the woodwork and the places on the stairs where years of footsteps had worn the treads. Just as Irena was about to turn away, she heard the soft footstep again, and a wrinkled hand held out a moist package quickly wrapped in a bit of paper. Touching her hand, it was warm and soft, and Irena took the offering. *Thank you,* she whispered. *Mrs. Sendler,* came the hushed reply, *you are welcome.*

Just as the sun began to light the streets of Warsaw that cool morning, an upstairs neighbor might have noticed a young woman walking out the front door of the apartment building, hand in hand with four well-turned-out small children. If Mr. Przeździecki in his garden saw them, he might have waved and wondered if they were local youngsters headed to Basia Dietrich's little kindergarten. The morning breeze blew at their coats, and the children moved a bit more briskly. The girl with the cap pulled them closer. In a few moments, all of them turned the corner and were lost to eyesight.

Neighbors in the building that day might have overheard a strange mid-morning conversation. Perhaps they had heard footsteps at dawn above them, a door open and shut, the creak of the staircase, the sounds last night of water running. Someone had been awake in the early hours of the morning. Now a woman was talking to Janina in a voice that drifted clearly down the stairwell. It was the old lady upstairs, and she said to someone there, commiserating, "I feel sorry for you, because your daughter is in a pretty bad way." A listener might have heard a quiet murmur. "It's clear she doesn't sleep at night," the old woman now said loudly. "Sure, [your daughter] has a husband in a camp, so crying at night over the thought of him is tough. But her getting up at three or four in the morning and doing the washing! And waking all the neighbors to borrow soap! Crazy!"

What no one could have seen was the small, silent nod and the thin smile before the door clicked shut again quietly. The neighbor understood exactly what had really happened.

The names of those four children were never documented by Irena, but they could have been any of a stream of youngsters who were in and out of her apartment and in and out of the apartments of all her conspirators. They might have been, for example, a young brother-and-sister pair saved from the ghetto and given new Polish papers as Bodgen and Irena Wojdowska. One of them might have been the little girl whose false Aryan papers gave her the name Halina Złotnicka. Halina, too, was saved by Irena's network and ultimately placed in Jaga's safe house, where she lived alongside Jaga's young girl, Hanna. "Jaga took care of me like her own daughter," Halina remembered decades later. Jaga was a bookworm and passed along to Halina her passionate love of reading. Perhaps Jaga also understood that the escape into a safer world of fantasy was just what a terrorized child needed.

The four youngsters that night in Irena's apartment might have been, in fact, any of hundreds of children. Strange messages came at all hours now, and Irena would have to act instantly. One day it would be a message from Jaga or Ala. A desperate Jewish mother had swaddled a baby in sofa cushions and thrown the infant over the ghetto wall, crying out for the mercy of strangers; a placement was in process. Increasingly now, however, word would come directly from Julian Grobelny, at the very top of Żegota. Irena was needed in the forest outside Otwock. A woman was hiding in a garbage bin with her infant daughter. The baby was dying: *Would Irena bring a doctor she trusted?* A child had survived the liquidations but her family had been murdered in front of her: *Would Irena travel to a village to fetch the baby?*

With thousands passing through the network, Irena and her team remembered many children best by small, heartbreaking details: the baby in the garbage can, the girl with the red bow, or the boy with the green jacket. Other times these were the children of friends. Many of the children Irena saved had some connection to someone in the group: they were friends of friends, the neighbors of families. It was an astonishing web of trust connecting strangers.

The winter of 1942–43 quickly proved a mad, exhilarating, and heartbreaking season. Many in the ghetto by late autumn were also set on armed resistance. Teenage girls smuggled in dynamite and guns, and in hidden rooms the young people manufactured Molotov cocktails. The fighters fortified the rooftops of buildings for defensive positions. The winter was frigid and punishing as usual in Warsaw, and all autumn there had been whispered rumors of something terrible coming. The Germans, no one doubted, would kill all of them, and the young people were determined to go down fighting.

On January 18, 1943, those fears were realized. That day the Germans initiated a new and long-expected mass deportation in the so-called "wild ghetto" in order to cull the weakened factory workers. But everyone feared it was the final, total liquidation — a "holocaust" of the ghetto. Few who survived the summer of 1942 were foolish enough to volunteer for this new "deportation." Everyone in the underground knew by now where the tracks from the Umschlagplatz led and what was waiting at Treblinka, and word spread quickly to anyone who was prepared to listen. The Germans, determined to make up the numbers, and not much caring who was deported, marched at gunpoint to the loading docks anyone they could lay a hand on, regardless of their health or work situation. Among those caught that day were a group of young people in the resistance, members of the Jewish Fighting Organization and Hashomer Hatzair, the Jewish paramilitary scouting movement. The youths were armed. They were organized. In hushed voices, they agreed: they were not going. For the first time in the ghetto, there were the cracks of explosives and Jewish gunfire.

Some of those who fired those first shots were friends of Arek and Ala's. Caught by surprise and astonished at the idea of a Jewish resistance, the Germans were flummoxed. For four days a battle went on, pitting a small, determined group of young people against the forces of the Nazi occupiers. The young rebels could not win, of course. The Germans had far greater firepower, and the resistance in the beginning was a small group of people. Nearly all of those who resisted were killed, and more than five thousand Jews were deported. But the atmosphere in the ghetto was electric.

Now everyone in the ghetto was looking for miraculously clever hiding places or trying to get out to the Aryan side of the city. On the Aryan side of the city Irena's friend and collaborator Janka Grabowska now received a frantic message from Regina Mikelberg, in hiding since her bold escape from the cattle cars destined for Treblinka. Since the ghetto was first closed, Janka had supplied Regina and her family with the food and medicine they needed to survive, using her epidemic control pass to ferry supplies back and forth across the checkpoints. Regina's parents were dead — they had never been nimble enough to jump from small train windows — but her younger sister was strong, and she had been assigned to a ghetto work detail on Bema Street since December. Regina thought she was now slave labor at the Strayer-Daimler factory. All the factory workers were herded in January to the Umschlagplatz, and Regina's sister had escaped detection only by hiding for days underneath a pile of corpses. Would Irena and Janka help her out of the ghetto? There was no question. Irena and Janka made preparations, and it was agreed: this would be Janka's operation.

All the plans were in place, and Janka was on her way out the door at her home on Karolkowa Street, when she was faced with disaster. At the sounds of a gentle tapping on the back door, Janka turned and opened the garden entrance. Her husband, Józef, a soldier in the Home Army, had been out on a mission, and he lay before her now, wounded and bleeding. As Janka hauled him over the threshold and out of the view of the neighbors, she now faced an agonizing decision: Should she take her husband to the hospital or keep her appointment in the ghetto? Józef gave a painful laugh when he understood the dilemma. *Wrap me up, Janka,* he said before drifting into darkness. What other choice was there? Janka checked Józef as best she could and decided he would have to manage. She would rush him to the hospital tomorrow.

That evening Janka brought the frightened

Jewish girl home with her, but the situation with Józef made hiding anyone too much of a gamble. Janka did what anyone would do. She called Irena. With the aid of Żegota, the Mikelberg sisters moved to a Jewish safe house run by Janka's mother. By spring, Adolf Berman's account books showed that the same secret courier was supporting the Mikelberg girls, the family of Jonas Turkow, and Adam Celnikier's mother, Leokadia. It was another curious link between the Mikelberg and Celnikier families.

Operations like this were possible only on account of the ghetto passes still in the women's possession. As the Germans pulled the noose around the quarter tighter in the days after the January uprising, those passes were at last canceled. Jaga and Irena would no longer be able to cross the checkpoints into the ghetto. From then on, Jews would have to get themselves out. But Irena would help them in hiding. Word had spread of underground cafés where Jews on the run could meet. Irena had postboxes — drop locations for notes — throughout the city where messages could be left if someone was in need of a safe house or an illegal doctor. She would go into the laundry and leave messages for her courier. But no one had any idea that she was anything other than a cog in a wheel. She acted like a foot soldier. No one suspected that she was the general. Her girlish looks were a great cover.

In the spring of 1943, disaster was looming ever closer, and there were a series of near misses with the children. One day that spring, Żegota leader Julian Grobelny sent urgent word to Irena and asked her to meet him at the train station. In the dingy railway station she scanned the crowds. Where was he? The train on the Otwock line was leaving shortly. Over the loudspeaker, a muffled voice read out track numbers and departure times, and behind her came the rattle of trains coming and going. When Irena caught sight of Julian coming at last, she was shocked. Julian's hacking cough and brightly stained hankerchiefs were telltale signs that the tuberculosis that he already knew would kill him was gaining ground now quickly. Irena tucked her arm in his as they scanned the train for an empty carriage. As the train pulled slowly away from the Warsaw station toward the rural Wawer district, Julian explained their mission. *I have a name,* he said, handing her a scrap of paper. *They are hiding in a village a Jewish child who witnessed her mother's murder. They say she is hysterical.* Irena understood. Moving a traumatized child was an especially high-risk operation.

But that afternoon disaster struck almost the instant they stepped off the platform at their first connection. Irena turned to lift down her supply bag. She never knew what a child's condition would be. By the time she turned back, the crowd was already surging forward. Someone barked orders in German, and somewhere a man cried out in pain as a baton hit him. Irena glanced at her bag. Julian's voice was urgent. *Roundup! Leave it.* Irena's eyes followed Julian as he slipped off the platform and scrambled between two carriages. Irena followed.

When Julian stopped, he leaned back against the carriage and tried to muffle the sounds of his coughing. This was too much for an old man with tuberculosis. She couldn't let him go on. On the platform, the voices of the roundup edged closer, and Irena and Julian crouched low beside the carriage. How long could Julian keep running? *Please, let me go alone. I can get the child. You should return to the city.* He looked down at her youthful face and saw her eyebrows knotted up in worry. No way was he abandoning this operation. "What is this," he retorted indignantly, "you have me for a loser who can not escape the Ger-

330

mans?" Julian flashed her a grin, and Irena realized with a start that the carriage had begun moving. As the train pulled away, in the direction of Wawer at last, Julian swung himself up and stuck out his hand to grasp Irena's.

But it was only the beginning. Irena knew that the hardest part was still ahead of them. Without an address, they looked for the girl late into the night. When they found her at last, Irena marveled at Julian. He tenderly pulled up a chair beside the weeping child and stroked her hair in silence that seemed to go on forever. At last the little girl turned to Julian and pulled herself onto his lap and clung to him. "I don't want to be here," she whispered into his shoulder. "Take me with you." Julian looked at Irena quickly and squeezed the child tighter. Irena smiled. She was glad to see she wasn't the only one who couldn't stop her eyes from watering.

In the spring of 1943, Irena was also still fretting over the safety of Katarzyna Meloch, the ten-year-old whom Ala and Jadwiga had led out of the ghetto the previous summer. In the ghetto, her grandmother, Michalina, and some of her family had eked out a precarious existence. In March that ended. Today, Katarzyna doesn't remember what she was doing the day her family was killed. "I cannot recall exactly what I happened to be doing on the 21st of March, 1943," she muses. "[Perhaps] I was seated on the school bench or running with friends through the forest. . . . [P]erhaps when shots were falling . . . I was singing with the other children in church."

By now, Katarzyna was in hiding at a convent orphanage in the isolated village of Turkowice, where Irena moved dozens of her children. But Katarzyna was a Jew, and there was no such thing as safety. She lived in daily terror of the other children discovering her secret. An older girl named Stasia frightened Katarzyna. Stasia looked at her strangely and was always watching her. If Katarzyna got her catechism wrong, if she mixed up matins and vespers, Stasia made a gleeful and knowing correction. When Katarzyna mentioned seeing a poster that warned residents to watch for pick-pockets, Stasia pounced. "My dear, this poster is in the ghetto," she said, delighted. "You are a Jew."

Then Stasia leaned in to whisper something else. "I know because I passed it one day in the ghetto with my parents. I am Jewish too. You must be more careful." The Germans were hunting for them both,

Stasia warned her. In the orphanages the children played a game: some pretended to be Germans hunting Jews, some were make-believe Jews who were hiding. For Jewish children, the games were all too real.

The Germans continued to hunt for members of Irena's network and Żegota. Stefania Wichlińska, the woman in Irena's office who had introduced her to Żegota, was arrested on April 4, 1943. Despite being tortured, Stefania did not betray her friend Irena. Stefania was gunned down on the streets of the ghetto in a mass execution. She left behind her husband, Stefan, and two children. Stefan, in time, would also risk his life to help save Irena.

But the nearest miss of all happened at the apartment of Jaga Piotrowska that spring. Jaga and her husband ran one of Irena's most important emergency shelters, and more than fifty Jewish people passed through Jaga's doors during the years of the occupation. Jaga was forty years old in 1943 — one of the older women in Irena's network — and her family's house was ideal because it had two entrances, one in the front and one in the back garden. Two ways in and two ways out were crucial in an underground operation. But Lekarska Street, which the house fronted, was divided down the middle and strung with barbed wire. On one side, the Polish residents had been turned out to make room for German doctors and nurses who worked at the nearby *Volksdeutsche* hospital. On the other side lived Polish families like Jaga's.

It meant German patrols went up and down the street at all hours. But the Germans, Jaga told friends with a laugh, were such an orderly, rule-bound people that they couldn't imagine anyone would do something as outrageously brazen as have fifty Jewish people coming and going in front of them.

But this day the barbed wire was part of the catastrophe. A German man had been murdered in the neighborhood. The resistance was stepping up now its targeted assassinations of the occupiers, and retribution was furious. German soldiers began door-to-door searches of the Polish houses looking for their suspect. It was early on a beautiful May morning, Jaga said. Long afterward she would remember that detail clearly. The patrols blocked both ends of the street, and the goose-stepping and barked orders worked their way toward the middle, where Jaga's house was located. She and her family were surrounded. There was no sneaking out the back exit. Jaga knew this was the end. "That morning in our apartment," she explained simply, "were several Jewish adults and children." They might have been Pola and Mieczysław Monar and their two children. One of the children might have been Halina Złotnicka. One of those present was, almost certainly, a teenager named Josek Buschbaum, who lived with Jaga from 1943 to 1946. Perhaps it was the Rapaczyński family, or perhaps the two sisters, Maria and Joanna Majerczy. Whoever Jaga's hidden Jews were, they were unlucky to be in the house on Lekarska Street that beautiful morning.

Jaga stood barefoot in the kitchen, cold with terror. Her daughter, her parents — how could she possibly save them? The shouts on the streets grew nearer, and Jaga whispered to herself the quiet words of the Hail Mary. One of the children watched, wide-eyed, and made a solemn pronouncement that rattled Jaga. *It's all because we are Jewish.*

Jaga's faith was ardent. What would happen to these Jewish children if they died unbaptized? The thoughts came rushing in quickly. Their souls would be lost to the God she even now prayed would save them.

Jaga turned to the Jews watching her. When someone was in extremis — when death was imminent — any Catholic could perform the baptism ritual. At moments like this, no priest was required. All it took was a faithful heart and some water. She turned to the water jug. She gestured to them and showed them how to put their hands together. "I did it myself," Jaga remembered: there in the kitchen, as her mother and her daughter looked on, as the sound of marching feet came closer. "I baptized them and I said that it is done." The Jewish child looked up at her and sighed. "So now we are just like the others?" But Jaga knew their baptism meant nothing to the Germans who were coming.

Jaga fell to her knees to pray in front of the kitchen stove, and the Jewish refugees fell to their knees beside her as Jaga led them in a prayer while they waited together for the Germans. Jaga clutched in her hand, poised before the open fire, a bit of paper. On it were the names of some of Irena's children. When the Germans knocked, she would toss it into the flames and would try to die bravely. Until then, Jaga would not stop praying.

The only sound in the room was the murmur of the Polish women's voices, and it came to Jaga suddenly. Where were the sounds of the Germans? She listened intently. They were becoming fainter now. The Germans were leaving! It was truly, Jaga knew, a miracle. The search squads had met in the middle of the block, just in front of Jaga's home. Each believed that the other had already searched that one. The Germans left Leskarska Street without ever knocking. Others on the street were not so fortunate. Five Jewish men were discovered hiding in a neighbor's home. The neighbors and their guests were shot dead at the crossroads.

As life on the Aryan side grew even more perilous, there were new children now, too — children with family ties to old friends especially. The parents of one Jewish child, Michał Głowiński, were Felicia and Henryk, and when the big *Aktion* started in the summer of 1942, Michał was seven. When they came for the family during the round-ups, his grandfather, Laizer, refused to go and instead jumped to his death from an upstairs window. But Michał and his parents were herded to the Umschlagplatz, destined for Treblinka. At the loading docks, a Jewish policeman showed them a hole in the fence, and the family fled to the relative safety of a ruined basement. For months the Głowiński family struggled in hiding inside the ghetto, and at last, in the first days of 1943, in exchange for a large bribe, a German officer let them hide under a tarp in a military truck at a checkpoint. Michał and his parents joined his aunt in a small attic hideout in the city.

Was this his aunt Theodora? Among Michał's aunts and uncles were Józef and Theodora Zysman, old friends of Irena Sendler's who had slipped out of the ghetto only a few weeks ahead of the Głowińskis. Michał's cousin, little Piotr, was already in safe hiding at an orphanage thanks to Irena. Michał passed long days that winter as a boy in the dusty attic, playing chess and learning his Catholic prayers quietly, until at last their hideout was uncovered by the blackmailing *szmalcownik*s. What choice was there but to flee? Michał's father — the hardest of them to hide and a danger to his family — fled to a nearby village. He would survive somehow, he said. And to help Michał and the women, the family, at last, turned to Irena. Irena found Felicia a position as a maid in the house of a rich Polish couple active in the resistance, people who ran one of the secret schools in Otwock and who hid some other Jewish people. Michał disappeared, first into a convent orphanage in Otwock, then to the distant Turkowice orphanage where Katarzyna Meloch was already hiding.

Decades later, Michał Głowiński would write of his childhood years in Warsaw. "I constantly think that I have encountered a real miracle: I was bestowed the gift of life," he said. The young woman who gave it to him and to his cousin Piotr — and to more than 2,500 other children — was "the great and wonderful Irena . . . the guardian angel of those in hiding. . . . Irena, who in the season of great dying devoted her entire life to saving Jews."

Irena brushed off these kinds of statements. Irena walked instead with the ghosts of those whom were missing — with the heart-break of losing Ewa and Dr. Korczak. With the loss of her thirty-two orphans and with the loss of the tens of thousands of other children who walked innocently, with a piece of soap in hand, into the "showers" that awaited them at Treblinka. Even surviving, she knew, "was a harrowing experience for the small heroes." Few of the children would ever be reunited with their families. Irena always said that the real courage belonged to them and to the fearless teenage girls who, now that the ghetto passes were gone, brought these children to her. To the streetcar drivers and janitors. To the young men who parachuted money into Warsaw and to nurses like Helena and Ala. To the nuns and the foster families across the city who cared for them and hid the children. Above all, it belonged to the mothers and fathers who let them go. She was, Irena always insisted, the least important part of a fragile but astonishing network that spread across Warsaw in the thousands that spring of 1943, just one part of a vast fraternity of strangers.

CHAPTER 13
ALA RISING

WARSAW, APRIL–JULY 1943

The Holy Week celebrations that led up to Easter Sunday took place that year in Warsaw in warm and welcoming spring weather. A funfair rose up that Palm Sunday like a gaudy spring flower in advance of the festivities, just along the Aryan side of the ghetto wall, and one of the star features was a "sky carousel." The Ferris wheel lifted young courting Polish couples high up into the air, and from the top there were long, slow-motion glimpses into the forbidden Jewish quarter. Vendors peddled hot pastries, and long into the evening carnival music blended with the squeals of children's laughter.

The opening of the Holy Week festival on April 18, 1943, also coincided with the Jewish holiday of Passover eve, and secretly throughout the quarter families were preparing celebrations. But long before midnight a terrible rumor swept the ghetto of a coming *Aktion.* No one any longer doubted such rumors, and the scanty feast tables were abandoned. Families instead spent the next few hours packing. Not for the east. Not for desperate flight across the ghetto wall. But to the hideout shelters in hidden attic rooms and to the underground bunkers that hundreds in the ghetto had spent the spring building.

While the children and the frail went underground, the ghetto's young people climbed the rooftops and took up posts in the alleys. Scouts manned observation posts and reviewed the codes for passing messages. Then the ghetto waited. Just after two a.m. SS troops stepping lightly surrounded the ghetto walls. The Aryan quarter dozed on peacefully.

But no one was sleeping in the Jewish quarter. Scouts spread the word throughout the district. It was happening. The residents knew that, when the next round of deportations came, it could only be a battle to the death this time. By two thirty a.m. the resistance had mobilized. At points along the battle line nearly 750 armed young men and women waited. Ala's friend, Jewish underground activist Marek Edelman, was one of their leaders. Irena's contacts at Żegota — Julian Grobelny, Adolf Berman, and Leon Feiner — were all awake as well and mobilizing support plans for the ghetto fighters. Adolf and Leon carried hand grenades and weapons for their Jewish comrades through treacherous tunnels dug underneath the ghetto walls. Julian, weaker than ever from tuberculosis, operated a bedside operational command headquarters and sent couriers here and there across the city, gathering information and passing it along. One of those first messages went out to Irena, who was en route to the front lines, ready to do anything needed. And that morning Ala Gołāb-Grynberg was also making her own preparations. Ala had survived these long, desperate last months by working as a seamstress in the Toebbens factory, but that was not her calling.

From two a.m. until just before dawn, everything was silent. The ghetto was watching. The Germans stood quietly at their posts until the darkest hours of the night and then, at four a.m., began to creep stealthily in small groups past the gates, confident of surprising the sleeping residents. At six a.m., as the sun rose brilliantly over the far horizon, two thousand SS troops were amassed and ready on the street corners and rooftops. An hour later engines fired to life, and the tanks and motorcycle artillery units swept into the district. The signal was given and the SS surged forward. The unseen Jewish fighters, however, were one step ahead of the Germans. Sliding into position, the resistance cut off the SS's path of retreat and opened a furious surprise fire.

The Germans had no idea it was coming. Jewish resistance on this scale did not fit with their preconceptions of what the *Untermenschen* were capable of planning. The resistance fighters — armed only with revolvers, homemade bombs, and a handful of rifles — struck hard and fast, and all that first day wild jubilation swept the quarter. The Jewish fighters weren't just doing battle. They were winning. Ala's old friend Marek Edelman — the slight twenty-year-old who had helped Ala and Nachum save hundreds from the Umschlagplatz in the summer of 1942 and was now leading a resistance battalion — remembered how they used incendiary bottles to attack the German columns. "[We] blew up German tanks and German troops [and by] 5 p.m. the Germans, surprised and shocked by Jewish resistance, withdrew from the ghetto," his diary entry that day boasted. Then, once again, the streets were silent.

The dead littered the streets of the ghetto. Nearly two hundred of the resistance fighters fell in the first fighting. But so did lots more Germans, they reminded each other. Old Jewish men came out from their hiding places to kiss the cheeks of the young heroes where they lay motionless on the sidewalks, and strangers embraced on the streets. Everyone knew it was a short-lived celebration, but this moment had been years in coming. On April 20, Germans delayed their return until the early afternoon and tried to reorganize. The fighting was as fierce as ever. A cheer went up as the ghetto fighters killed a hundred Germans in one fell swoop as a strategically placed mine exploded under them. To the shock of the Germans, teenage girls, fearless and ready to die, carried hand grenades hidden "in their bloomers up to the last moment" in order to get close enough to kill more of their enemies. And their spirits were soaring on the second evening. "We were happy and laughing," fighters remembered. "[When] we threw our grenades and saw German blood on the streets of Warsaw, which had been flooded by so much Jewish blood and tears, a great joy possessed us." Amid the ruins of the Jewish hospital, where Ala was living in a crumbling basement at number 4, Gêsia Street, she and Nachum Remba joined forces once again with the other nurses and doctors and swiftly set up a makeshift emergency medical station to help the fighters.

As word spread across the Aryan side of the ghetto revolt, there was also cheering from that quarter. But the cheers had a sinister undercurrent. Residents of the Aryan side now flocked to the carnival and stood in long lines to buy tickets to be lifted up to watch the fantastic battle unfolding. With picnics and in boisterous parties, Poles lined the bridges overlooking the ghetto. And it seemed to those fighting for their lives inside that those who gathered to watch were not cheering *for* the Jewish fighters so much as they were reveling in the welcome spectacle of the Germans losing. At rooftop parties, people said that it was "the first real entertainment the Germans had provided in all this sad time," and their callous remarks carried on the breeze as far as the ghetto. German airplanes soon swung low over the city, dropping bombs on the walled quarter and exploding houses. As apartment buildings exploded, eager bets were laid on how long it would take the quarter to burn and on whether there would be any Jews left inside afterward.

Irena could hardly bear it. Her ghetto pass was gone, and no Aryan was allowed any longer in and out of the ghetto. Each day she went and stood at the wall, racking her brain to imagine some action, some way, to show Ala that she was still with her. Among her prewar Jewish friends, only Ala remained inside now, fighting. But there was nothing Irena could do to help her or the other fighters.

By Sunday, the sixth day of the insurrection, the tide inside the ghetto was turning. The Germans, furious and determined, lit fires building by building. Smoke poured from behind the walls of the ghetto, and large flakes of gray-white ash floated in the springtime air across central Warsaw. Julian Grobelny sent Irena a message and asked her now to come quickly to the secret Żurawia Street apartment that morning. As Irena stood on the threshold of the front entrance, she remembered later that at that moment the Easter church bells were ringing out across the city. Women floated past in holiday hats and flower-print dresses. From the open windows came the sounds of families sitting down to their joyous Easter breakfast. But in his small room at the back of the apartment, Julian was depressed. It was urban guerrilla warfare inside the ghetto, his contacts were reporting, and the attacks were coming at the fighters from all directions. It was not a question of winning against the Germans. It had always been impossible. Now it was only a matter of helping any survivors who could make the dangerous passage out of the inferno.

"You have to help them," Julian said. Irena's answer was instant: *What do you need? Tell me.* Julian replied, "Give me some addresses where we can take people who make it to the Aryan side." From there, Żegota could help them. Irena considered. Which addresses could she use? There was her apartment. She knew she could count on Zofia and Stanisław. She could count on Janka and her sister Jaga. *We have our "emergency rooms,"* Irena replied. *They are open to anyone who flees the ghetto. Can Żegota transmit the addresses to the Jewish combat organization?*

Irena also considered further. She knew it was a daring risk — even more daring than some of their old operations. But if the Germans were hell-bent on destruction street by street, Irena spotted opportunity. Were the Germans distracted enough that she could perhaps get back into the ghetto? she wondered. And if she could get in, surely she could get out with some people. Irena had made it in — and out — of the ghetto that day, and brought with her a youngster. It could be done!

She mobilized her team, and for the next few days the women were once again in and out of the ghetto. Irka Schultz fearlessly rushed into burning buildings and pulled out crying toddlers. Irena waited at sewer manholes and tunnel exits, directing refugees to safe-house addresses. At Janka's apartment, members of the resistance came and went, depositing secret documents being ferried out of the ghetto. Shut off from her friend, Irena was desperately worried for Ala. As the blaze grew fiercer with the passing days, Irena hoped that, somehow, Ala would be one of those to make it to the shelters. Julian shared her worry for Ala. Ala was working directly with him and with the others in the Jewish resistance, and Julian knew her well as a woman of immense resourcefulness and courage. If anyone could survive, it would be Ala.

For a week or two the ruse worked, and families crawled through the sewers to safety. But soon the Germans grew wise to the escape routes. They now shut off all the city utilities and pumped poison into the water and gas mains to kill those escaping. By early May, for those left behind, there was no easy exit. Ala was among those who stayed on, fighting. From burnt-out shelters on opposite sides of Gėsia Street, Ala, Nachum, and Nachum's wife, Henia, tried to help the wounded ghetto fighters with medical services.

On May 8, 1943, close to the end, the German patrols raided the bunkers on Gėsia Street. All around Ala, the ghetto was burning. "There was no air, only black, choking smoke and heavy, burning heat radiating from the red-hot walls, from the glowing stone stairs," her fellow activist, Marek Edelman, wrote in his diary. "The flames cling to our clothes, which now start smoldering. The pavement melts under our feet." Mothers jumped with their small children to their deaths four or five stories below, amid a hail of German gunfire. Charred corpses lay on the streets, and buildings were reduced to rubble. In the underground dirt cellars, the hospital team crouched together fearfully, piling rocks carefully to hide from view their children. But the Germans hunted with dogs now, and one of those dogs betrayed Ala. She could taste the dirt and ash in her mouth, and her legs trembled as they crawled out into the open at gunpoint.

They were marched that day together to the assembly point at Nalewki Street. The path led to the Umschlagplatz. Ala knew what awaited them on the other end of the train line. For two days they waited for the train to come. German and Ukrainian soldiers probed the bodies of young men, searching their body cavities for hidden weapons, and around Ala young men were disemboweled and dying. Ala tried not to watch, too, as the prettier girls were raped in turn by a gang of laughing soldiers, followed by the unmistakable ricochet of the gunfire. Perhaps Henia Remba was one of those women. She was young, and there is no known record to show that she ever left Warsaw. Murmurs of pain were silenced with iron cudgels, and then Ala and Nachum were wired into one of the cattle cars destined for Treblinka.

On the Aryan side, the burning of the ghetto could be clearly seen from Świętojerska Street and from Krasiński Square, and there, despite it all, the carnival continued.

The partisans did battle until there was no longer a ghetto left to hide in. By May 9, their number dwindling, the top leader of the Jewish Fighting Organization — one of several resistance groups in the ghetto — was Marek Edelman. But by May 10 or 11, there wasn't any drama left for curious Poles to watch, just relentless execution and death by fire. Jewish fighters raised a makeshift plea, scrawled on a bedsheet, over the wall toward the Aryan side: "Brother, Please Help! We Fight for Our and Your Freedom!" But no help ever came from the Polish masses. Marek and his partisans, men and women, retreated to the buried hillside bunkers and, in a desperate change of tactics, only came out after darkness for nighttime street fighting. During the days, the ghetto was eerily quiet, and the ever-present whisper of flames and sometimes beams crashing were the only sounds heard. The fighters ran out of water and ammunition. The only goal in the last days was not to be taken alive by the Germans. Trapped in hideouts that would be their crypts, families and resistance leaders pulled out from their last, precious possessions their cyanide pills and committed suicide together.

Only a handful of the Warsaw ghetto fighters escaped death and transport to the camps. These were the fighters who managed to slip, undetected, to the Aryan side in the last days of the revolt. There were fewer than two hundred of them. But Marek

Edelman was one of them. He remembered later how, with the ghetto collapsing around them, a few strong and lucky fighters — men and women — "half-walked, half-crawled for twenty hours" through sewers booby-trapped by the Germans, squeezing themselves through fetid pipes just over two feet in diameter in darkness. On the other side, trucks and comrades, ready to rush away to the forests or safe houses, waited for them. At one of those grates, Irena stood sentinel.

At 8:15 p.m. on May 16, just as dusk settled over Warsaw, a colossal blast of dynamite shook windows as far as the Aryan quarter. The great synagogue shuddered for a moment and then crumbled. It was the last symbolic defeat of the Jews of Warsaw. The battle for the ghetto was over. The German governor-general of the city informed his superiors in Berlin that his mission was accomplished. "Jews, bandits, and subhumans were destroyed. The Jewish quarter of Warsaw is no more." Only the bombed-out steeple tower of Saint Augustine's church rose up forlornly in the center of a sea of concrete and brick rubble. The governor-general proudly reported that the total number of Jews destroyed in the *Aktion,* at the death camps or by fire, totaled 56,065 out of a population of perhaps 60,000.

And for those Jews in hiding on the Aryan side of the city, life now became — though it was hard to believe it — infinitely more precarious.

Many in hiding outside of the ghetto now despaired of survival. Constant terror took a psychic toll from which some would never recover. Faced with the chance of fleeing, some Jewish men and women now took fantastic gambles. One of those men was Irena's old friend, the attorney Józef Zysman.

When Józef and his family escaped the ghetto at the end of 1942, the Hotel Polski was a seedy four-story building at number 29, Długa Street, located just outside the ghetto boundary. On the ground floor was a restaurant, and the stairs above led to rooms with narrow rectangular windows overlooking the cobbled avenue. Since his escape, Józef had been moving from one apartment safe house to another, and the family had separated for safety. Irena was looking after little Piotr, and Theodora was living now with false papers.

By the late spring of 1943, Józef was lonely and tired. *Szmalcownik*s stalked the city, ferreting out hidden Jews for extortion and the German bounty. They searched for small clues of someone in hiding: the play of shadows against an attic window at twilight or an extra loaf of bread in a housewife's basket. Then his guardians would come to Józef, frantic, and he would flee to the streets at a moment's notice, again homeless. Józef wandered, trying to think of where he could go to sleep just for a few hours. He missed his family. He missed his life. He knew that he could not carry on in this state of constant terror.

It was sometime in the second or the third week of May that Józef first heard a wild rumor. The occupiers, someone whispered to Józef, were willing to exchange Jews for German citizens abroad, and the Jews would be sent out of Poland on regular train service. Soon the rumors took on an even more fantastic dimension. People said now, at the underground cafés where Jews on the run learned to go for news and coffee, that a long-awaited ration of visas and passports for foreign-born Jews and Jews wanting to emigrate to South America and Palestine had arrived in Warsaw from the embassies abroad. The papers arrived too late to save their intended recipients. The Umschlagplatz had claimed nearly all of them. But that didn't mean these visas and passports couldn't save someone — although salvation would come at black-market prices.

Behind it all were an unscrupulous Jewish profiteer named Adam Żurawin and a ghetto gangster named Leon "Lolek" Skosowski. No one quite knew how, but during the ghetto uprising they had come into possession of an astonishing cache of undelivered mail, which included hundreds of emigration papers. Adam, the whisperers at the underground cafés said, managed a small hotel at number 29, Długa Street. You could go there to buy a passport. The fees, naturally, were staggering. Only rich Jews who had saved something of their prewar fortunes would be able to pay Adam Żurawin's prices, although that did not stop desperate and impoverished families from trying. Rumor had it, too, that the hotel was being set up as a kind of neutral staging ground — a place where Jews could register for emigration and wait safely until the papers were processed and the deportations out of Poland started.

Józef watched and waited. But it was true! The first arrivals registered for visas, and they were told that they would have to be patient. They checked into sunlit rooms on the upper stories, and the Germans didn't come to arrest them. In fact, it seemed like some kind of paradise. Inside the confines of the hotel corridors and rooms, the residents were granted unimaginable freedom. Here, Jews didn't have to wear the Star of David, and the Gestapo studiously — too studiously, some said — ignored the building. A small patch of cobblestone in front of the main entrance was declared a patio for the café-restaurant, and from the street corner Józef could plainly see for himself well-dressed Jews enjoying coffee unmolested in the late spring sunshine. People came and went, and at night the neighborhood rang with the sounds of the wildest, most joyous parties at the Hotel Polski. Women pulled out their hidden fur coats and their mothers' pearls and walked the corridors with a swish of satin. Amorous couples, desirous of nothing as much as life and this freedom, staggered tipsily through the corridors, oblivious to the fate of others.

At the Hotel Polski, it was miracle after miracle. Still, Józef was watchful. But he was also growing desperate. On May 21, even the naysayers and the doubters were silenced. That morning sixty-four Jews from the hotel — with no SS guards and with great politeness from the Germans — boarded a well-equipped and comfortable train destined for the camp at Vittel, on the eastern border of France, where conditions were known to be civilized. On the train, even the children had their own seats and waved a cheerful good-bye to Warsaw from the gleaming windows.

Those who boarded inevitably included those willing to pay the largest bribes. Some families paid 750,000 złotych — something over $2 million — for one of the precious passports. Many families paid 20,000 or 30,000 złotych for single documents that might help in an application. When letters arrived from Vittel that the recipients knew were authentic, confirming safe arrivals and good conditions, things went crazy. More than 2,500 Jewish people rushed from their hiding places on the Aryan side. Some figures put the number as high as 3,500. They all came to jockey for a place on the list of emigrants — to roll the dice in what even those going there understood was the war's most spectacular and dangerous lottery.

Irena's friend, the Jewish attorney Józef Zysman, was among them. It wasn't that Józef believed the Germans so much as he had lost faith in his chances of survival on the run, for hiding Jewish men was much, much harder than hiding mothers or children. And for some reason — perhaps it was pride, perhaps it was the sense that he had already asked too much by giving her Piotr — Józef didn't reach out to Irena. He didn't believe he could last on the Aryan side much longer, and if there was any chance, it was worth the wild gamble.

The Polish underground tried to warn Jews that it was a trap. Urgent messages buzzed across all their secret networks. But the Jews who went could not be persuaded. Hope was too powerful. For months a fantasy world had taken hold at the Hotel Polski, and the party went on until the gangsters were confident that the last pockets of hidden wealth were exhausted. The Hotel Polski was nothing more than a cruel opportunity — arranged between the Gestapo and a handful of Jewish collaborators — to strip Warsaw's Jewry of its last remaining resources. Among those Jewish collaborators and the architects of this tissue of rumor was a woman whom Irena and Józef knew well from the ghetto. She was the sultry cabaret singer who crooned old love songs at the smoke-filled Café Sztuka, and she was Ala's cousin: Wiera Gran. Irena was convinced that Wiera was a Gestapo informer.

Irena wasn't the only one. Many of those

closest to Irena saw evidence of Wiera's treachery. Secret files of the Home Army warned its agents that Wiera Gran, "Jewess, before the war, a cabaret dancer, now leads an office of the confidants of the Gestapo, who are occupied mainly [in] hunting for Jews." At Żegota, Dr. Adolf Berman saw her as a Nazi collaborator. So did Ala's young friend, the now-celebrated ghetto hero Marek Edelman. Jonas Turkow, the Jewish actor whom Ala and Nachum had saved at the Umschlagplatz, claimed to have witnessed her betrayals directly. Asked later to describe the singer, whom she had watched perform that night with Ala in the ghetto nightclub in the days before the great *Aktion,* Irena was blunt in her assessment of Ala's cousin: "Wiera Gran, a cabaret actress . . . worked for the Gestapo alongside Leon Skosowski. . . . It hurt me a great deal that among the list of great people of the Jewish Nation, Wiera Gran was among them — a criminal, who sold out her own people."

One of those Wiera was rumored to have sold out that year was Józef Zysman. He presented himself that spring, along with those thousands of others, at the shabby front desk of the Hotel Polski. He handed over whatever sums that registration required. And for weeks Józef passed his days

360

pacing up and down the tired hallways, his last resources dwindling rapidly amid the scenes of jubilant chaos. At last, one morning in July, someone excitedly spread the word. They were leaving! The trains were coming! It seemed so civilized to Józef in the beginning. Jews calmly boarded the trains, expecting to head west, to life and freedom. How long was it before those on board realized that the tracks only led to the concentration camps at Bergen-Belsen? And when the trains could not take them all and the Gestapo was eager to be done with the affair, those who remained — several hundred — were taken to the notorious Pawiak Prison in the ruins of the ghetto. Some were lined up against the elm tree in the courtyard and executed in a hail of gunfire. Others were led opposite the prison gate to Dzielna Street, to where a rough wooden platform stretched out over the abyss of a burnt-out foundation. As shots rang out, bodies tumbled from that parapet into a mass grave filled with jumbled quicklime-covered bodies. Among the victims of the Hotel Polski was Józef Zysman. "A wonderful man died a martyr's death, dishonorably deceived by barbarians" — that was Irena's indictment. Irena and her friends would not forget the role of Wiera

Gran in his murder. Wiera protested her innocence. Irena was not persuaded. After the war, there would be consequences and more allegations. There would be trials and recriminations, and Irena would bear testimony against Wiera personally.

Something else astonishing and heartbreaking made its way that summer back to Warsaw through the channels of Żegota and the underground, too, and surely its leader, Julian Grobelny, shared the news with Irena. A determined group of Jewish fighters, caught up in the deportations to Treblinka in the last days of the ghetto uprising, had been sent on to a slave labor camp at a place called Poniatowa. There the prisoners were set to work fabricating German military uniforms for the textile magnate Walter Toebbens, and most of those saved from the gas chambers were Jews who had been assigned to his factories inside the ghetto. Henia Koppel, the mother of baby Bieta, was one of them. Now word was coming that a dozen or so among them were organizing within the camp a resistance cell and an underground railroad. Someone among them got word to Marek Edelman's organization. They needed urgent help to keep on fighting. Someone in the cell got a message to Julian Grobelny at Żegota as well. Among their number, Julian learned, was a woman, a nurse, who had already set up at the camp a secret medical clinic and a children's youth circle. Her team needed false identity papers, money, and, once again, weapons. Operations had begun to smuggle out the children with the aid of local Żegota operatives. Then they planned to stage a mass prison escape and another Jewish uprising. That nurse was Ala.

Nineteen forty-three was a year of great tragedy and moral darkness in Warsaw, but there were also amazing stories of survival and struggle — Ala's and others'. That autumn there was another dramatic rescue of a child whose life would be tied forever to Irena's story. Chaja Estera Stein was the first of Irena's own two foster daughters. Once again it was Julian Grobelny who made the connection.

Estera came from the village of Cegłow, not far from Warsaw, and in 1940, the year Estera turned thirteen, she was interned in the ghetto in Mrozy with her parents, Aron and Faiga, and her little sister, Jadzia. In 1942 the Mrozy ghetto was liquidated. Aron, Faiga, and Estera fled the roundups with their lives and huddled together that first night in an old garden shed on a farm outside the village. But little Jadzia had been left behind in the chaos alone, and her mother was frantic. Aron laid his hand on his wife's shoulder and promised: he was returning to the ghetto. He would find her. For days the mother and daughter waited in the shadows. Then Faiga understood that Aron and Jadzia were never returning.

Faiga looked at her hungry and tired daughter. They couldn't stay in a garden shed forever. In the darkness, Faiga crept for help to the only person in the village she could think might help them. Aron owned a factory, and his business was making soda water. Julian Grobelny owned one of the large farms in the village — perhaps even the farm where Estera and her mother were hiding. Julian and Aron were great friends, both with each other and with the local priest in the parish church. Estera's image of her father was always one of him and the priest walking together, her Orthodox Jewish father with his long beard and black garbardine coat and the priest in his swaying cassock. When Faiga knocked on the door of the parish house, the old priest gave her food and water and promised he would help her. But Faiga did not survive the return journey. She was captured and murdered.

The priest sent urgent word to Julian that they would have to hurry if they were to save Estera.

Julian turned, as always, to Irena, the director of Żegota's child welfare cell, who sent a courier to the priest with new identity papers. Estera's new Aryan name was now "Teresa Tucholska," and she would have to travel alone on the train to Warsaw. Anything else was too dangerous. The priest walked Estera to the train station and showed her which compartment to enter, and when the Germans asked to see her papers, Estera remembered what to say perfectly. The railway station in Warsaw was crowded and noisy, but on the platform a small blond woman waited for her patiently. Irena touched the girl's shoulder reassuringly. *Come along, then, Teresa.* And the next few days Estera stayed with Irena and her mother in the small apartment in Wola, during those dangerous first hours of transition. Estera was an independent and clever girl, but in the space of weeks she had lost her entire family, and Irena found herself wishing for the first time that she had babies.

Despite what Irena wished, Estera could not stay on in her apartment. Liaisons and resistance couriers came and went, and it was too dangerous for a child already. At last, Irena hit upon the perfect solution. She would send Estera to Zofia and Stanisław, her old friends from the Polish Free University and both activists in the cells of Dr. Radlińska's underground networks. Zofia and Stanisław had four children of their own, and they were already hiding in their apartment at number 9, Lekarska Street, in the Ochota district, three additional Jewish youngsters. Of course they would hide Estera, they assured Irena — and "Teresa" would become the eighth child in their wartime family. It was just in time. Soon, Irena wouldn't be in a position to safely take care of anyone. It was Irena who, in the fall of 1943, would desperately need saving.

CHAPTER 14
ALEJA SZUCHA
WARSAW, OCTOBER 1943–JANUARY 1944

Bracka Street was just off a main thorough-
fare to the east of where the ghetto had
stood, and its busy storefronts included a
laundry shop where housewives could get
some relief, if they had the money to spare.
Women came and went all day there, picking up neatly wrapped brown paper parcels
or linens piled in baskets. Sometimes,
though, the women came and went bringing something else, a note, or a message,
tucked among the folds of garments. In
October 1943 the Gestapo arrested the
woman who ran the shop, accusing her of
aiding the resistance by passing parcels and
messages. Taken to Szucha Avenue and
tortured, brutalized at Pawiak, and interrogated again with iron bars and truncheons, the broken and wretched woman
gave the Gestapo what information she
knew. She was almost certainly executed
afterward. There was no way to blame

367

someone in these circumstances. No one knew whether they would be able to withstand torture until faced with one's executioners. When she cracked, she named at least three women who used her shop as an underground postbox. One of them was Irena Sendler.

On the evening of October 19, Irena and her family gathered for a small party. One of her aunts had come and spent the night with her mother. So, too, had Irena's friend — and her underground liaison — Janka Grabowska. Janka and her husband, Józef, were a couple whom many people trusted to keep their secrets. They were hiding for some members of the Jewish Fighting Organization important files and archives, and they were also still hiding their friend — a woman who was, perhaps, something even more to Adam and his family: Regina Mikelberg, along with her sister. Neither Janka nor Irena had forgotten Regina's dramatic escape from the railcars rolling toward Treblinka or the old ties of college friendship that connected them to each other and to Adam, no matter how complicated Irena's most private emotions.

After the cakes and cordials, the mother and aunt retired to bed, but Janka and Irena stayed up talking until long after curfew. It was nearly two in the morning, in fact, before the younger women settled down to sleep on makeshift beds in the living room. Before letting herself drift off to sleep, Irena carefully did what she always did as a precaution: she placed the current card files with the names and the addresses of dozens of Jewish children in the center of the kitchen table, underneath the window. She tucked her weathered workbag, which held some blank identity papers and a large sum of money, by the side of her bed for safe-keeping. Then she dozed lightly.

At just after three a.m. the pounding started. Her mother, Janina, suffering from a heart condition that left her tossing fit-fully, had awoken moments earlier, and her whispered alarm had given Irena the pre-cious few moments she needed to clear her fuzzy head and spring into action. The agents roared at the door, screaming: *Open! Gestapo!* A pry bar scratched at the door, and there was the sound of cracking. Irena had practiced her routine many times. She had prepared for this eventuality. She grabbed the lists and moved swiftly toward the window. As she was about to lift the sash, her heart stopped. Below were more Gestapo agents, gazing malignantly up at

her. *Jesus. Jesus. Jesus.* What was she going to do now? Irena scanned the room
hopelessly. There was nowhere safe to hide
the lists. As the pounding on the door grew
more furious and the door began to give
way, she tossed them desperately to Janka:
*This is a list of our children; hide it somewhere.
Save it! It cannot fall into the hands of the
Gestapo!* She had time to see Janka stuff
the list into her bra before the door clattered open.

Eleven Gestapo agents swarmed forward,
and behind them Irena saw the horror-
stricken face of Mr. Przeździecki, the building manager. The men went wild. The
agents stood above her, inches away, and
screamed threats and orders at her. In their
frenzy they destroyed the apartment. They
tore apart the insides of the stove looking
for hidden materials, pulled up the floorboards, threw dishes from the cupboards. It
was all calculated for maximum effect, and
Irena had to admit that it worked. She was
frightened. The search went on for three
heart-stopping hours, and there was something almost surreal about how it all unfolded. Irena didn't believe in miracles, but
as the Gestapo began tearing apart the mattress of her makeshift bed, she watched in
awe as the rickety frame collapsed on top of

the bag, sitting there in plain view, with all the identity documents and cash inside. Irena could not believe it. The Germans had just hidden from themselves the most incriminating of all the evidence.

All the while, they battered Irena and her visitors with questions. Irena at last convinced the agents that Janka was an innocent out-of-town visitor like Irena's aunt, although in fact Janka was practically a neighbor. Her mother, the agents saw plainly, was too ill to be engaged in the underground. So that left only Irena.

At six a.m. the agents wrapped up their search, and the agent in charge barked at Irena to dress quickly. Pulling on her skirt in a rush and trying to quickly button up her sweater, Irena's heart felt lighter than she ever could have imagined. If they were letting her get dressed, they were done searching. If they were done searching, they hadn't discovered the lists. And if they weren't there for Janka, they didn't know about Jaga's apartment or the sisters' collaboration with her. Her eyes met Janka's, but Irena didn't risk a smile. All she wanted was to get out of the apartment before the Gestapo could reconsider.

As the agents led her into the corridor, their heavy boots echoed in the stairwell.

Along the hallway, Irena knew that the neighbors were listening at their doors in silence. A few moments later it would be chaos and gossip.

A prison car waited outside, its engine already running. Janka dashed down the walkway at the last moment — a dangerous impulse. In her hands, Irena saw her shoes. *She will need them. Please.* The men just nodded, bored, and gestured to Irena to get on with it.

Irena knew her destination. The sedan was cramped, and Irena was pressed inside, onto the lap of one of the young Gestapo agents. The doors slammed closed and the car lurched into motion. She supposed she had always known this moment would come, but she realized suddenly she hadn't been prepared for it.

The sun wasn't yet up over Warsaw, and in the half-light of morning the agents closest to her dozed lightly. Irena tried to think calmly, rationally. Janka knew how important the lists were and she would surely hide them. She understood how things stood. There was no chance, realistically, of Irena surviving.

As the car turned south to join the broad boulevards, Irena thought of Dr. Radlińska and her dozens of sleeping conspirators scattered across the city. At least, she desperately hoped they were sleeping. She thought of Adam. Would she be strong enough to keep his secret? There was no point in pretending. Something terrible was coming next. She knew that. Was there pain enough in the world that would lead her to betray Adam's hiding place? Was there enough to make her betray Jaga or Janka or the children? What about Adam's Jewish wife? Would she die to protect her also? Irena thought she could bear it. But most could not stand the torture. She must steel her nerves. She would die in silence. As long as her friends and the children survived, she told herself, she could suffer anything. That was what everyone said at the beginning.

As they approached the final turn, Irena slipped her hands into her coat pockets to warm them for a final few moments. The jolt of fear came like a knife in her heart. A list. Addresses. She had forgotten last night to take it out of her jacket. On a small roll of cigarette paper was scratched the details of one of the safe houses.

Irena rode the rising tide of panic for a moment. There was no time left. They were nearing Szucha. The young man on whose lap she was perched, surely his breathing meant he was dozing? Quietly, gently, she rolled and shredded the tissue paper into balls in her pocket. Its flimsy texture gave way quickly. If nothing else, it would smudge the writing. Watching the heads of the nearest agents bobbing and swaying with the car's motion, she was nearly certain they were sleeping. What else could she do but this one last gamble? She lifted her hand gently to the open window and let the tiny bullets flutter free. The agent beneath her twitched and snorted, and then nothing.

Irena leaned her head against the window and closed her eyes, too, but with tears streaming down her face.

The slaughterhouse. That was what people on the streets of Warsaw called the squat gray compound on Szucha Avenue. Steel chains and locks studded the iron gates that rose up before Irena, and the guards wore ugly whips slung at their hips and high black boots with a glossy polish. A bored officer brusquely hustled Irena toward the anteroom. Beyond the doorway, she could make out the contours of a large room where interrogations were conducted. She was pushed along quickly for registration, into a small room where a typewriter clanged and the radio played German music.

She waited. Soon she was led into another

room where a tall German man asked her questions in perfect Polish. His manner was smooth and gentle. Irena knew that the intention was deadly. *What was her name? Where did she live? Who was her family?* Those were easy questions — questions to which the Gestapo already had the answers. But before long the questions moved on to more perilous ground. *We know you are helping the resistance and the Jews, Pani Sendler. What organization are you working for? It will be better for you.* They knew about Julian Grobelny. They were hunting for this elusive man "Konrad Żegota." They knew about the underground postbox at the laundry. The thickness of the man's file made her start feeling very frightened. She prayed they did not know about Adam.

She protested that she knew nothing. It was all a misunderstanding. She was a social worker, and that brought her into contact with many people. Naturally. But if someone in her circle was doing something wrong, she knew nothing about it. The agent gave her a thin smile and arched his eyebrow. He had seen it all before. These people always protested their innocence in the beginning. Torture had a way of getting them talking. She was choosing the hard way. *So be it, Pani Sendler. We will talk further, I promise.*

Another guard pushed Irena along the corridor afterward. The tunes still drifted from the radio. It was early and everything else was silent. Before long the transfers from Pawiak would be arriving and the hallways would echo with footsteps and weeping. The ceilings there were low and the corridor narrow. Irena passed four cells, each with iron grates and a row of narrow wooden benches, and at one of them the door was pushed open. Others sat silently, with slumped shoulders, and no one turned as she entered, stumbling. *Sit,* came the stern order. *You are to look only at the back of the head in front of you. No speaking.* Irena smelled fear and dampness. They were all new arrivals, sleepless and worried.

The narrow bench was hard and too low to be comfortable. The ground beneath her shoe was sticky. Blood. A wave of dizziness flooded over her. For a time Irena and the others sat motionless. Just after eight a.m. the transports arrived and the benches around her filled with strangers. The radio stopped playing, and now names were called. Soon cries of terror came from the hallway, the distant sounds of things being thrown, dull thuds, and then the cries of bodies being broken. Sometimes there was gunfire. Interrogations took place on the upper floors or in the basement, but the doors and windows were left open as an inducement to the others waiting to assess their options carefully. Said one survivor of those morning rituals at Szucha Avenue, "One could hear curt questions, the murmur of low answers and again and again, the sound of blows, after which came a shriek, often a woman's sob, clutching at our hearts and impeding our breathing."

There was another prison tradition. On the first day of their arrest, prisoners were severely beaten. Often, one savage session did the trick. By the second or third day, many proved more pliable and willing. Irena would never talk of the abuse she suffered that day or in the days that followed, but others remembered the abuses at Pawiak with horror. There were blows to the face with fists and boots that left eyes hanging from sockets, and bone-shattering strikes with rubber truncheons. Soldering irons burned the flesh of breasts and faces. Shoulders were dislocated. Afterward the limp and bloodied inmates were thrown back into the cells and ordered to sit at attention until the covered prison trucks that would transport them to Pawiak rolled through the gates. On October 20, 1943, Irena was among those bruised and beaten bodies. Inside the darkness of the transport van that first afternoon, she tried to push the pain and fear from her mind as the truck sped across the city, its horns blaring a disconsolate refrain — but every movement was agony.

At Pawiak, a prison guard marched Irena down broad stone stairs. Those who could not stand were hauled along, and a handful of grim-faced nurses and doctors pulled the most dangerously beaten from the truck and loaded them, moaning, onto canvas army stretchers. Officially, Pawiak was the prison for political figures, academics, students, doctors, and those in the resistance and illegal universities — the intelligentsia. But in practice, it was a notorious black-site prison, and there was no legal process. One-third of those who arrived that afternoon with Irena would face execution. Most of the others would perish after being sent away on the late-night transports that left the prisoners at Pawiak in a constant state of terror. Those destined for the concentration camps of Ravensbrück and Auschwitz were hauled into the prison courtyard after lights-out and, in the darkness, pummeled with rifle butts by furious guards, then loaded on coaches handcuffed to one another. Irena understood. Death was how this ended.

At Pawiak, Irena was shocked to see old friends and conspirators among the inmates. In her cell that first night, Irena and her neighbor Basia Dietrich grasped hands silently in the darkness. In an urgent whispered conversation, long after lights-out, Basia told Irena that another friend, Helena Pęchcin, had also been arrested. Helena was a history schoolteacher. Basia and Irena had lived nearby for years in the same apartment complex in Wola, where Basia was a Scout leader and still ran the community kindergarten. Irena had known Basia since those first days as a young newlywed with Mietek. Unofficially, though, Basia was a captain in a resistance movement known as the Powstańcze Oddziały Specjalne "Jerzyki" — the Insurgent Special Forces "Swifts" — a group of dedicated men and women who ran, in parallel to Irena's network, an operation rescuing several hundred Jewish children from the ghetto. Helena was Basia's operational partner. By the spring of 1943, when the Insurgent Special Forces were combined with Home Army operations and became part of the sprawling and diffuse underground movement that included Żegota, their group was in regular contact with Irena.

The next morning Irena made contact with another friend inside the prison. Jadwiga Jędrzejowska was alive! She could not believe it. Jadwiga Jędrzejowska was another of Dr. Radlińska's girls from before the war, a few years older than Irena and her close circle, but Irena recognized her instantly. Jadwiga and her Jewish boyfriend, Horak, joined the resistance immediately after the occupation started, working in the underground press movement, and for three years they eluded the Gestapo. But in 1942 the two were arrested. Horak was shot, and for a year Jadwiga languished in prison, assigned at first, despite her medical training, to cleaning latrines and offices. But in the prison there was an astonishing resistance taking shape, and soon Jadwiga was pulled into the network. Two husband-and-wife teams were at the heart of this underground cell: Dr. Anna Sipowicz, a dentist, and her medical doctor husband, Dr. Witold Sipowicz; and Dr. Zygmunt Śliwicki, a physician, and his wife, the prison head nurse, Anna Śliwicka. All four were members of the Polish resistance; like Irena, the women were in their early thirties and fearless.

At nine a.m. on the second day of her incarceration, Irena stood with the others at attention. Breakfast — a bit of moldy bread and ersatz coffee — was over. So were the eight thirty a.m. calls for the day's executions. As the stricken women were led out for the last time, Irena dropped her eyes to the ground. She could not bear to watch this. Above her scuffed shoes, she felt the red welts rising along her ankles where bedbugs crawled over her in the night, and even moving her head made her face throb where the first German blows had fallen. The nine a.m. roll calls were for patients ordered to the medical clinics. Irena's mind wandered. Her head jerked up as she heard Jadwiga Jědrzejowska's voice call out Irena's name for the dentistry office. Dentist? Irena started to say, *I don't need to see the dentist . . .*

Then it flashed upon her: *it was a message.* Irena stepped forward wordlessly and followed.

The window of the cramped office into which she was led looked out over the ruins of the ghetto. It was hard to forget what she had witnessed there. Ewa. Dr. Korczak. Rachela. Ala. Józef. As far as she could see, it was a sea of rubble and stone and burnt-out ruins of foundations.

When the prison dentist, Dr. Anna Sipowicz, slipped into the room, Irena realized she also knew Anna from prewar activist circles. What a relief to be among friends! Irena started to speak, but Anna quickly put up a finger and gestured to the dentist's chair before her. Irena nodded. In order not to raise suspicion, Anna would have to drill a hole and fill a cavity that had never existed. But Irena, in the dentist's chair, understood at last when Anna passed her a *gryps* — a secret wadded prison message. It was from Julian Grobelny — "Trojan" — and the message was simple: "We are doing everything we can to get you out of that hell." On the tissue-thin paper that Anna held out to her, Irena scribbled back the only return message that mattered. *The lists are safe!* As long as Irena did not break under the torture, no one knew the location of the hidden children. What Irena didn't tell Julian Grobelny, of course, was that the lists were with Janka. It would have been too great a risk if the message were intercepted. It would turn out to be an amazingly lucky decision.

Over the next days and weeks, there were more trips to Szucha, just as her German interrogator had promised. Some mornings when the rolls were read after breakfast, calling forward those destined for transport and torture, Irena's heart clenched to hear her name among them. Before long, the bones of Irena's legs and feet were broken, and there were scars and ugly open wounds running in jagged strips across her body that would mark her forever.

All that saved Irena from being beaten to death on those days was the fact that the Germans didn't have any idea whom they had captured. The Gestapo thought Irena was a small player, a foolish young woman dabbling at the periphery of the Polish resistance. They had no inkling yet that they had captured one of its most senior leaders or a woman responsible for hiding thousands of Jewish children across the city. But they would not be ignorant of this fact forever. Through the pain, Irena reasoned with herself silently. Some days the torture seemed bearable, and with enough concentration she could sometimes float away from her poor, miserable body. Other times the beatings were fierce, and the darkness lapped at the edges of her consciousness. Was she prepared to die to save the others? She knew she had it in her power to bring about the deaths of thousands. She repeated over and over her story. She was just a social worker. She knew nothing. She refused to let herself think of Adam. To even think of

Adam might mean his name would slip out unbidden as she fell to the floor under the blows.

Twice a day, at noon and in the evening, the vans carted the broken bodies back to Pawiak. "One could have an impression that this was an ambulance carrying victims of a disaster," one of the doctors remembered. "Their faces were pale and covered in blood, with black eyes, clothes crumpled and soiled, often with sleeves and pockets torn off." Some days Irena was among them. Other days she worked in the prison laundry, standing long hours on fractured and painful limbs that were healing badly, scrubbing feces from stained German underwear in between the torture. She limped painfully now, and the daily walks around the prison courtyard were an agony. When the job in the laundry was not done to the Germans' satisfaction, the punishments were sadistic. One afternoon a furious guard lined the laundry women up against the wall and, walking down the row, put a bullet through the head of every other person. Irena, that day, was one of the survivors.

On the morning of Irena's arrest, as word spread, there was panic. Julian Grobelny and the leadership at Żegota faced one set of concerns, the most important of which was the lists and the addresses of the children. If Irena were executed, the information about the lists would perish with her. Thousands of children, many of whom were too young to remember their own identities, would be lost forever to their families and to the Jewish nation. But there was also a far bigger risk that Irena posed to those children. Irena put it bluntly: "They weren't just worried about me . . . they didn't know whether I could stand the torture. After all, I knew where all the children were." If Irena broke, it would be an unparalleled disaster. But saving her was an immense challenge. It would mean bribing someone at the very highest levels of the Gestapo.

At Maria Kukulska's house in Praga, the problems were different. And the residents were asking themselves the same questions: Could Irena withstand the torture? What did the Germans know already? Janka Grabowska passed word of the arrest to Maria and Adam, but she could only advise them to be prepared for what might happen.

Jurek was still courting Maria Kukulska's daughter, Anna, and, the moment he stepped through the door of the apartment that day, he knew something was terribly wrong. Maria's home was usually a place of laughter and a warm welcome. But Adam sat slumped in a chair staring ahead blankly. Jurek wasn't sure that he even saw him. Adam did not turn. He said nothing. Jurek knew in a flash that it was Irena.

Anna quickly signaled for Jurek to follow her. *Irena?* he asked. Anna nodded. "She's at Szucha, and perhaps already in Pawiak," she told him. "There are efforts to get her out." Jurek felt close to collapsing. Irena had guided everything, kept all of them safe. What now?

When Adam roused himself at last, it was to insist against all reason that they *would* save Irena: *We will get her out. That's all there is to it.* Head in his hands, he said it over and over. Maria didn't dare to tell him that it was surely hopeless. People didn't leave Pawiak. Not in the way that Adam wanted.

Gently, Maria broached at last an even more painful problem, a more urgent question that she needed Adam to consider. Would Irena betray them under torture? How much did the Gestapo know already? The apartment here was "burnt" — no longer safe for hiding. Adam would have to flee now to another hiding place. *Adam, we need to go now.* Worried about Adam and unwilling to leave him alone anywhere, Maria could see only one solution. Adam would need to travel to the safe house on Akacjowa Street in Otwock, where Żegota leader Julian Grobelny and his wife Halina were hiding. The boy, Jerzy, would stay with them also.

Moving a man who looked as strongly Jewish as Adam was perilous. It was risky for him to be seen too close to the window. Now he was going to walk through the streets of Warsaw? Take a streetcar to the suburbs unnoticed? There was no option. That autumn afternoon, for the first time in more than a year, Adam Celnikier walked with Maria Kukulska down the stairs of the apartment and onto the streets of a changed Warsaw. Maria insisted on traveling with Adam personally on the journey to Otwock. The streets of Praga were quiet, but as they neared the depot the crowds grew thicker, and Maria felt only rage when at her side two Polish men blocked their way forward. *A Jew. Here's a Jew.* One of the men held out a hand for money. *I hope you are rich, Pani. Otherwise it's the Gestapo.*

Maria turned on the man with wild fury. *Leave us alone,* she hissed. *Or I will have the Home Army execute you.* It was not an idle threat in the autumn of 1943, although admitting that one had contacts in the resistance was also an immense danger. The Polish underground state had a mirror justice system that was running at full tilt now, and judicial executions of collaborators and blackmailers were common. The blackmailers exchanged a quick look and slid away in search of easier targets. Maria's bluster, astonishingly, had succeeded.

At the safe house in Otwock, Julian and Halina Grobelny welcomed Adam as an old friend, and at the hideout people were always coming and going in secret. Julian was quiet in the eye of the storm, but around him constantly were movement and urgent whispers. By now Julian was bedridden and struggled for words. His cheeks had been hollowed out by tuberculosis. Halina tended him carefully, with a cheerful smile, but he was dying.

Beyond Pawiak, things were changing quickly for the others in Irena's network at the end of October, too, and it would not take long for word of this to reach Julian Grobelny. Southeast of Warsaw, at the slave labor camp at Poniatowa, where fifteen thousand prisoners struggled for survival, the prison resistance movement was growing stronger. Baby Bieta's mother, Henia

Koppel, was still alive and laboring as a seamstress. So was the indefatigable Ala Gołąb-Grynberg. Ala was already part of a small camp cell working in direct contact with Marek Edelman's fighting organization and Żegota. The ringleaders were carefully planning a daring escape. Camp uprisings were now plaguing the Germans. In August the arrivals at Treblinka revolted, and there were incursions even at Auschwitz that autumn. The revolts were put down with brutal force, but by the fall of 1943 things were not going so well for the Germans in the war, and Berlin was nervous.

At the end of the month, their attention turned to Poniatowa. Suddenly a couple of hundred laborers were pulled from the textile factories and set to work in the fields building deep zigzagging defensive trenches, two meters deep, to fortify the compound. Work went on for days, and word was that the next detail would be the construction of air raid towers. Ala and those in her cell, however, grew increasingly suspicious and watchful.

Ala and her cell already had a small arsenal of weapons, smuggled into the camp with the help of Żegota, and when the Germans ordered a dawn roll call of all the prisoners on the morning of November 4,

Ala knew with a sinking heart that something terrible was coming. The cell leaders — men and women who had fought together in the ghetto uprising and members of the Jewish resistance — huddled together and quickly made a bold decision. The fighters would not report for the roll call. They gathered instead in one of the barracks and set up the barricades, ready for defensive military action. The cache of weapons was tiny, but these were already men and women who had seen firsthand what was possible.

Along the trenches, in freezing November morning temperatures, the Germans now called the prisoners forward in groups of fifty. At gunpoint they stripped off their clothing and placed their valuables in small baskets. Then nearly fifteen thousand slave laborers lay down together, amid machine-gun fire and barking dogs, in the trenches and were executed in mass graves in an action the Germans had code-named "Erntefest" — the Harvest Festival. The executions went on for days. Henia Koppel was twenty-four when she died in the "harvest." Bieta was now an orphan.

Ala, however, did not die in the trenches. She was thirty-nine that year and yearned to live. She was fierce and fearless. She and the others who had fought in the Jewish uprising that spring banded together inside their barracks, and when the Germans came for them with the dogs, they opened fire on the SS. Guards fell to the ground. The casualties first stunned the German officers, and then they turned murderously furious. There was nowhere to run inside the barbed wire of Poniatowa. The Jewish fighters weren't interested in running anyhow. The Germans set fire to the building and torched the barracks. Ala and her friends died inside, trapped in the blaze but still resisting. In those final hellish moments, as the world exploded in flames around her, she surely thought of her husband, Arek, perhaps still somewhere out there fighting, and of her precious little daughter in hiding.

For Irena's circle of friends, the winter of 1943–44 was a killing season. There was no way to look on the bright side during those months. It was loss after loss. That the children were safe was the only possible consolation.

By the second week of November, as the ripple effects of the laundress's denunciation of Irena spread throughout the network, there was more bad news. Now, in the cells at Pawiak, Irena caught sight of a beaten and brutalized Helena Szesko. Helena's role as a nurse and courier in the network was a crucial one. Helena was, Irena always said, "full of initiatives," and she brought to their underground network dozens of contacts in hospitals and "clandestine circles" across Warsaw. Would Helena be strong enough to stay silent too? Like Irena, Helena held in her hands the lives of Irka Schultz, Jadwiga Deneka, and Władysława Marynowska — and the lives of hundreds of children in the orphanages. The women were herded together each day to the courtyard for daily walks at Pawiak, and sometimes she and Helena exchanged a careful glance, a look of solidarity and determination. However, Helena's husband and their collaborator, Leon — the man who had arranged for children to be smuggled out through the Muranów streetcar and saved so many — was beyond reach already. He was shot in a public execution by firing squad on November 17.

The next to fall was Jadwiga Deneka. The network was unraveling. On November 25, Jadwiga was checking in on some Jewish refugees hiding out in a basement safe house and underground press distribution point on Świętojerska Street, in the Żoliborz district, when the Gestapo raided. Jadwiga was twenty-four that year, and it was only because she did not break during the torturous interrogations at Pawiak, where she now joined her comrades-in-arms in the cells, that Katarzyna Meloch and dozens of other children were not discovered. Like Ala and Irena, Jadwiga also would not be broken.

All the women did their best to keep their spirits up in prison, despite the constant aching hunger and daily abuses of mind and spirit, and despite capricious executions and beatings. Death could come to each of them any morning at roll call. They lived with that knowledge at Pawiak. They also lived with boredom and sorrow. In Irena's cell, some of the women secretly crafted playing cards from scraps of bread and paper, and in the evenings, when the guards retreated and left them all in darkness, the cells often resounded with the sound of sad Polish music — sweet women's voices echoing off the concrete chambers, singing children's lullabies and old folk tunes. Irena and Basia, assigned to the same cell, slept crammed together, along with a dozen or more others, in the small, dank room. But when Basia sang, it felt like freedom. She was one of the most beautiful of all the singers.

One night in early December, Basia leaned against the cool cell wall and turned her face away from Irena. Irena was sure her friend was crying. *Basia, what's the matter? Shall we sing something?* she suggested. Basia shook her head slowly and said, *No, I can't sing.* She paused. *Irena, they are going to execute me tomorrow. I have a feeling.* Irena whispered quiet words of reassurance, but Basia stopped her. *No. We saw Zbigniew Łapiński today. Coming out of the chapel. He had been beaten.* Zbigniew was eighteen, only a boy, and a courier in the children's underground. Basia and Helena Pechin watched the guards drag him, limp and broken, along the corridor after interrogation, and Basia berated the young German lieutenant. *I gave away that we knew him, Irena.*

All that night Irena lay quietly and traced over and over with her eyes the patterns on the ceiling, thinking. Next to her, she knew that Basia was also awake. As they left the cell for roll call at dawn, Basia grasped Irena's hand and squeezed hard. Irena tried not to cry at the roll call. When the names were read out for the morning execution, as Basia had known would happen, she was among them. Basia and Zbigniew were executed that day in a public firing squad at the corner of Ordynacka and Foksal Streets.

Irena went carefully through Basia's possessions in the cell that night, and her hand fell upon a small keepsake. It was a small handmade portrait of Christ, with the words "I trust in Jesus." Irena held it to her and did not try to stop crying now. For the rest of her life, Irena would guard that small treasure.

There were deadly roll calls every morning. On January 6 they called the name of Jadwiga Deneka. Jadwiga was executed in the ruins of the ghetto, just beyond the prison gates, alongside the eleven Jewish women she had been caught hiding. She had divulged nothing.

Irena knew that her turn was coming.

In January, Irena was once again called in the morning lineup to the dentist's office, and in the chair, as the drill whirled, Anna Sipowicz handed Irena a last message from Żegota. It no longer spoke of escape or freedom. It read, "Be strong. We love you." In a matter of just another few weeks, it would be too late to get any prison messages to Irena. "One day, I heard my name," Irena said. It was January 20, 1944, the day of her execution.

CHAPTER 15
IRENA'S EXECUTION
WARSAW, JANUARY 1944

They took her to Szucha.

The inmates called the death van "the hood," and the sturdy canvas cover that left the prisoners unable to look out added to the mounting sense of terror. There were twenty, perhaps thirty women that morning, herded by Polish prison guards with green caps and sympathetic looks into the waiting truck for their final destination. Many at Pawiak were summarily executed outside the prison gates, in the ghetto ruins, perhaps on flimsy boards above that gaping pit of ruined basement foundations. This truckload was destined for the firing squads at Szucha. And although the women were in the dark, they were not spared the knowledge of what was coming. Irena knew this was her final hour.

The women were led into a waiting room with doorways on all sides, and most were crying. One by one a woman's name was called, and she was led to a door on the left that led to a courtyard. One by one came the sound of shots. The sobs in the room grew louder. Irena heard her name called, and that short walk across the room felt like falling. The clock ticking off the seconds seemed strangely loud, and the world narrowed down to footsteps and thoughts of her mother and Adam. She walked left. But the guard signaled to her to take the door on the right. Further interrogation. Irena's heart sank. She wanted the torture to be over. She had no doubts about how this would end. Inside the room was a Gestapo agent in his tall black boots, a florid-looking German. *Come,* he instructed her. Irena followed. He led her out into the thin winter sunlight. Irena wished for cyanide to end this gently. Would he shoot her at the crossroads, like so many others? He led her now away from Pawiak, toward the parliament buildings, and at the intersection of Aleja Wyzwolenia and Aleja Szucha, he turned to her.

"You are free. Save yourself fast." Irena's mind stumbled to process the information. Free? She couldn't register at first the word's meaning. All she could think next was that there was no way to live in occupied Poland without identity papers. "My

Kennkarte," Irena insisted. "I need my *Kenn-karte.* Give me my papers!" Rage flashed in the German's eyes. "You lousy thug, get lost," he snarled, and he pounded his fist into her mouth with fury. Irena's mouth filled with blood, and she staggered away, dizzy. When she looked back, the German was gone.

She stumbled. A stranger on the street turned to look and hurried past. She was too bloodied and bruised to go far, and her half-healed bones were not sturdy enough for running. "I could not go on," she said later of those first few moments. "I went into a nearby drugstore. The owner took me to the back room, where I washed, [and] she gave me a few pennies for the tram ticket." The owner's name was Helena, and she gently bathed Irena's shattered face and found something to cover her telltale prison uniform.

Irena admitted afterward that it was fool-ish — reckless and stupid, even — but she couldn't think of anything to do except go home to her mother. She boarded the number five streetcar in the direction of Wola, stunned and frightened. Suddenly there came a cry from one of the teenagers on the streetcar, and everyone rushed for the doorways. *Gestapo at the next stop! Get off quickly!* The Germans were checking papers ahead. Women with shopping bags and men in limp fedoras rushed past her and disappeared into the crowds, but Irena was half-crippled and slow-moving. An old man with sad eyes turned and stopped and waited for her. She wanted to cry for gratitude when he offered her his hand to help steady her as she stepped from the platform. The intensity of his sorrowful gaze said that he knew she was in the resistance. Irena stepped from the streetcar and disappeared quietly into the crowd, trying not to stumble. Her broken leg burned with a white pain, and she willed away the darkness that nibbled at the edges of her consciousness again. How easy it would have been to faint away and let oblivion carry her. When she arrived home at last, she was hardly able to stand. The limp would stay with her forever.

"I was so naïve," Irena said afterward, "that I spent several nights at home, in the same apartment where the Gestapo had arrested me." Across the city that afternoon, trucks with bullhorns blared out the names of those executed that day for crimes against Germany, and posters tacked to billboards announced her death in bold letters. *Obwieszczenie! Irena Sendlerowa. 20. i. 1944. Crime: Providing Aid to Jews.*

Sooner or later someone who had seen that poster would realize that she was still living in the apartment, and the Gestapo would come looking. That realization slowly dawned on Irena. Staying was too dangerous. But leaving was impossible. Her mother, Janina, was dying. She had suffered for years from a heart condition. A daughter in Pawiak and nights of endless worry had taken a worse toll, and Irena struggled with guilt and remorse. However unwittingly, what other conclusion was there except that she was responsible?

In the day or two after her release, another thought nagged at Irena. Why had they set her free? Was it some kind of trap? Her first worry was what would happen if one of her liaisons — nearly all of them friends — came near her now. But soon a note came from a young courier who immediately scampered off. When she saw her code name, "Jolanta," she had her answer. Żegota had arranged it. Żegota wanted her to leave the apartment now. She knew the safe-house location.

But Irena couldn't go. She couldn't leave her mother. Another message came. Julian Grobelny tried to warn her. Janka came and pleaded. Irena put it off. It meant disappearing. A cousin who had come to nurse

Janina during the months of Irena's incarceration promised to stay on; everyone urged Irena to flee. But Irena couldn't bear to leave her mother. She moved the next night into the apartment of a neighbor one flight up, who agreed to let her stay there just for a short while. Hiding in a place so nearby meant that, for a few minutes each day, Irena could slip down the stairs to see her mother.

Even this was a foolish gamble. She was inviting disaster, and Julian was growing impatient. One night in the last week of January, that disaster struck. Just after the eight p.m. curfew passed, when the streets were quiet and the Gestapo raids started, the tramp of heavy boots once again filled the staircase of the apartment building, and Irena heard voices with German accents shouting. Her heart froze. She knew what it meant. The Gestapo had realized she was missing. They were searching the building. Doors slammed on the first floor. Irena looked around the small apartment hopelessly. A closet? The bed? There was no point in hiding. It was stupid to die like this. Stupid. She could not believe she had been so foolish. She knew that this time it would kill her mother. The look on the face of her stricken neighbor told her that the woman understood for the first time that it was her own death sentence as well. "We died inside from fear," Irena said simply.

"I do not know how long it took — minutes seemed like an eternity — until we heard the sound of running shoes, moving away," Irena said later. When the corridors were quiet again, a tap came on the neighbor's door, and Irena's cousin passed her a message and quickly embraced her. *Goodbye. You must go, Irena.* And then she turned and retreated down the hallway.

Irena held the thin sheet of paper, and her hand was shaking. She read her mother's heart-wrenching message: "They were looking for you again, you must not come near even to say good-bye to me. Get out as soon as possible." The Gestapo had searched all the lower floors of the building. They had stopped just one floor below where Irena was hiding.

Irena relented at last. What other option was there if it meant the murder of her mother? An awful knowledge crashed upon her now: she had been a terrible daughter. Julian Grobelny swiftly arranged Irena's new identity papers, and the woman who had spirited thousands away to safety would herself now go into the deepest hiding. For a short time, while she was healing, she was allowed to stay with Julian and Halina and Adam in Otwock. But staying in one place for long was not an option for a woman who had now shot to the top of the Gestapo's most-wanted list, and for Adam's safety as much as her own she had to keep moving as soon as she was able. With her stunning escape came the belated realization at Szucha Avenue that she had not been a small player in the resistance. The Gestapo hunt for Irena was on.

Irena's new papers gave her a fresh identity, and suddenly, like the thousands of children she had helped to save, there were a dozen new details for her to learn completely. Her name now was Klara Dąbrowska. Irena dyed her hair red as a disguise, and in Home Army files on her there was a description of her as she looked then: about 160 centimeters tall, slender, with a "slightly aquiline nose," bright blue eyes, and a short haircut. After the first few weeks Irena moved constantly. There were other safe houses in Otwock. She stayed for a time with her uncle near Nowy Sącz. When things got too hot, she spent some time back in Praga, as a hidden resident at the Warsaw zoo, where some of the Żegota leadership, including Dr. Adolf Berman, had gone underground in the autumn of

Irena's arrest. Moving was a fact of life in this dangerous evasion, but Irena missed her mother and Adam.

In Otwock, Irena learned at last the heroic story behind her eleventh-hour rescue. When Janka brought the news of Irena's capture to Adam and Maria Kukulska at the apartment in Praga, all three were wildly determined to save Irena. At the safe house in Otwock with Julian, Adam's grief and worry was a constant reminder. Julian promised that Żegota would supply any sum needed to bribe the Gestapo, if such a thing could be done. For Irena's release, they paid the highest ransom ever in their history as an organization. No one knows quite how high the figure was, but it was something close to 35,000 złotych — the equivalent today of more than a hundred thousand dollars.

But could it be done, at any price? Only a bribe at the highest ranks of the Gestapo could bring about such a brazen prison break, and who among them had those kinds of contacts? The obstacle was finding someone with contacts close enough to the Gestapo to make it happen. You didn't just go up to Germans on the street and start asking — especially not if you were a Jewish man in deep hiding. What the friends needed was someone Polish and someone with connections inside the Gestapo. What they needed was someone like Irena's office conspirator Maria Palester, with her weekly bridge games. Several years now into the German occupation, Maria amiably chatted up Gestapo informers each week and more than once had used her charms in the service of Irena's network. She had an extensive network of contacts in the underworld, but there was no way to minimize the risk Maria was taking now to save Irena. She was calling in her chips and risking the lives of her family.

After all, Maria's Jewish-convert husband, Henryk, was no less in danger now than when the war had started. Her teenage son, Kryštof, was in an elite resistance squadron and in constant danger. And the family was still helping to hide Jewish friends in their apartment. But Maria did not balk at a bold gamble. Irena had made it possible for her family to survive. If she could, she would now save Irena. Maria reached out to a friend, who reached out to someone else. Somewhere along the way, a bargain was struck at last with the German officer who took Irena to the crossroads on the morning of her execution. Lured by the fantastic sum, he agreed to enter in the official records that Irena Sendler had been executed.

The drop-off was the stuff of cloak-and-dagger spy novels. Finding someone to deliver a bribe to the Gestapo was a fantastically high-risk proposition. Maria's fourteen-year-old daughter, Małgorzata Palester, undertook the operation. She calmly carried the rolls of cash buried in the bottom of her school backpack to the rendezvous with the courage of a seasoned resistance agent. It would have been an easy thing to take the cash and shoot the girl on the street. Germans answered few questions when it came to Polish corpses. He might have taken the cash deposit even more easily and still led Irena to her execution. For whatever reason, he didn't.

Adam now explained to her another secret. Żegota had gone to such lengths to free Irena — a single agent in a large and sprawling network with a hundred different cells — in largest part because of the lists of children. While Irena thought she had been keeping the lists to protect the children, it turned out that the lists had saved her life also. "Żegota sent me letters so that I would be assured that they were doing everything possible to get me out," Irena recalled, "but all the prisoners got these letters." Sure, Julian Grobelny and Adolf Berman, the organization leaders, cared for Irena and Adam personally. "But their great efforts to keep me alive were due to something greater than sentiment," Irena now realized. "They knew that if I died, the only trace of the children would die too. The index was the only chance of finding the children and returning them to Jewish society. And Żegota did not know that my liaison officer hid the index. They only knew from my letters that the Germans did not find the index."

What to do with the lists now? It was another pressing question, as members of their cell kept falling into the clutches of the Gestapo. Janka was still hiding the tissue-paper rolls that Irena had tossed to her the morning of the arrest, but there were other parts of the list also stashed away for safekeeping. What if Irena were again arrested? What if something happened to Janka? Janka's husband, Józef, was a resistance soldier in the Home Army, and their home was exposed and vulnerable. The lists needed to be gathered together and hidden properly. In the winter of 1944, Irena and the two sisters, Jaga and Janka, now agreed on a new location. They buried their papers in a bottle under the apple tree in Jaga's wild backyard on Lekarska Street.

Irena was living on the run, and she could wait a little while longer to be with Adam, if that was how to keep him safe. But breaking her ties with her mother was impossible. Janina did not have much time left. She was dying. And the Gestapo knew it. Irena's old Wola apartment, where Janina still lived, was under surveillance, and the trap was set to spring on Irena. She now struggled with the realization that she had risked her mother's life at every moment, but only in hindsight did Irena see how great the danger had been. She stayed away, but it felt like a betrayal.

Irena pushed those thoughts away. Stopping to rest now felt like failure. Within weeks after her release, despite her badly healed bones, she returned to dangerous underground work as "Klara." She was determined to continue delivering her support funds to the families and checking in on her children. There is no record of the precise visits Irena made in the winter of 1944. Although she and Adam kept careful records of all "her" children, those account books would not survive the coming tumultuous summer of 1944 in Warsaw. But it is almost certain that she made one of her first trips to the Ochota district to visit her old friends Zofia Wědrychowska and Stanisław Papuziński and to check in on three of her Jewish children — including her favorite, Estera.

Ochota was still more of a village than a part of the city in the winter of 1944, and Zofia and Stanisław's house — number 3 — was the last home in the development there, before Matwicka Street gave way to fields and farmland. Stanisław worked in a medical clinic and traveled each day to the Old Town of Warsaw, but Zofia was a public librarian in the neighborhood. There was a willow tree swing in the overgrown backyard and bright flower gardens that Zofia tried to tend amid the flurry of more than a half dozen children. When Irena came up the front step, they greeted her with a chorus of happy screams, because Pani Irena was a favorite. Zofia and Stanisław had five children of their own: a son, Marek, who would turn thirteen that year; ten-year-old Eve; nine-year-old Andrzej; four-year-old Joanna; and an infant born just that year named Thomas. Often, when Irena came, Zofia was away working, and then the children's grandmother greeted her warmly and offered her tea and cakes, the ubiquitous gesture of Polish welcome. Along with an older man in the neighborhood, Mr. Siekiery, their grandmother looked after all the children on the street when the parents were working, and there was a tribe of them, children with names like Sławek, Julia, Adam, and Hania. There were also the four or five Jewish children whom the family was hiding for Irena and for Dr. Radlińska's network. The eldest among them was "Teresa Tucholska" — Estera — who acted the part of a little mother to baby Thomas.

It was great luck that Irena was not visiting on the afternoon of February 22, 1944, a blustery winter Tuesday. That day tragedy struck the family. Stanisław was out of the house — perhaps at work at the clinic or perhaps, some say, at a clandestine meeting of the resistance. But Zofia was at work, and there were so many little ones underfoot that the older children on the street, mostly boys who were thirteen and fourteen, were left to their own devices. The boys went out into the barren fields behind the house to play at being resistance fighters. The children may even have had a gun. They had certainly absorbed the silent lesson from their parents that it was brave to fight the Germans. Like Irena, Zofia and Stanisław both still worked in the underground with their old professor, and their sister-in-law, Halina Kuczkowska, was a senior underground operative.

While the neighborhood boys were playing at killing the occupiers in the fields, some actual Germans spotted the youngsters, and the boys howled with glee at the adventure. But the Germans gave chase for real, ordering them to surrender. Pursued by German soldiers, the children were too frightened to stop, and they ran for home. The first home on the street belonged to Marek's parents, Stanisław and Zofia. The boys clattered through the front doorway. The Germans stormed the threshold behind them. Inside the house there was a fight with the soldiers. Little Eve hid under the bed crying. The Germans chased the boys in a hail of gunfire. A bullet hit one of the older boys, wounding him badly, and he fell with a cry in the stairwell. The other children jumped out of the window and fled to the fields, and the soldiers gave chase. But, of course, it was only a matter of time before they returned for the boy and his parents.

When a frantic neighbor fetched Zofia from the library, the Germans were gone and the children were terrified. They watched wild-eyed as Zofia tried to stop the boy's bleeding and started quickly burning sheets of papers. Zofia's first thought was to hide the children in the attic. She knew the police would be coming soon with reinforcements from the Gestapo. Then she thought better of it. Turning to the children, Zofia put Estera in charge. *You must take them to my friend's house on Krucza Street,* she told Estera. Estera knew the one. *Go quickly. Do not come back; I'll come to get you.*

Estera fled with the little ones immediately. Zofia stayed with the bleeding child, and found him a spot in the attic to hide in. But the stairs were covered with his blood, and she had to remove the trail that led right to him. While a neighbor tried to tidy up the ruined living room, Zofia got on her hands and knees with a pail of water and started to scrub the blood away.

That was where the Germans found her when they stormed the house: on her knees, scrubbing and crying. She had not been able to complete the job before their arrival. A German soldier towered over her. He held a gun to Zofia's head and told her to get the boy quickly. On the way to Pawiak, in the back of the van, she cradled the boy for as long as they would let her. But he was dead before they reached Szucha Avenue. Zofia — whom the Gestapo had on their list of those they wanted to interrogate for other reasons — was taken inside alone for questioning and torture.

When Stanisław heard, he turned to Irena — their old friend and fellow collaborator. Not only would the Jewish children whom Zofia and Stanisław were hiding for her network need new homes, and quickly, but the Gestapo was searching for Stanisław too. He would have to go into hiding as well. But he couldn't take his own children with him. Would Irena help him? She would, of course, without a moment's hesitation. Irena swung into action and moved Estera to a "holiday camp" that was hiding Jewish children near the town of Garwolin, some forty miles southeast of Warsaw. She found homes for the other children in orphanages and in several cases with friends from their prewar social work network. She turned especially to old contacts from the Polish Free University, more former students of Dr. Radlińska. A number of the youngsters went to the countryside near the village of Anin. Some of Zofia's children ultimately found homes at the camp in Garwolin and in the orphanage in Okęcie with Estera.

Stanisław made heroic efforts to have Zofia released from the Gestapo interrogation center and later from Pawiak Prison. He reached out to every contact he knew in the Home Army. But with the children's lives at stake and in hiding himself, it was perilous, and Halina's work in the underground was Zofia's death sentence. Zofia was executed at Pawiak in the spring of 1944, in the same fashion the Germans had intended for Irena. She was in her late thirties. To the end, she also kept silent.

Bribing the Gestapo — or trying to — was becoming all too common in their network that spring. Julian and Halina Grobelny owned a small country house with a garden in Cegłów, a village not far from Mińsk Mazowiecki, and for more than a year the cottage had been used as a Jewish safe house where at-risk children could be hidden away until Irena could obtain new identity papers and make a permanent placement. It was there one day in March that the Gestapo captured Julian, whom they had pegged not as the leader of Żegota but as a minor leftist partisan. Now Julian Grobelny was taken to Pawiak and was the one in need of saving. Julian was already hopelessly ill from tuberculosis. Even if he escaped execution, the harsh and damp conditions in the prison were for him a certain death sentence. Irena turned to old friends and once again to Dr.

Radlińska's underground circles. Dr. Juliusz Majkowski, the director of the health offices at number 15, Spokojnej Street, and the man who in the beginning had given Irena, Irka, Jaga, and Jadwiga their ghetto passes, came to the rescue. Working with the medical underground at Pawiak, Dr. Majkowski smuggled extra food and supplies into the prison to try to preserve Julian's precarious health. At last, the prison staff obtained for Julian a medical furlough and a transfer to the Warsaw hospital, where he would remain a prisoner in a care unit. But the patient never arrived at the hospital. Żegota — for another immense bribe — arranged for Julian's escape from the ambulance as it roared across the city that morning.

Julian's dramatic escape now gave Irena an idea, and she again turned to Dr. Majkowski. By March the situation with her mother's health was critical. Janina's strength was failing fast, and Irena could not leave her mother to die alone in her old apartment. Would Dr. Majkowski help her smuggle her mother out of Wola? Dr. Majkowski agreed, and a daring plan was made. Dr. Majkowski would come by ambulance to spirit Janina away to a local hospital on a false emergency. Janina's Gestapo watchers would give chase, of course, but in the manufactured chaos there would be a brief window of a few precious minutes between the time of Janina's arrival and the time it took for the Gestapo to locate her inside the hospital. As Janina was wheeled to a brightly lit room on one of the upper stories, nurses in the medical resistance stood waiting. Helping the frail woman to step out an open window, they assisted her gently down the fire escape. There, in the alley, another ambulance waited with its engine running to ferry her to a Żegota safe house at the apartment of Stefan Wichliński, the widower of Irena's murdered coworker Stefania.

As Irena said later of that desperate adventure, "I had to steal my dying mother from our home and take her to unknown persons until she ended life several weeks later." When Janina died in the days that followed, on March 30, 1944, Irena was there with her. As they sat together quietly on those final days, Janina took her daughter's hand and extracted from her child one deathbed promise. *Don't go to my funeral, Irena. They will be looking for you there. Promise.*

And Janina was right. At Janina's funeral, the Gestapo was wild with fury. A scowling Gestapo agent accosted friends and family.

"Which is the dead woman's daughter?" he demanded. Mourners shrugged. "Her daughter is in Pawiak Prison," they replied.

"She certainly *was* [in Pawiak]," came the tight-lipped reply, "but she inexplicably *isn't* any longer."

By the spring of 1944, Irena was, instead, running her operations from the apartment safe house of her old friends and conspirators, Maria and Henryk Palester. From his hideout in Otwock, where Irena risked capture to see him, Adam fretted. Irena struggled that spring to set aside her grief and threw herself into work with a vengeance, but Adam could see that there was something brittle in her now. It was no wonder: Irena — still only in her early thirties — had lived on the edge of death every day for nearly five years. She had buried her mother and more than a dozen friends, and she had survived her own execution. She held in her hands the lives of thousands, and the psychic burden was unbearable. And, from his bedside retreat in Otwock, Żegota leader Julian Grobelny, too, was giving Irena greater and greater responsibility. She was the general to his field marshal. Irena would not stop. But Adam also knew that she could not go on like this forever.

At the weekly Żegota leadership meetings, it was no longer the leadership delegating to Irena. Irena was, increasingly, setting the agenda. By July, word was coming through underground channels that the Soviet army was approaching from the east. Inside occupied Warsaw, the Gestapo nets were closing tighter and tighter around the resistance — a movement that now included a larger part of the Warsaw population than ever before. The city was on the brink of explosion. In the last days of the month, Irena learned of a group of Jewish refugees fighting for survival in the forests. "It was a desperate SOS, brought to me by someone who had managed to escape Treblinka," Irena remembered. "I presented the problem to the entire presidium," and the Żegota leadership instantly authorized Irena to run the dangerous mission of delivering funds for the camp survivors. As always, in Adam's careful account books, which he pored over alone in isolation, he meticulously recorded the figures. "I knew that the friend from Treblinka (I can not recall the names) handed over the money," Irena said, "because the next day, before the uprising started, he wanted me to let [Żegota] know."

Irena also still safeguarded her "indexes" of the children. She and Janka knew that a battle for Warsaw was coming. In those final days of peace, the women dug up the lists buried in Jaga's garden, repackaged the entire archive in two glass soda bottles, and under the same apple tree reburied all the names that since 1939 their network had collected. By the time Warsaw exploded into street warfare on the first of August, the lists held the names of nearly 2,500 Jewish children.

CHAPTER 16
WARSAW FIGHTING
WARSAW, JULY–DECEMBER 1944

The general uprising in Warsaw had been planned by the Home Army to begin at five p.m. on August 1, 1944, and it was based on a tragic miscalculation. The Germans were losing ground by the summer of 1944, and the Home Army gambled that, in the face of a sustained military revolt, the occupiers would retreat and Warsaw would be liberated. Soviet troops were amassing just outside the city, across the Vistula River in Praga, and they were poised as allies. The Poles assumed that the Soviets would support them, and the Soviets made noises of warm assurance. What the residents of Warsaw could not know was that the Germans, faced with the sweeping advance of the Red Army from the east, had decided to hold Warsaw as a strategic retreat at any cost. The residents did not know, either, that Himmler's orders from Berlin instructed his troops to kill all the city's inhabitants and to bulldoze the entire city. And they did not know — although they might have guessed — that the Soviets had their own divergent political motives, which did not include Polish independence.

That summer in Warsaw, there were several resistance organizations ready to do battle in the city, including the remnants of Marek Edelman's Jewish Fighting Organization and any number of small resistance cells. But the Home Army, supported by the Polish government-in-exile, was the largest and best equipped of the resistance movements, and by July it boasted a volunteer military corps nearly forty thousand strong in Warsaw alone, out of a population of about one million in the city. Among those militia recruits were as many as four thousand battle-ready young Polish women. The number would grow rapidly in the next few weeks as average civilians joined the battle. For five years the Germans had made it a capital crime for a Pole or a Jew to own a weapon. As a result, there were firearms in the corps for fewer than three thousand. But what the Poles lacked in weapons, they made up for in organization and raw courage. The army had ranks and a chain of command, and districts of the city were divided into orderly fighting units.

With the battle for Warsaw looming and the city anticipating a siege and street fighting, Adam left the hideout in Otwock and joined Irena at last in the Palesters' apartment on Łowicka Street, in the Mokotów district, sometime in July, in a strange and bittersweet reunion. They naïvely thought they were safe there, Irena admitted later, and those days seemed like a kind of honeymoon to the young couple. But danger surrounded them, and only afterward did Irena understand that they had been extraordinarily lucky. The Germans, determined to ferret out and crush all resistance, now went from house to house in the neighborhood, searching apartments and demanding identity papers, and somehow they missed the door of the Palester family.

The first day of the uprising, Adam and Irena shared in the euphoria that swept across the city. It looked to the residents like a victory of sorts in the beginning. That day and the next, several thousand Poles were killed, and they learned only later that Janka Grabowska's husband, Józef, had been among them. There were Polish casualties. But the militia had also killed on the first day more than five hundred German soldiers, and that counted as success in an occupied city.

The Home Army turned to the Soviets. With the aid of the Red Army, surely the Germans would flee Warsaw, whatever their orders. The Soviets, however, quickly made a cynical strategic decision. Although they were on the side of the Allies by 1944 and the Poles desperately needed support, the Soviets instead retreated to let the Poles and the Germans battle themselves into mutual exhaustion. Ultimately, the Soviets also refused to allow the other Allies — who were slow to act anyhow — to use the airfields outside the city to help the people of Warsaw, even for drops of food and equipment.

It was a foolish error of judgment, and the senior leadership in the Home Army realized it quickly. In the words of one general, Władysław Anders, "You can never trust the Soviets — they are our sworn enemies. To hold an uprising whose only success depends on either the collapse of your enemy or help from another enemy is wishful thinking beyond reason." But by then it was too late. Within days, Luftwaffe planes, marked on their underbellies with ominous black crosses, swept over the city in bombing squadrons, and the Poles had no air defense. The bombings would continue without interruption, and, to the despair of the city's residents, on the ground the tide turned just as quickly.

By August 5, the Germans had the upper hand, and troops rampaged through the city, perpetrating the mass murders of civilians. There were stark orders to kill every inhabitant of Warsaw, down to the smallest children. In the next two weeks no fewer than sixty-five thousand residents were executed on the streets. Soldiers entered hospital wards and, row by row, discharged single bullets into the heads of bedridden patients. Some of the worst atrocities took place in the Wola district, just beyond Irena's now-empty apartment, where the street fighting was fierce. Buildings exploded in bomb blasts, and tanks rolled down the streets firing shells, crushing under their weight cars and fallen horses and bodies. People quickly gathered together what water and food they could find and retreated to the city's basements to hide.

The German governor of Warsaw, Hans Frank, recorded with satisfaction that "almost all Warsaw is a sea of flames. To set houses afire is the surest way to drive the insurgents out of their hiding places. When we crush the uprising, Warsaw will get what it deserves — complete annihilation." As their homes burned around them and heavy beams crashed from all directions, residents who were driven from their basements were herded into the open squares at gunpoint and mowed down with machine-gun fire. "They drove us from the cellars and brought us near the Sowiński Park at Ulrychów," said one heartbroken survivor. "They shot at us when we passed. My wife was killed on the spot: our child was wounded and cried for his mother. Soon a Ukrainian approached and killed my two-year-old child like a dog; then he approached me together with some Germans and stood on my chest to see whether I was alive or not — I shammed dead, lest I should be killed too." Some of Irena's hidden children and their courageous foster parents disappeared that summer, and there is little doubt that they were among those who perished — after so many had risked so much to save them — in these indiscriminate street massacres. For Irena and her friends, it was all a terrible reenactment of those last days in the ghetto, and the Poles understood at last what it meant to be, in the eyes of the occupiers, *Untermenschen* — subhumans.

Soon the Germans came to the Mokotów district, where Adam and Irena were hiding with Maria and Henryk Palester, and began clearing the houses. Like the ghetto, Warsaw was being liquidated and burned, street by street, in preparation for a final cultural annihilation. Adam and Irena fled together, along with a woman from a neighboring apartment, Dr. Maria Skokowska, and a young Jewish woman named Jadzia Pesa Rozenholc, who had been hiding with the Palester family. But where should they go? Homeless, the friends anxiously debated their next step. One thing was absolutely certain: none of them were about to report, as ordered, to the German checkpoint for deportations. One did not get on trains when the Germans were directing.

At last they hit upon a hiding place together in the ruins of a tattered construction site at numbers 51–53, Łowicka Street. Huddled in the darkness, they held a quick conference. Henryk Palester and Maria Skokowska were both physicians. Irena and Maria Palester had trained nurses and social workers. The next day they went to work setting up an emergency field hospital for wounded resistance fighters and civilians caught up in the turmoil. The hospital quickly became — like anything Irena put her hand to — a sprawling operation. The need was immense, and unsurprisingly it was well organized and efficient despite the almost complete lack of equipment or medicine.

Adam, on the other hand, was a lawyer and a philosopher; he would be no use to them wrapping bandages, he told Irena. By that summer he had been cooped up in hiding for two years, and Irena understood. He was desperate to be out there fighting in this battle. So Adam threw in his lot with Maria and Henryk's courageous teenage son, Kryštof, and two other youngsters, and first they battled the Germans from a nearby cemetery. Adam fought alongside the boys again in the battle for the Old Town, where they lost two of the three young men in the action. Kryštof Palester disappeared to rejoin his old "Parasol" battalion and died in a gunfight in the streets not much later. Adam's heart broke for Kryštof's disconsolate parents and little sister.

On the streets of the Mokotów district, Irena was now stunned but overjoyed by a different kind of chance encounter. From behind a rubble barricade, a familiar voice called out, *Over here! Over here!* Startled, Irena turned, and saw before her a dusty young woman with her blond hair tucked in a cap, raising in warm welcome an arm on which Irena could plainly see the red badge of the Home Army. *Rachela!*

It was Rachela Rosenthal, the Jewish friend whom Irena had thought had died in Treblinka in the summer of 1942. Irena rushed toward Rachela, and crouching behind the barricades together they embraced, laughing. Irena had counted Rachela among those lost to the Umschlagplatz, but here she was, alive and as beautiful as ever. But Rachela's entire family, including her small daughter, had all perished; she was the last survivor. Rachela shyly looked at Irena and then turned to introduce her as well to a fair-haired Polish soldier. *My husband.* The man grinned, and embraced Irena like an old friend. At last Irena turned: *I need to go. I'm at the field hospital.* Rachela's husband laughed and told her she had better get going. *We'll give you cover if you hurry!* Irena couldn't get over the transformation in her old friend. "She was a totally different person," Irena remembered. "She was now a soldier, sharp, determined, fighting with a gun in her hand. Her extraordinary bravery was recognized by everyone in her group."

In Mokotów, if the days were hard, the nights were a time of terror. Drunken SS officers made forays into basement shelters and gang-raped Polish women and children hiding there. A German soldier ran his bayonet through Irena's leg when she stumbled upon him, and soon Irena's wound festered from a dangerous infection that made standing agony. Food was running out and so was water, and civil order was breaking down all around them. At night Irena lay in the shelter beside Adam, listening to the quiet breathing of Henryk and Maria and worrying endlessly about the fate of her hidden Jewish children. Many of those youngsters had been moved months earlier to orphanages or rural safe houses as the street-by-street Gestapo searches of attics and basements intensified. But some were still concealed by trusted families in Warsaw — families who, like all of them in the city, were in unremitting danger. Irena's leg throbbed hotly. Between the pain of her wound and the perils of the streets, delivering support was impossible, and she struggled to make contact with the foster guardians and the children. They were still uniquely vulnerable. Even in the chaos of the uprising, anti-Semitic blackmailers roamed the streets, threatening to denounce anyone who might have a bit of change in their pocket and who "looked" Jewish. Irena worried about Adam and the girls who lived in hiding with them, and danger seemed to be coming at them from all directions. And it wasn't only in Mokotów either. Across town, Irena's old friends would later tell the same terrible stories. Stanisław Papuziński fought in the street battles as a soldier. Jaga Piotrowska rushed into burning buildings during the destruction of her street and pulled to safety unconscious survivors. The razing of Warsaw included the destruction of Jaga's own house, where the lists of children's names were now buried deeper under the rubble in the back garden.

By September 9, the fate of the city was sealed. Luftwaffe planes circled slowly over Warsaw, and the residents looked up from their bomb shelters in basements to see paper leaflets falling. The leaflets fluttered onto rooftops, and people caught them in midair from their balconies. On the thin printed sheets was a final German warning. All residents were ordered to leave the city and report to German processing centers on the penalty of execution.

Together in Mokotów, the friends delayed. By now thirty refugees were hiding in the makeshift medical clinic with Irena and Adam and the Palester family, among them two young Jewish children. The Umschlag-platz loomed large in Irena's unsettled dreams. She wanted nothing to do with

German processing centers. But on September 11 the Germans arrived on their street with flame-throwers and incendiary devices, intent on burning to the ground every last structure, and there was no longer any option. The air was thick with smoke and dust, and when soldiers discovered them crowded in the basement refuge, the Germans were angry and impatient. Had the resistance fought this long and this hard to be sent now to the concentration camps? They were forced to join a bedraggled convoy of other civilians being marched at gunpoint to the deportation center.

They were all in bad shape by this point, but Adam and Henryk were increasingly worried about Irena, who was limping and struggled to keep up. The bayonet wound to her leg had still not healed. It oozed pus, and Henryk worried about sepsis. But Irena wasn't focused on her leg. She was focused on what to do about the young Jewish child traveling with them, a girl named Anna, and how to get them all out of this death procession.

In the end, the friends agreed that the best solution was the most expedient. They turned out their pockets quietly and offered a bribe to a German guard if he would send their entourage in another direction. The

German considered. There were empty army barracks in Okęcie, out by the abandoned airfields, where Soviet POWs and Jews used to be incarcerated, he finally offered, placing the roll of bills carefully in an inside pocket. *It will be better if you head in that direction, out of the city.* With a jerk of his head and a shrug of his shoulders, he ambled on in another direction.

Maria, Małgorzata, and Henryk Palester, along with Dr. Maria Rudolfowa, Irena, Adam, and the girl Anna, made the dangerous trek south out of the city as Warsaw burned around them. "She treated me like a daughter," Anna said of Irena later. Lice and bedbugs chewed them in their sleep, and they combed the ruins for something to eat and for water. Then, undeterred, they threw themselves into starting up their hospital again.

Mokotów was among the last districts in Warsaw to fall, and Adam and Irena left behind them fighting that continued for several weeks. By October 4, 1944, it was all over in Warsaw. The uprising had been defeated. The final death toll was catastrophic: 200,000 residents, most of them civilians, were killed. As the German occupation continued into the winter, another

150,000 were ultimately transported as slave labor to camps in Germany, and the concentration camps claimed another 55,000. Some historians say that the total number of Jews to survive the war in Warsaw was fewer than 11,000. Adam and Anna were among them. Henryk Palester, struck down by a German truck in December, did not make it. And by winter, just as Hitler had wanted, Warsaw lay in ruins.

The Soviet and Polish armies at last entered the wasted city on January 17, 1945. By then eighty percent of Warsaw was stone and rubble. All that winter, Irena and Adam — living under false papers still as Klara Dabrowskå and Stefan Zgrembski — stayed on at the hospital station in Okẻcie, and from her southern outpost Irena carried on working for Żegota up until the final moment. That winter, at last, Irena's leg wound healed, one of the injuries treated at the hospital station, although she was still limping from the damage to her legs inflicted by her Gestapo torturers.

Despite the Soviet "liberation" of Warsaw, the war, of course, would go on for months across Europe. But in Warsaw all that was left was to count the losses and fear what would come next. Hundreds of thousands were in labor camps and prisoner-of-war compounds far from home. A staggering fifteen percent of Poland's prewar population — six million people — had perished. So had ninety percent of the country's Jewish population. In late 1944, Dr. Adolf Berman's wife, Basia, wrote in her diary about what it meant to understand at last the scale of that destruction: "Even after the final liquidation [of the ghetto], we clung to fairy tales about underground bunkers and sophisticated shelters in which thousands of people are supposedly living. Then we deluded ourselves that they were in the camps and when the nightmare ends will return with a fanfare of victory to the ruins." There were perilously few survivors. Many of the victims had been the children. At the start of the war, there were an estimated 3.4 million Jews in Poland, one million of whom were children. According to Yad Vashem, only five thousand children out of that million survived the war in Poland and the final massacres of the uprising. The number may be low, historians quibble. Double it. Triple it, then. The numbers are still shatteringly small.

And there was, in fact, one very "sophisticated shelter" in which thousands of Jewish boys and girls *were* still living: a shelter, staffed by dozens of volunteers who were often nothing more than immensely decent and brave people, that spread across the city and safeguarded Irena's children. Of those youngsters who survived in Warsaw, Irena and her network saved the greatest proportion.

In the first weeks after the Soviet liberation, Irena once again encountered Rachela by chance on a street in Warsaw. It was a moment that afterward defined something essential for Irena about what it meant to try to piece together a life in the decades that followed as witnesses and survivors. When they met in the midst of the wasteland that had become Warsaw, the two women embraced for a long moment on the street. *We survived that hell,* they said to each other, laughing. Then Irena saw that Rachela was crying. "I'd never seen Rachela cry before," Irena remembered. She reached for her friend, and Rachela looked at her sadly. *My name now,* she explained to Irena, *is Karolina. Only Karolina. Rachela died in the ghetto, Irena. Stanisław knows nothing of her existence.* Irena nodded gravely. She understood. Part of her had died in the ghetto too. So had part of all the surviving fighters.

Now, Rachela told her, she and Stanisław had a baby — a little girl — and all there was to do was try to make a future. Dwelling on the past could only mean reliving the intense sorrow. Rachela was a vibrant young woman, and the hardships and deprivations had not destroyed her spirit. She was by nature cheerful and resilient. But, like so many in Warsaw, Rachela buried that other life completely. "She never talked about those things again," Irena said later. But, as the women parted on the street, hands touching lightly, her friend turned to her. *Sometimes, Irena, will you remember Rachela?* Irena promised she would.

CHAPTER 17
HOW THE STORIES ENDED
WARSAW, 1945–1947

Adam and Irena stayed on in Okęcie with Maria Palester and Dr. Rudolfowa until the spring of 1945. It would be months before the war in Europe finally ended, but by March the mission at the barracks was changing. What was needed now was not a field hospital but a home for the thousands of war orphans. Maria and Dr. Rudolfowa opened the doors of the facility to homeless youngsters and stayed on as the new directors.

In March, Adam and Irena went home to Warsaw together. For them the end of the war was — after so many false starts and interruptions — the real beginning of their life together and their long-awaited love story. That love story had been untidy and chaotic. The human heart is not symmetrical or neat, either, but turns back on itself in folds and knots. And the ties that connected Adam and Irena and the passion that still burned between them were as strong as ever. There were challenges ahead. War had left its scars and traumas, some of which marked the mind and some of which marked her body. And there was the question of what she was going to tell Mietek if he made it home to Warsaw. But Irena loved Adam, and this was what she wanted. So, in making a home together at last, their life began anew. Adam — who would never again go by that name but would instead call himself Stefan, the name in the false identity papers that Irena had found to save him — returned to work in earnest on his doctoral thesis and immersed himself in his books and the study of ancient history. Irena, in contrast, directed her energies outward. She returned to her job at the city welfare office and devoted herself to rebuilding it from the ruins. She was quickly appointed director of the citywide welfare services. One of her first acts as director was to establish a formal bond of cooperation with the orphanage in Okęcie and with Maria Palester.

After a long, dark season, there was good news at last. The losses were behind them, and Adam and Irena could now rejoice together in stories of survival. Helena Szeszko was alive when the Ravensbrück camp was finally liberated, and she made it home to Warsaw. Dr. Hirzsfeld and Dr. Radlińska were survivors. Izabela Kuczkowska, Irka Schultz, Władysława Marynowska, Janka Grabowska, Stanisław Papuziński — they all lived to see the liberation of Poland. Stanisław reclaimed his motherless children from the foster homes and orphanages and reconstituted his family. Marek Edelman — the young man who worked beside Ala and Nachum at the Umschlagplatz medical clinic and who led a heroic uprising in the ghetto — was lauded as a hero. He went on to become a doctor. One likes to imagine that, in doing so, he was remembering Ala and Nachum.

Irena and Adam now added to their new family two Jewish foster daughters, including Irena's favorite, Estera. It made for a full house, and they had a small apartment, but Irena now wanted desperately to be a mother. Estera stayed on with them for several years, and she remembers of her adolescence that Irena and Adam were affectionate and protective. Adam spent hours with Estera, coaching her on her homework and acting as a tutor. He had always loved teaching.

What of Irena's other "children"? Theodora,

the wife of Irena's old friend Józef Zysman, retrieved little Piotr from the orphanage where he had been safely hidden. Irena never forgot Józef's words when he gave her Piotr to save: "Let him grow up to be a good man and a good Pole." Theodora kept that promise for Irena. Piotr's cousin, Michał Głowiński, was another small survivor, and his mother also found him at the orphanage where Irena had protected him.

Stanisława Bussold and her husband had grown to love fiercely baby Bieta — now a toddler — and adopted her. "My birth certificate is a small silver spoon engraved with my name and birth date, a salvaged accessory of a salvaged child," she says. But she today honors, too, the beautiful childhood her foster parents gave her. Bieta has searched for but never found that numbered bank account in Switzerland where the Koppel family fortune may still be waiting.

Katarzyna Meloch, the ten-year-old girl whom Julian Grobelny and the old priest passed into the care of Irena, lost her mother and her father long before the war was over. But after the war an aunt found her. "If the aunt had not seen the address on a package sent to me to the care center," Katarzyna says, "she would not have found me so easily." Many decades later, Katarzyna remains haunted by memories of the ghetto. After the war, Katarzyna made her career as a journalist. "[But] I am still unable to write about my stay in the Warsaw ghetto," she says. "I saw bodies covered with sheets of paper. They were a permanent part of the landscape." And she always remembers the heroism and the tragic loss of her wartime "guardian," Jadwiga Deneka.

After the war, Ala's small child, Rami Gołąb-Grynberg, was reunited with her uncle, Sam Gołąb (Golomb), and his wife, Ana, and went on to become both a nurse and a mother too. Today she is a grandmother. She remains friends with Elżbieta, the daughter of her wartime protectors, Jadwiga and Janusz Strzałecka, who helped Irena in her children's network.

These were a handful among thousands. And while many, like Rachela, coped by burying the past, there was one thing that Irena knew had to be excavated. In the spring of 1945, not long after Adam and Irena returned to Warsaw together, Irena and Janka met on a warm sunny afternoon in the ruins of Jaga's old back garden to look for the buried records on which the names and addresses and true identities of as many as 2,500 Jewish children had been

441

recorded. They had a large, unwieldy shovel. It was just midday, and the women wore sturdy boots as they picked among the bricks and rubble. The house had been destroyed in the uprising and since then looted, and the garden was a tangle of twisted metal and brush. In 1945, Warsaw was bleak and treeless. They searched that day for hours, but it was hopeless. The lists, along with Irena's wartime journals and account books, like so much else in the city, were lost forever, destroyed in the inferno and destruction of the Warsaw uprising.

However, Irena and her team were undaunted. The women set about to re-create large portions of the list from shared memory. The lists were never complete. Irena freely admitted that there were almost certainly children whose names they could not remember. The lists they could reconstruct were carefully punched out on Jaga's old typewriter, salvaged from the ruins. When the names were neatly catalogued, Irena gave the list to Dr. Adolf Berman, her colleague in Żegota and now the postwar head of the Central Committee of Jews in Poland. In 1945, Adolf Berman took the list to what was then Palestine, and they rest today in an Israeli archive to respect the privacy of those thousands of families.

"Let me stress most emphatically that we who were rescuing children are not some kind of heroes," Irena insisted to those who wanted to celebrate her actions. "Indeed, that term irritates me greatly. The opposite is true — I continue to have qualms of conscience that I did so little." And Irena worked for decades afterward helping reunite "her" children with their families.

Jaga Piotrowska and Jan Dobraczyński made their own lists of the Jewish children who had passed through the Catholic orphanages during the war and been given new identities, but here their stories diverged from Irena's. "The awareness that I behaved in a decent manner and with dignity" was something Jaga afterward said she treasured. More than fifty Jewish people passed through her home during the years of the occupation, and she acted with immense and true courage. But there was also, Jaga said, "a deep wound in my heart. . . . When Poland was liberated in 1945, a Jewish community was established," Jaga explains, "and Janek Dobraczyński and I went over to it to give them the lists of the saved children." Jewish community leaders still remembered those old conversations with Jan Dobraczyński. Dr. Adolf Berman quoted back to Jan what he had said when the Jew-

443

ish parents were powerless, how the children themselves would have to decide their faith when they were old enough. *You baptized them and made them Christians,* came the retort. "During the conversation," Jaga said, "we were told . . . that we had committed a crime by stealing hundreds of children from the Jewish community, baptizing them, and tearing them away from their Jewish culture. . . . We left completely broken." Forty years later Jaga was still grappling with this on her conscience.

The end of the war also raised for Adam and Irena some other pressing questions. What to do about her marriage with Mietek? What to do, for that matter, about Adam's wife?

By the end of 1946 the question took on a special kind of urgency. When Mietek returned to Poland from a prisoner-of-war camp in Germany, Irena was five months pregnant with Adam's daughter. What else could Mietek do? A divorce went ahead quickly. Adam had some complicated matters to attend to himself before they could focus on new beginnings. All that is known for certain of his private matters today is that he and Irena remained good friends with his wife after their divorce and that, for reasons one can only guess may have been connected to his unorthodox love life, his Jewish mother, Leokadia, was furious.

In 1947, after having loved each other sometimes passionately and sometimes hopelessly for more than a decade, Adam and Irena were at last married in a small Polish ceremony. On March 31, 1947, Irena gave birth to their first child, a little girl named Janina after her mother. In 1949 there was a second child, a son, Andrzej, who died as an infant, and a few years later another little boy, Adam.

Irena remained unwavering in her commitment to her work. She threw her passion as zealously as ever into the social welfare department. She worked hand in glove in the years that followed with Maria Palester at the orphanage in Okęcie, and until the end of her very long life, she always kept her door open to any of her 2,500 children. She had been, said one witness, "the brightest star in the black sky of the occupation," and that star was undiminished.

Coda:
The Disappearing Story of
Irena Sendler, 1946–2008

In a fairy tale or motion picture, this would be the end of Irena Sendler's astonishing biography. We would read that the traumas of the war only touched her lightly. We would read of how her quiet heroism was celebrated across Poland, and I would tell you that it is only because this happened in a distant country that you have not heard this story.

But life after the war in communist Warsaw was not easy, especially for those who had fought for Polish freedom in the resistance; throughout the 1940s and 1950s the Soviet state persecuted those who had participated in the Warsaw uprising and those who, like those of Żegota, had turned to the Western Allies for their resources. Many of those people Irena had worked with most closely were now targeted, and Irena herself was under perilous and constant suspicion. It was not the end of anti-

Semitism, and there were reasons why many of the Jewish survivors kept their silence. Names were changed. History was rewritten.

And so the story was buried except among the innermost circle of collaborators. It was too dangerous to speak of what they had done together. Irena was devastated when — after decades as a left-wing activist and lifelong socialist — the ruling communist party punished her by targeting her children, who were denied educational opportunities in postwar Poland. Only among her old friends would Irena speak freely of the past. Sometimes she would look for Rachela — the only one of her Jewish school friends, besides Adam and Regina, to survive the ghetto revolt. "There are times when she avoids me," Irena wrote of that long postwar friendship. "Sometimes we go two or three years without seeing each other. During those periods she manages to forget the past, at least a little, and enjoy the reality of the present. But sometimes, she's overcome with a longing for her lost loved ones, her parents, her brothers and sisters, and the surroundings in which she grew up. That's when she visits me." On those days, Irena was flooded by her own memories of Ewa and Józef and Ala and Dr.

Korczak and all the lost children. And in her sleep, even decades after the war, Irena was haunted by nightmares about those who perished and nightmares about the children. "In my dreams," Irena said, "I still hear the cries when they were leaving their parents."

When Adam Celnikier died of heart trouble in 1961, only in his late forties, their tumultuous love story — which had already ended in divorce and seen the infant death of one of their three children — was also part of what Irena buried. Devastated by a string of post-war losses, Irena turned passionately to religion for the first time since her adolescence, and her return to Catholicism was almost certainly a motivating factor in her decision to remarry Mietek Sendler that decade. It was also one reason why, in her eighties and nineties and as a devout elderly woman, Irena glossed over certain complex parts of their bohemian wartime romances.

It was impossible to speak of Irena's stories in communist Poland. But many of the infants and toddlers whom Irena and her network of friends helped to save from the ghetto lived after the war in Israel, the United States, or Canada, and by the mid-1960s the youngest of them were in their twenties. In the West, the stories of Irena's children were taking hold and growing. In 1965, based on that burgeoning body of testimony — and especially on the wartime testimony of Jonas Turkow — Yad Vashem, the Holocaust memorial organization in Israel, awarded Irena Sendler its highest honor. They added her name to the list of those who are "Righteous Among the Nations" and planted in her honor an olive tree on the Mount of Remembrance. According to Jewish tradition, there are in every generation a tiny number of people whose goodness renovates the entire world in the face of evil, and Irena was named among them. So, too, in time were Jaga Piotrowska, Maria Kukulska, Irka [Irena] Schultz, Maria Palester, Jadwiga Deneka, Władysława Marynowska, Janka Grabowska, Julian and Halina Grobelny, and even Jan Dobraczyński. The Soviets, however, refused to authorize Irena's passport so she could travel to Jerusalem to accept the award. Irena had been branded a decadent Western dissident and a public menace.

So the story in Poland again faded from memory. By the late 1970s, many of those who had survived the war were disappearing. One day in 1979, Irena, Iza, and Jaga met, along with another woman in their old

449

network, and they jointly authored a statement that recorded for posterity the history of their astonishing collaboration as young women. That statement reads, "We estimate (today after 40 years it is difficult to determine it exactly) the number of children which Żegota helped in various ways to be around 2,500." Irena was always emphatic that she did not save them alone. "Every time people said that she saved 2,500 Jewish children's lives," Yoram Gross — the wartime boy known as Jerzy — recalls, "she corrected this by saying that she doesn't know the exact number and that she was saving the children together with friends that helped her." And, as Irena said late in life, "I want everyone to know that, while I was coordinating our efforts, we were about twenty to twenty-five people. I did not do it alone." After the war, when Irena made a list of all the people in Warsaw who took part in her network to help Jewish families and save their children, it was fourteen pages long, and the names in fact numbered in the dozens upon dozens. What Irena never forgot was that she was simply one member of a vast collective effort of decency. She did not want the world to forget either.

That same year, in 1979, at an international conference on Holocaust rescuers and their stories, just as research into the buried history of the "Righteous" was being unearthed and debated, a Professor Friedman stood up before a room of listeners and said that, in time, he believed there would be hundreds of inspiring stories coming to light in Poland. "If we knew," he told the crowd that day, "the names of all the noble people who risked their lives to save Jews, the area around Yad Vashem would be full of trees and would turn into a forest." But it was not until the beginning of glasnost in the late 1980s, when she was in her seventies, that Irena was able to meet, face-to-face again in Israel, many of the children whose lives she saved. Those scenes of reunion were inspiring and heartbreaking. These children only knew her — if they knew her at all as toddlers or infants — as "Jolanta." But she was the last face of their childhood.

It wasn't until the 1990s, after the end of the Cold War, that the story was finally able to be told in Poland. The story was recovered in the mainstream press by a group of American schoolchildren and their history teacher in Kansas, whose story is told in the memoir *Life in a Jar*. By the turn of the millennium, when the truth was being reported, celebrated at last, and remembered collectively, Irena was among the last living survivors of that network, already in her nineties. And parts of the truth were already lost to history. "I only have recourse to the memories burned into my mind by the events of those days," Irena said when she turned, decades after the war, to putting down her story on paper.

In 2003, some of the children she helped to save wrote a joint letter nominating Irena Sendler for the Nobel Peace Prize. They nominated her again in 2007, and momentum was building. Press around the world began to notice. The committee awarded the honor that year instead to Al Gore for his work on global warming, but few doubted that in time Irena Sendler would be a laureate. However, Irena herself crossly brushed aside this talk of awards and honors. "Heroes," she said, "do extraordinary things. What I did was not an extraordinary thing. It was normal." She walked with the spirits of those they could not save, with the faces in her dreams of those who perished.

And time now was scarce and precious. In 2008, at the age of ninety-eight, having borne witness not just to the better part of a century but also to the lives of thousands who survived because of her unwavering moral compass, Irena Sendler died peacefully in Warsaw, surrounded by several of "her" children. She is buried in a wooded cemetery in Warsaw, amid a small copse of trees where the leaves fall gently in the autumn, and perhaps it is a mark of her fame now that on November 1 her simple tombstone is ablaze with candles and awash with small bouquets of flowers. And it is not only in November that one finds small votive candles burning there. In the hush of a Polish forest, where songbirds still speak their welcome to those who listen, the flame of her memory burns on quietly in the shadows, remembered. On her gravestone are only the dates of her life and the names of her parents. But if we could choose a more elaborate epitaph, perhaps we would engrave the words of Mahatma Gandhi, who once said, "A small body of determined spirits fired by an unquenchable faith in their mission can alter the course of history." Such were Irena and all her friends, and this is their story.

AFTERWORD:
AUTHOR'S NOTE ON THE
STORY OF *IRENA'S CHILDREN*

What happened in Warsaw during the German occupation and what this group of people — led by Irena Sendler — achieved is, by any measure, an astonishing tale, with all the elements of great fiction. This book, however, is a work of nonfiction in all its essentials. My sources for this book have been the extensive record, which includes Irena Sendler's handwritten memoirs and her recorded interviews, the testimony of the children she saved and those with whom she worked (and their children), memoirs and biographies of those whose stories intersect with hers, published interviews, private conversations, academic histories on occupied Warsaw, firsthand visits to many of the sites described, and extensive research at archives in Warsaw, Berlin, London, New York City, and Jerusalem.

Frequently, however, as with any secret "cell," the historical record is conflicting or some of the connecting threads of the story are missing. There are aspects of this story that were too dangerous to record in the years after the war, especially during the communist period in Poland, and there are cases where testimony was necessarily selective. Irena herself sometimes wrote — especially about Adam — using coded names that have to be deciphered, and there is the question of how we balance the truth of youthful indiscretions with cases of late-life religious conversions. There are the stories we want to tell of the glorious dead for our own emotional purposes. Above all, there are the competing memories, recounted decades later, of multiple witnesses to singular events that were, by necessity, only dimly understood even in the moment of living them, and in the news reporting and published transcriptions of interviews, there is the trace of everything that is lost in translation.

Not everyone wanted his or her story told — no matter how heroic — in the complicated years that followed the liberation of Warsaw, and in this account I do not pretend to be encyclopedic. I gesture toward some of the untold stories and the names lost to this history (although not always lost to other stories) in the notes with which this book concludes. Some of Irena's most important collaborators — men and women like Wanda Drozdowska-Rogowicz, Izabela Kuczkowska, Zofia Patecka, Róża Zawadzka, Wincenty Ferster, Jadwiga Bilwin, and Helena Merenholc, among others — are mentioned here either only in passing or not at all. It is most often for the simple reason that I was not able to find enough information about their lives and wartime activities to tell their stories. It is also because there is no way to tell in one book the story of twenty or thirty heroes and do them any justice. But Irena considered these men and women among her most fearless collaborators.

I should note as well that this is the biography only of the early part of Irena Sendler's life. I do not attempt to document here the very complex family, romantic, and political experiences that shaped her long life after 1945, except in a very brief coda. The story of Stalinism and post-Stalinism in Poland was its own kind of Holocaust, and Irena faced during that period another set of dangers and repressions entirely.

In all these instances, I have had to weigh the veracity of one set of details over the other and drawn reasonable inferences based on common sense, my assessment of private motives, and the entire body of evidence. When it has seemed clear to me, despite the lacunae, that there is only one way to make sense of the disparate facts and how they are connected to each other, based on what is known of the context and the character of the person in question, I have told the story, without further qualification, as I believe it must have happened. That has included, in some instances, extrapolating from historical context to establish the order of events and the particular details of connections and meetings between individuals within the cell whose identity was left unspecified. The details are, in all cases, based on the scaffolding of known facts, but where there are gaps in that scaffolding — and some gaps are significant — I have made the leap of inference based on my best judgment and larger knowledge of the period and the people about whom I am writing. Another writer might have told a different story based on this same scaffolding. For any readers interested in following in my footsteps and drawing their own, perhaps different, conclusions, my research can be tracked in the notes in the final pages, or I welcome correspondence from readers to my email address at my academic institution.

In order to tell this story, I have taken only one other significant liberty with the archives and historical sources. In several instances, I have offered insight into a character's own thoughts or feelings, or I have offered reframed dialogue. Where material is presented in italics, it represents speech that is not present or is not present in this same form in the historical record. These passages, instead, are based on historical records of a conversation or experience, based on extrapolation from factual scaffolding as noted above, or based on my comprehensive sense of the character and personalities of these individuals after extensive research and gathering of recollections about them. Often this work of extrapolation and historical reconstruction has been necessarily piecemeal. In describing, for example, New Year's Eve in 1942, the materials used in assembling that scene range from an old snapshot of the friends taken that night and recollections of the Kukulska apartment by one of the witnesses to historical information on Polish New Year traditions, other World War II–era memoirs, and an overarching sense of what we know about the personalities of the individuals present and the relationships among them. In other cases, Irena recorded in her memoirs the precise words of what others said to her in a conversation (words placed in quotation marks here) but only summarized the content and not the precise language of her response to those words. Where the summarized content has been presented as speech in this book, the extrapolated speech (or thoughts) have been presented in italics. I have in a few instances also modified past-tense eyewitness testimony to the present tense in order to tell the story as these people experienced it. And in writing from an individual character's perspective to describe what he or she would have seen and experienced, especially in scenes narrating events and places in Warsaw, I have relied extensively on historical photographs, other eyewitness accounts, maps, and oral history interviews. My major sources are noted throughout, and all sources are listed in the bibliography.

This is history, through a glass darkly, with all the attendant perils of the great darkness that was the Holocaust in Poland both during the Second World War and in the decades of communist rule that followed. I have used in all cases my best judgment as a historian and scholar and then proceeded to get on with telling the story of an aston-

460

ishing group of men and women who saved from the darkness thousands of children.

ACKNOWLEDGMENTS

Perhaps more than any other book I have written, this is a story in which I am conscious of the immense debt that I owe to others in the telling of it. I would like to begin by thanking the children — who are not now children at all — for revisiting this past with me and for sharing their experiences. I would like to thank, at the Association of "Children of the Holocaust" in Poland, Elżbieta Ficowska, Marian Kalwary, Katarzyna Meloch, and Joanna Sobolewska for speaking with me. The late Yoram Gross, who passed away just as this book was entering production, shared with me by email his recollections of Irena and his boyhood, and Janina Goldhar shared with me her recollections of the Palester family and her youth in Poland. In Warsaw, I was fortunate to speak with Andrzej Marynowski and Janina Zgrzembska. My thanks to the family of Ala Gołąb-Grynberg, who generously shared information and photographs. I also wish to thank, for information, conversation, connections, or critiques that contributed to this book, all the members of that much-loved tribe, the "Cockneys" (you know who you are), as well as Mirosława Pałaszewska, the Nalven family, Aviva Fattai-Valevski, Avi Valevski, Warren Perley, Les Train, David Suchoff, Anna Mieszkowska, Aleksander Kopiński, Emmanuel Gradoux-Matt, Erica Mazzeo, Charlene Mazzeo, Mark Lee, Halina Grubowska, Mary Skinner, Stacy Perman, Axel Witte, Mark Anderson, and Klara Jackl at the Museum of the History of Polish Jews. For research assistance and translation work, I am grateful to Marta Kessler, Zofia Nierodzinska, Olek Lato, and Phillip Goss, and I must offer an immense acknowledgment and thanks to my primary research partner and Warsaw-based translator, University of Warsaw doctoral student Maria Piåtkowska, without whom this book simply could not have been written.

Once again I owe warm thanks to my literary agent, Stacey Glick, who makes all things possible; to my fabulous film agent, Lou Pitt; and to my editor at Gallery Books, Karen Kosztolnyik, whose vision has made this book possible. I'd also like to thank from Gallery Books: Louise Burke, Jennifer Bergstrom, Wendy Sheanin, Jennifer Long, Jennifer Robinson, Liz Psaltis, John Vairo, and Becky Prager for their incredible support.

And last but certainly not least, I offer my deepest gratitude to my husband, Robert Miles, to whom this book is principally dedicated. The quote with which this book begins is from Shakespeare's *King Lear,* a drama — like the story of Irena Sendler — at its heart about that which we gain and that which we lose and precarious ripeness that is living in the midst of dying. It is a rare man who can balance out the darkness of the long days that I have spent reading and writing about death and the persecution of children with the radiant brightness of love and family, and it is my great fortune to share my life with a husband who is the best of them.

This book was supported by the generosity of Colby College and the Clara C. Piper named professorship, which it is my privilege to hold as a faculty member, and I have been aided in the research for this project by the staff at institutions including, in Warsaw, the Jewish Historical Institute, the Museum of the History of Polish Jews, and the Institute of National Remembrance; in

Jerusalem, Yad Vashem; in Canada, the University of British Columbia libraries; and in the United States, the New York Public Library.

CAST OF CHARACTERS

IRENA'S NETWORK

Irena's Radlińska Circle
These people were former students of Dr. Helena Radlińska, students in the professor's department at the Polish Free University in the 1930s, or faculty in social welfare departments in Warsaw. They were all part of Irena's network of collaborators.

Dr. Helena Radlińska, the celebrated Jewish-born professor at the Polish Free University, was an innovator in the field of social work and welfare services in Poland. She inspired intense loyalty in her students, many of whom were women, and when the war began mobilized resistance cells for the underground — perhaps even Irena's.

Ala Gołąb-Grynberg, Jewish, was the chief

nurse in the Warsaw ghetto and a wartime heroine of the first order; her husband, Arek Grynberg, was an operative in the Jewish resistance; her cousin by marriage, **Wiera Gran**, was rumored to be a traitor to the Jewish people. She and **Nachum Remba** rescued hundreds from deportation to Treblinka in the summer of 1942, earning her the title of the "Good Fairy of the Umschlagplatz" among grateful families. Ala also worked closely with **Jan Dobraczyński, Helena Szeszko**, and **Władysława Marynowska** at the Father Boduen children's home and collaborated directly with Irena and Adam on smuggling Jewish children to safety. Sent to the labor camp at Poniatowa after the ghetto uprising, Ala kept fighting: she was part of a network, aided by Żegota, planning a mass prison break and uprising.

Ewa Rechtman, one of Irena's closest friends from the Polish Free University, worked with orphans in the ghetto and ran the youth circle on Sienna Street. During the deportations of 1942, Irena and her network mounted a desperate effort to save Ewa.

Dr. Janusz Korczak, a lecturer at the Polish

Free University and a civic leader in social work and children's education in prewar Warsaw, ran an orphanage in the ghetto where Irena was a welcome guest and frequent visitor; the "old doctor" perished at Treblinka with nearly two hundred Jewish children — including most of the thirty-two children that **Jan Dobraczyński** had returned, against Irena's wishes, to the ghetto.

Zofia Wędrychowska, a public librarian, left-wing radical, and unmarried mother of four, was a former student of **Dr. Radlińska** and, with her life partner and children's father, **Stanisław Papuziński**, was a key player in one of the professor's cells in the resistance. Their home hid several of "Irena's children," placing the family in constant danger.

Irena "Irka" Schultz, a senior colleague in the welfare offices and one of **Dr. Radlińska**'s prize former students, was one of the original conspirators in Irena's network and helped to save the lives of dozens of Jewish children; no one, it was said, was better at smuggling children out of the ghetto than Irena Schultz.

Józef Zysman, a Jewish pro bono attorney for **Dr. Radlińska** and an early friend of Irena's. Józef was trapped in the ghetto with his wife, Theodora, and their young son, **Piotr Zysman**. From inside the ghetto, Józef and Irena conspired together at secret meetings of the resistance.

Izabela Kuczkowska, one of Irena's old friends from the Polish Free University and part of a cell run by **Dr. Helena Radlińska** during the occupation, worked directly with **Zofia Wędrychowska, Stanisław Papuziński**, and, ultimately, Irena to save the lives of dozens of Jewish children and to support the Polish resistance.

Rachela Rosenthal, Jewish and trained as a teacher at the Polish Free University, was trapped in the ghetto with her husband and small daughter. When she alone survived the summer of 1942, Rachela became "Karolina" — one of the great women warriors of the Warsaw uprising and the lover of a Polish resistance fighter.

Maria Kukulska was a schoolteacher and activist who was part of the social welfare networks in Warsaw tied to the Polish Free

University. A trusted member of Irena's network and skilled at giving Jewish children "makeovers," she hid **Adam Celnikier** and a Jewish doctor in her apartment safe house after their escapes from the ghetto.

Jaga Piotrowska, a social worker, colleague of Irena's, and a former student at the Polish Free University, risked her life and the life of her family to hide more than fifty Jewish people during the occupation. Jaga was one of the original conspirators in Irena's network and one of Irena's bravest liaisons; but as a devout Catholic like **Jan Dobraczyński**, Jaga's faith ultimately led to conflict with the Jewish community despite her unquestioned valor.

Dr. Witwicki, a psychologist and one of the professors close to **Dr. Helena Radlińska**'s circle, wisely fled into hiding when the occupation started. Irena brought him secret support funds from his old friends, and in return he gave her gifts for the ghetto children: Jewish dolls that he spent his days in hiding sculpting.

Dr. Ludwik Hirszfeld, an infectious disease specialist and the cousin of **Dr. Helena**

Radlińska, worked closely with **Ala Gołąb-Grynberg** in the ghetto teaching clandestine medical classes to stop the epidemics.

Jadwiga Deneka, trained as a teacher at the Polish Free University, was one of the original members of Irena's network, responsible with her brother, Tadeusz, for saving the lives of numerous Jewish families and their children. Captured by the Gestapo in 1943, she was executed in the ruins of the ghetto.

Jadwiga Jędrzejowska was another of Irena's friends from their days at the Polish Free University. Irena reencountered Jadwiga inside Pawiak Prison, where Jadwiga was part of the resistance that helped to save Irena.

Social Welfare Colleagues and the Father Boduen Team

These people were Irena's colleagues, coworkers, and conspirators in the Warsaw municipal social services.

Janka Grabowska, a fellow social worker and an underground liaison for Irena's network, was with Irena on the morning that Irena was arrested by the Gestapo. On the table were the lists with the names and addresses of dozens of Jewish children. Janka's quick thinking and her generous brassiere proved a salvation.

Jan Dobraczyński, a senior administrator in the Warsaw social services, was a member of a far-right political party and an ardent Catholic; despite his prewar anti-Semitism, Jan ultimately joined Irena's network to save Jewish children. His zeal for baptizing Jewish children, however, placed him, along with his close conspirator **Jaga Piotrowska** in conflict with the Jewish community.

Władysława Marynowska, the housemother and a social worker at the Father Boduen children's home in Warsaw, joined Irena's network as the deportations accelerated, and bravely hid children in her apartment. She worked closely with **Helena Szeszko, Jan Dobraczyński**, and **Ala Gołąb-Grynberg**.

Dr. Henryk and Maria Palester, he a Catholic-born convert to Judaism: when the doctor was banned from his position in the health ministry, Irena supported the

473

family's decision to stay on the Aryan side in open hiding and found Maria the job in the social welfare offices that she needed to support her family. Daughter **Małgorzata Palester** played a heroic role in the rescue of Irena from Pawiak Prison and survived the war, and the family's teenage son, **Kryštof Palester**, was part of an underground assassination cell in the resistance called "Parasol," which famously fought in the Warsaw up-rising. Irena and Adam stayed with the Palester family and fought together throughout that last battle for survival in Warsaw.

Żegota, the Resistance, and the Medical Underground

These people joined Irena and her network from other branches of the resistance in Warsaw.

Dr. Anna Sipowicz, the dentist in the prison underground at Pawiak, helped Irena smuggle messages back and forth with Żegota.

Dr. Adolf Berman, a Jewish psychologist and one of the leaders of Żegota; after the war, Irena returned the lists of saved Jewish children to him as the leader of the Jewish community.

Stanisława Bussold was the middle-aged midwife and nurse whose apartment was one of Irena's emergency shelters for children smuggled from the ghetto, including the baby **Elżbieta Koppel**.

Stefania Wichlińska, one of Irena's colleagues in the social-welfare offices, was the underground liaison for Żegota's cofounder and the agent responsible for bringing Irena to Żegota; she was murdered by the Gestapo before the war ended. After her escape from Pawiak, Stefania's widower husband helped hide Irena from the Gestapo in the first weeks after her escape from the firing squad.

Julian Grobelny, one of the leaders of Żegota: despite suffering from debilitating tuberculosis, Julian and his wife, **Halina Grobelny**, together walked numerous Jewish children out of the ghetto long before joining forces with the indomitable Irena.

Marek Edelman, a young Jewish man who became one of the joint leaders of the ZOB, the Jewish fighting organization that led the ghetto uprising: Marek worked alongside **Ala Gołåb-Grynberg** and **Nachum Remba** at the Umschlagplatz in their furious trackside rescue mission.

Dr. Juliusz Majkowski, part of the medical underground in Warsaw and a conspirator with **Dr. Radlińska,** gave Irena and her first collaborators epidemic-control passes that allowed them in and out of the ghetto.

Basia Dietrich, one of Irena's neighbors in the apartment complex in Wola district, also ran an operation to save Jewish children. Arrested with Irena and sent to Pawiak, the women shared a cell until that final morning.

Dr. Leon Feiner, one of the Jewish leaders of Żegota, recruited Irena into a secret ghetto mission during the famous ghetto visit of Jan Karski.

Jan Karski, a secret agent of the Polish underground, toured the ghetto in the summer of 1942 and tried to tell the world about the genocide happening in Poland; Irena was one of the signposts on his tour of the ghetto.

Helena Szeszko, a Polish nurse in the medical underground, helped save children from the Warsaw ghetto as part of Irena's network; she and her husband, Leon, were both senior operatives as well in the Polish resistance, responsible for forging identity papers.

Jerzy Korczak, wartime name "Jurek," was one of the two Jewish teenagers living on the Aryan side who became part of the household at Maria Kukulska's apartment and witnessed the intimate life and work of Irena and Adam.

Yoram Gross, wartime name "Jerzy," was one of the two Jewish teenagers living on the Aryan side who became part of the household at Maria Kukulska's apartment and witnessed the intimate life and work of Irena and Adam.

Irena's Family

Irena Sendler, "the female Schindler," who organized across Warsaw an astonishing network of former classmates and coworkers, saved the lives of thousands of Jewish children and created one of the most important underground cells anywhere in occupied Europe.

Adam Celnikier, Irena's Jewish boyfriend from their days at the University of Warsaw and later Irena's second husband, fled the ghetto with new identity papers in the name of Stefan Zgrembski and survived the war by hiding in the apartment of Irena's friend **Maria Kukulska**. From his hiding place Adam aided Irena in her activities for Żegota.

Dr. Stanisław Krzyżanowski and Janina Krzyżanowska: the early death of Irena's father, a passionate activist, set firmly Irena's moral compass; the fate of her ailing mother during the occupation was one of Irena's greatest wartime worries.

Mieczysław Sendler, "Mietek," was Irena's first husband, whom she divorced after the war in order to marry **Adam Celnikier**.

Ghetto Encounters
These were people Irena and her network met inside the ghetto — one of them was a Gestapo collaborator but most of them were rescued Jewish adults or children.

478

Chaja Estera Stein, a Jewish girl saved by the collaboration of **Julian Grobelny**, a kind but unnamed parish priest, and Irena. After the war, under the new Polish name "Teresa," she lived with Irena and **Adam Celnikier** as a foster daughter.

Wiera Gran, the stage name of the sultry Jewish cabaret singer Weronika Grynberg, the cousin of **Ala Gołąb-Grynberg**'s husband, Arek. Wiera's alleged collaboration with the Gestapo and betrayal of the Jewish people earned her a secret death sentence from the resistance and the eternal enmity of the Żegota leadership and Irena.

Jonas Turkow was a Jewish actor and a friend of **Ala Gołąb-Grynberg** and Irena. Ala saved Jonas at the last possible moment from deportation to Treblinka.

Nachum Remba, a clerk at the *Judenrat* who, along with **Ala Gołąb-Grynberg**, became one of the heroes of the Umschlagplatz, where, by brazenly playing a Jewish doctor, he saved hundreds from deaths at Treblinka.

Henia and Josel Koppel were Jewish parents

who gave their infant daughter, **Elżbieta Koppel** — baby "Bieta" — to Irena in the last days before the deportations to Treblinka.

Regina Mikelberg, a former university classmate of **Irena Sendler, Adam Celnikier,** and **Janka Grabowska,** Janka and Irena saved Regina and her sister from the ghetto, where the Mikelberg family lived cheek by jowl with members of the Celnikier clan.

Katarzyna Meloch was a Jewish girl saved from the ghetto and the death camps by Irena's network; **Ala Gołąb-Grynberg** led her out to safety; **Jadwiga Deneka** cared for her after.

Michał Głowiński was one of the Jewish children saved, along with his mother, by Irena's network.

Halina Złotnicka was one of the Jewish children saved by Irena's network. Halina lived for much of the occupation in the home of **Jaga Piotrowska,** who treated her as a second daughter.

NOTES

Prologue

Twice a day, just before noon and in the early evening: Pawiak Museum, public exhibition, 2014; see also Leon Wanat, *Za murami Pawiaka*, Warsaw: Książka i Wiedza, 1985.
They pulled up floorboards and broke furniture: Testimony of Irena Sendlerowa, Association of "Children of the Holocaust" in Poland, www.dzieciholocaustu.org.pl/szab58.php?s=en_sendlerowa.php.

Chapter 1: Becoming Irena Sendler

At the edge of the sky, the forest grows dark: Imagery drawn from Yiddish folk tale; see, for example, Ḥayah Bar-Yitsḥaḥ, *Jewish Poland: Legends of Origin: Ethnopoetics and Legendary Chronicles,* Detroit: Wayne State University Press, 1999, 44.

Otwock, home to a large impoverished Jewish community: Miriam Weiner, "Otwock," Routes to Roots Foundation, www.rtrfoundation.org/webart/poltownentry.pdf; see also Chris Webb, "Otwock & the Zofiowka Sanatorium: A Refuge from Hell," Holocaust Education & Archive Research Team, www.holocaustresearchproject.org/ghettos/otwock.html.

Irena Stanisława Krzyżanowska — for that was her maiden name: "Irena Sendlerowa," Geni database, www.geni.com/people/Irena-Sendlerowa/6000000019948138463.

"If someone else is drowning, you have to give a hand": Magdelena Grochowska, "Lista Sendlerowej: Reportaž z 2001 Roku," *Gazeta Wyborcza,* May 12, 2008, n.p.; also David Barré and Agata Mozolewska, *Elle, elle a sauvé les autres . . .* Paris: Éditions du Cosmogone, 2009.

Dr. Krzyżanowski, with the aid of his brother-in-law: Aleksander Kopiński, personal correspondence.

He welcomed everyone kindly: Grochowska, "Lista Sendlerowej."

Since Jews made up nearly fifty percent of the local population: Yoram Gross, personal correspondence.

She was accustomed to the sight of Jewish

mothers: Grochowska, "Lista Sendlerowej." Generally the reluctance to have Catholic and Jewish children play together was on the Jewish side; see Mark Paul, "Traditional Jewish Attitudes Toward Poles," January 2015, www.kpk-toronto.org/archives/jewish_attitudes.pdf.

"I grew up with these people": Irena Sendler, "O Pomocy Żydom," *Lewicowo,* October 6, 2011, http://lewicowo.pl/o-pomocy-zydom. The article is a reprint of material originally published as *This Is My Homeland: Poles Helping Jews, 1939–1945,* eds. Władysław Bartoszewski and Zofia Lewinówna, 2nd ed., Kraków: Znak, 1969. That text is based on two earlier statements, an early article by Joseph Goldkorn, "He Who Saves One Life," *Law and Life,* no. 9 (1967), and the written testimony of Irena Sendler, first published as "Those Who Helped Jews," *Bulletin of the Jewish Historical Institute* 45/46, 1963.

"Don't spoil her, Stasiu": Ibid.

large, square house at number 21, Kościuszki Street: Anna Legierska, "A Guide to the Wooden Villas of Otwock," August 10, 2015, *Culture.pl,* http://culture.pl/en/article/a-guide-to-the-wooden-villas-of-otwock.

Jewish culture was familiar to Irena: Grochowska, "Lista Sendlerowej."

Irena felt more at home with the Jewish mothers: Marjorie Wall Bingham, "Women and the Warsaw Ghetto: A Moment to Decide," *World History Connected,* http:// worldhistoryconnected.press.illinois.edu/ 6.2/bingham.html.

Uncle Jan and Aunt Maria were rich: Grochowska, "Lista Sendlerowej."

"I was constantly drawn back to those areas": Legierska, "A Guide to the Wooden Villas of Otwock."

Scout's pledge "to be pure in thinking": "Rediscover Polish Scouting," Polish Scouting and Guiding Association, http:// issuu.com/zhp_pl/docs/rediscoverpolish scouting.

The boy's name was Mieczysław "Mietek" Sendler: "Piotrków: Pamiątkowa tablica ku czci Sendlerowej," *ePiotrkow.pl* www .epiotrkow.pl/news/Piotrkow-Pamiatkowa -tablica-ku-czci-Sendlerowej-,2801. See also Paweł Brojek, "Piąta rocznica śmierci Ireny Sendlerowej, Sprawiedliwej wśród Narodów Świata," *Prawy,* May 12, 2013, www.prawy.pl/wiara/3049-piata-rocznica -smierci-ireny-sendlerowej-sprawiedliwej -wsrod-narodow-swiata.

Adam was married to a Jewish woman: Anna Mieszkowska, *Prawdziwa Historia*

Ireny Sendlerowej, Warsaw: Marginesy, 2014, 21–22.

"My father," she explained, "was a doctor": "Fundacja Taubego na rzecz Życia i Kultury Żydowskiej przedstawia Ceremonię Wręczenia Nagrody im. Ireny Sendlerowej," October 23, 2013 program, Museum of the History of Polish Jews, http://nagrodairenysendlerowej.pl/dir _upload/download/thumb/9b515fb73c99 cb31408f589b0b27.pdf.

Dr. Radlińska quickly offered her newest acolyte not just a student internship: Museum of the History of Polish Jews, 2010, "Irena Sendler," *Polscy Sprawiedliwi* (Polish Righteous), www.sprawiedliwi.org .pl/en/cms/biography-83/.

Another neighbor, Basia Dietrich: Testimony of Barbara Jankowska-Tobijasiewicz, "Irenę Sendlerową i Barbarę Ditrich: niezwykłe sąsiadki z ul. Ludwiki wspomina," *Urząd Dzielnicy Wola,* January 28, 2010, www.wola.waw.pl/page/341,internet owe-wydanie-kuriera-wolskiego—-ws zystkie-numery.html?date=2010-01 -00&artykul_id=394.

"Everyone here was dedicated and true to their goals": Grochowska, "Lista Sendlerowej."

Chapter 2: Dr. Radlińska's Girls

The end of his raised cane shimmered in the light: Joanna B. Michlic, *Poland's Threatening Other: The Image of the Jew from 1880 to the Present,* Lincoln: University of Nebraska, 2006, 113.

"Because," she snapped, "I am Polish": Robert Blobaum, ed., *Antisemitism and Its Opponents in Modern Poland,* Ithaca: Cornell University Press, 2005; also Grochowska, "Lista Sendlerowej."

a seating area in the lecture halls for Jewish students that was set apart: Mary V. Seeman, "Szymon Rudnicki: Equal, but Not Completely," *Scholars for Peace in the Middle East,* book review, June 7, 2010, http://spme.org/book-reviews/mary-v -seeman-szymon-rudnicki-equal-but-not -completely. Note that throughout this book I use the term "Aryans." Both Jews and gentiles used that word freely throughout the occupation of Poland, and it has been retained as historically accurate.

Other professors supported the students: Ibid.

"The years at the University were for me very hard": Yoram Gross, personal correspondence.

The third member of their circle was Ewa

Rechtman: Here and throughout on Irena's youth circle friends, see Irena Sendler, "The Valor of the Young," *Dimensions: A Journal of Holocaust Studies* 7, no. 2 (1993), 20–25.

"I met a few, illegal members of the Polish Communist Party": Grochowska, "Lista Sendlerowej."

He planned, he told her boldly, to give it all away to charity: Anna Mieszkowska, *Irena Sendler: Mother of the Children of the Holocaust,* trans. Witold Zbirohowski-Koscia, Westport, CT: Praeger, 2010.

"I fit right in with my political past": Museum of the History of Polish Jews, 2010, "Irena Sendler," *Polscy Sprawiedliwi* (Polish Righteous), www.sprawiedliwi.org .pl/en/cms/biography-83/.

Adam had already qualified as an attorney: Sendler, "The Valor of the Young."

Adam began doctoral work in political history: Andrzej Biernacki, *Zatajony artysta. O Wacławie Borowym 1890–1950,* Lublin: Norbertinum, 2005.

By July, Warsaw buzzed with rumors: John Radzilowski, "The Invasion of Poland," *World War II Database,* ww2db.com/ battle_spec.php?battle_id=28.

From the sky came nothing — no bombs, no sounds: British Broadcasting Corporation, "On This Day: 1939: Germany Invades Poland," http://news.bbc33.co.uk/onthisday/hi/dates/stories/september/1/newsid_3506000/3506335.stm.

Hitler's attack on Poland had already started: "Directive No. 1 for the Conduct of the War," Avalon Project: Yale Law School, www.yale.edu/lawweb/avalon/imt/document/wardir1.htm.

direction of her office on Złota Street: Barré and Mozolewska, *Elle, elle a sauvé les autres.*

"faraway surf, not a calm surf but when waves crash onto a beach": Diane Ackerman, *The Zookeeper's Wife: A War Story*, New York: W. W. Norton, 2008, 32.

Doctors and nurses helped rush moaning residents to aid points: Irena Sendler, "O Pomocy Żydom."

a pro bono Jewish lawyer named Józef Zysman: Sendler, "The Valor of the Young."

He was also in a regiment, out there somewhere: Sendler, "The Valor of the Young." See also Irena Sendler, "Youth Associations of the Warsaw Ghetto: A Tribute to Jewish Rescuers," ZIH archives (Materialy Zabrane w Latach, 1995–2003, sygn. S/353), trans. Stanisław Barańczak and Michael Barańczak.

Irka Schultz was the office boss: Irena

Schultz's name has been shortened throughout to the Polish nickname for Irena, Irka, in order to avoid confusion between Schultz and Sendler in the narrative. This is the equivalent in English of differentiating, say, between one character as "Jennifer" and another as "Jenny."

senior administrator in a branch of the social welfare office: Louis Bülow, "Irena Sendler: An Unsung Heroine," www .auschwitz.dk/sendler.htm.

"Corpses of men and animals are heaped in the streets": Details paraphrase material from the Polish Ministry of Information, *The German Invasion of Poland,* London: Hutchinson & Co. Ltd., 1940, excerpted at http://felsztyn.tripod.com/german invasion/id1.html.

Exhausted, Irena and her boss, Irka, sat together in an office: Barré and Mozolewska, *Elle, elle a sauvé les autres.*

Some 40,000 people died in the bombings of Warsaw: For a contemporary account of the Siege of Warsaw by a Żegota survivor, see Władysław Bartoszewski, *1859 Dni Warszawy,* Kracow: Wydawnictwo Znak, 1974.

While the Germans considered how best to arrange a mass forced migration: Ellen Land-Weber, "Conditions for the Jews in

Poland," *To Save a Life: Stories of Holocaust Rescue*, Humboldt State University, www2.humboldt.edu/rescuers/book/Makuch/conditionsp.html.

Of course she must help!: "Irena Sendler Award for Repairing the World," program description, Centrum Edukacji Obywatelskiej, www.ceo.org.pl/pl/sendler/news/program-description.

"The sole goal of [their] schooling is to teach them simple arithmetic": "Poles: Victims of the Nazi Era: Terror Against the Intelligentsia and Clergy," United States Holocaust Memorial Museum, www.ushmm.org/learn/students/learning-materials-and-resources/poles-victims-of-the-nazi-era/terror-against-the-intelligentsia-and-clergy.

Dr. Borowy, immediately joined the underground university: Mieszkowska, *Irena Sendler: Mother of the Children of the Holocaust,* 26.

Dr. Radlińska, hobbled but resolute: "Life and Activity of Helena Twóczość Radlińskie," http://sciaga.pl/tekst/69744-70-zycie_twoczosc_i_dzialalnosc_heleny_radlinskiej. See also Zofia Waleria Stelmaszuk, "Residential Care in Poland: Past, Present, and Future," *International Journal of Family and Child Welfare,* 2002/3, 101.

So did Ala's mentor and medical research partner, Dr. Hirszfeld: Thomas Hammarberg, "2007 Janusz Korczak Lecture: Children Participation," Brussels: Commissioner for Human Rights/Council of Europe, 2007, https://rm.coe.int/CoERMPublicCommonSearchServices/DisplayDCTMContent?documentId=09 0000168046c47b. See also Bogusław Filipowicz, "Nadzieja spełniona: dzieło Ireny Sendlerowej w ratowaniu dzieci żydowskich," *Quarterly Research* 1, no. 1 (2010), www.stowarzyszeniefidesetratio.pl/Presentations0/09Flipipowicz.pdf.

Aleksander Rajchman, a prominent mathematics professor: Antoni Zygmund, "Aleksander Rajchman," *Wiadomości Matematyczne* 27 (1987), 219–31, excerpted at www.impan.pl/Great/Rajchman.

Some fifty thousand other members of the "intelligentsia": On this history, see Richard Hugman, ed., *Understanding International Social Work: A Critical Analysis,* New York: Palgrave, 2010.

Later, hundreds of Catholic priests were rounded up: Ewa Kurek, *Your Life Is Worth Mine: How Polish Nuns Saved Hundreds of Jewish Children in German-Occupied Poland, 1939–1944,* New York: Hippocrene Books, 1997, 17, 45.

Her husband, Arek, had left Warsaw: personal correspondence.

Restrictions required Jewish property to be registered: Kurek, *Your Life Is Worth Mine,* 18.

Hundreds of thousands of Jews — nearly one in ten in Poland: Laura Jockusch and Tamar Lewinsky, "Paradise Lost? Postwar Memory of Polish Jewish Survival in the Soviet Union," *Holocaust and Genocide Studies* 24, no. 3 (Winter 2010): 373–99.

ten Poles in Warsaw were murdered for every Jewish resident: Kurek, *Your Life Is Worth Mine,* 17.

"In reference to today's conference in Berlin": Ibid., 18.

Chapter 3: Those Walls of Shame

Rudnicki was the false name under which Helena Radlińska was working: Internetowy Polski Słownik Biograficzny, "Helena Radlińska," www.ipsb.nina.gov.pl/index .php/a/helena-radlinska.

"There were families where one herring was shared amongst six children": Grochowska, "Lista Sendlerowej."

"has large Polish contacts, especially on the left": Government Delegation for Poland, Department of the Interior, folder 202/II-

43, reprinted in Krzysztof Komorowski, *Polityka i walka: Konspiracja zbrojna ruchu narodowego, 1939–1945,* Warsaw: Oficyna Wydawnicza "Rytm," 2000.

"She would also eventually develop her own independent clandestine Jewish welfare program": Stelmaszuk, "Residential Care in Poland."

Irena's colleague and friend Jadwiga Piotrowska: Jan Dobraczyński, private diary, 1945; courtesy of Mirosława Pałaszewska, personal communication.

Her father, Marian Ponikiewski: Tadeusz Cegielski, "Liberum Conspiro, or the Polish Masonry between the Dictatorship and Totalitarianism, 1926–1989," *Le Communisme et les Elites en Europe Centrale,* March 31, 2004, École Normale Supérieure, colloquium presentation, www1.ens.fr/europecentrale/colloque_elites 2004/4Documents/Resumes/Cegielski _resum.htm.

She and Janusz Piotrowski had a young daughter: "Jadwiga Maria Józefa Piotrowska," Geni database, www.geni.com/people/Jadwiga-Piotrowska/600000001 5472386167.

She lived on Karolkowa Street in Warsaw's Żoliborz district: Museum of the History of Polish Jews, 2010, "The Stolarski Family," *Polscy Sprawiedliwi* (Polish Righteous), www.sprawiedliwi.org.pl/en/family/123,the-stolarski-family/; see also "Józef Dubniak," Museum of the Polish Uprising, www.1944.pl/historia/powstancze-biogramy/Józef_Dubniak.

team was providing public welfare support to thousands of Jews: Irena Sendler, "O Pomocy Zydom."

It was based on nothing more than faking files: Ibid. See also Barré and Mozolewska, *Elle, elle a sauvé les autres.*

"The basis of receiving social assistance was collecting data": Museum of the History of Polish Jews, 2010, "Irena Sendler," *Polscy Sprawiedliwi* (Polish Righteous), www.sprawiedliwi.org.pl/en/cms/biography-83/.

By January, young Polish ruffians: Yisrael Gutman, Ina Friedman, *The Jews of Warsaw, 1939–1943: Ghetto, Underground, Revolt*, Bloomington: Indiana University Press, 1989, 28.

Germans were making plans to establish a Jewish quarter: Leni Yahil, *The Holocaust: The Fate of European Jewry, 1932–1945*, Oxford: Oxford University Press, 1991, 169.

Those living on the wrong side of the boundary would have to move: Yad

Vashem, *This Month in Holocaust History,* "Warsaw Jews During World War II," www.yadvashem.org/yv/en/exhibitions/this_month/resources/warsaw.asp.

wartime property records show that some members of the Celnikier and Mikelberg families: Kawczyński and Kieszkowski, Dekret Bieruta, database, www.kodekret .pl/Dekret-Bieruta.pdf. The Bierut Decree, passed in 1945, was an effort to restore real estate confiscated during the German occupation, making it an important immediate postwar record of property ownership.

Regina Mikelberg, though, was not among them: Museum of the History of Polish Jews, 2010, "The Stolarski Family," *Polscy Sprawiedliwi* (Polish Righteous), www .sprawiedliwi.org.pl/en/family/123,the -stolarski-family/.

But already in October work started on a ten-foot-high brick wall: Harrie Teunissen, "Topography of Terror: Maps of the Warsaw Ghetto," July 2011, www.siger .org/warsawghettomaps.

"In Warsaw, there were several thousand Jews who practiced professions": Kurek, *Your Life is Worth Mine,* 15.

She was a fellow social worker named Maria: Janina Goldhar, personal correspondence; see also Museum of the History of Polish Jews, 2010, "Maria Palester," *Polscy Sprawiedliwi* (Polish Righteous), www.sprawiedliwi.org.pl/en/family/434,palester-maria/; and "Irena Sendlerowa," Association of "Children of the Holocaust" in Poland, www.dzieciholocaustu.org.pl/szab58.php?s=en_sendlerowa.php.

It was the fact that Henryk: Museum of the History of Polish Jews, 2010, "Maria Palester," *Polscy Sprawiedliwi* (Polish Righteous), www.sprawiedliwi.org.pl/en/family/434,palester-maria/.

Jewish families, slowly walking to clandestine Shabbat services: "Spiritual Resistance in the Ghettos," *Holocaust Encyclopedia,* United States Holocaust Memorial Museum, www.ushmm.org/wlc/en/article.php?ModuleId=10005416.

It came like a thunderbolt, residents said afterward: Emanuel Ringelblum, qtd. Monica Whitlock, "Warsaw Ghetto: The Story of Its Secret Archive," January 27, 2013, British Broadcasting Corporation, www.bbc.com/news/magazine-21178079.

Polish residents — both friends and strangers — arrived in huge numbers: Władysław Bartoszewski, *The Warsaw Ghetto: A Christian's Testimony,* trans. Stephen J. Cappellari, Boston: Beacon Press, 1987.

496

Soon the boundaries were guarded with ruthless determination: Ringelblum, *Notes from the Warsaw Ghetto,* 228–29. See also Stanislaw Adler, *In the Warsaw Ghetto: 1940–1943, An Account of a Witness,* trans. Sara Philip, Jerusalem: Yad Vashem, 1982.

official rations allotted to her Jewish friends amounted to a paltry 184 daily calories: "Warsaw," *Holocaust Encyclopedia,* United States Holocaust Memorial Museum, www.ushmm.org/wlc/en/article.php?ModuleId=10005069. Historical descriptions of Warsaw throughout this story have benefited from the following additional sources: Karol Mórawski, *Warszawa Dzieje Miasta,* Warsaw: Wydawnictwo Kxiåžka i Wiedza, 1976; Robert Marcinkowski, *Warsaw, Then and Now,* Warsaw: Wydawnictwo Mazowsze, 2011; Olgierd Budrewicz, *Warszawa w Starej Fotografii,* Olszanica: Wydawnictwo Bosz, 2012.

The Germans responded by adding loops of barbed wire: Ringelblum, *Notes from the Warsaw Ghetto,* 228–29.

Now residents scuttled along the edges of the buildings: "Nożyk Synagogue, Twarda Street 6," Virtual Shtetl, www.sztetl.org.pl/en/article/warszawa/11,synagogues-prayer

-houses-and-others/5,nozyk-synagogue
-twarda-street-6/.

One in five of her admitting staff would succumb to the disease: Naomi Baumslag, *Murderous Medicine: Nazi Doctors, Human Experimentation, and Typhus,* Santa Barbara: Praeger, 2005, 107.

As Polish residents hurrying to work looked on in astonishment: Michael A. Grodin, ed., *Jewish Medical Resistance in the Holocaust,* New York: Berghahn, 2014, 70.

In December the Jewish hospital was closed: Commission of History at the Polish Nurses' Association, "The Nursing School at the Orthodox Jew Hospital at Czyste District in Warsaw," Virtual Museum of Polish Nursing, www.wmpp.org.pl/en/nursing-schools/the-nursing-school-at-the-orthodox-jew-hospital-at-czyste-district-in-warsaw.html.

"the first prerequisite for the final aim is the concentration of the Jews": *The Einsatzgruppen Reports,* eds. Yitzhak Arad, Shmuel Krakowski, Shmuel Spector, Jerusalem: Yad Vashem, 1989.

"cities which are rail junctions should be selected": Ibid.

Chapter 4: The Youth Circle

Her daughter, Rami, was five that year: "Mlawa Societies in Israel and in the Diaspora," *Jewish Mlawa: Its History, Development, Destruction,* ed. and trans. David Shtokfish, Tel Aviv, 1984, 2 vols., www .jewishgen.org/yizkor/mlawa/mla449.html, see especially chapter 14, "Modern Times." See also Jonas Turkow, *Ala Gólomb Grynberg: La Heroica Enfermera del Ghetto de Varsovia,* trans. Elena Pertzovsky de Bronfman, Buenos Aires: Ejecutivo Sudamericano del Congreso Judío Mundial, 1970.

She was also in charge of leading the youth circle at number 9, Smocza Street: Sendler, "Youth Associations of the Warsaw Ghetto."

"Don't you people understand yet?": Ibid.

"I was a frequent visitor to the walled district": Ibid.

Prices for smuggled food were astronomical: Samuel Kassow, translated and co-edited by David Suchoff, *In Those Nightmarish Days: The Ghetto Reportage of Peretz Opoczynski and Josef Zelkowicz,* New Haven: Yale University Press, 2015.

"Abuses — wild, bestial 'amusements' — are daily events": Bartoszewski, *The War-*

saw Ghetto.

Above all, Irena's friends were watching hungry small children die each day from typhus: "Irena Sendler," Association of "Children of the Holocaust" in Poland.

"the population density [inside the Jewish quarter] is unimaginable": Bartoszewski, *The Warsaw Ghetto,* 9.

"The Jews will die from hunger and destitution": State University of New York at Buffalo/Jagiellonian University, "Slow Extermination: Life and Death in the Warsaw Ghetto," *Info Poland,* http://info -poland.buffalo.edu/web/history/WWII/ ghetto/slow.html.

"I want to steal, I want to rob, I want to eat, I want to be a German": Ringelblum, *Notes from the Warsaw Ghetto,* 39.

Ewa Rechtman was an increasingly important figure at CENTOS: Sendler, "Youth Associations of the Warsaw Ghetto."

Ewa ran the youth center at number 16, Sienna Street: Ringelblum, *Notes from the Warsaw Ghetto.* See also Virtual Shtetl, "Janusz Korczak's Orphanage in Warsaw," trans. Ewelina Gadomska, www.sztetl.org .pl/en/article/warszawa/39,heritage-sites/ 3518,janusz-korczak-s-orphanage-in -warsaw-92-krochmalna-street-until -1940-/.

"orgy of parties": Ringelblum, *Notes from the Warsaw Ghetto*, 249. On the archives kept by Ringelblum and his collaborators inside the ghetto, see *The Warsaw Ghetto: Oyneg Shabes–Ringelblum Archives: Catalogy and Guide*, eds. Robert Moses Shapiro and Tadeusz Epsztein, Bloomington: Indiana University Press, 2009.

The Sienna Street complex where Ewa worked housed one of those cafés: Ringelblum, *Notes from the Warsaw Ghetto*, 119.

the café was only a stone's throw from the relocated Czyste Hospital's main ward: Grodin, *Jewish Medical Resistance*. See also Barbara Góra, "Anna Braude Hellerowa," Warsaw: Association of "Children of the Holocaust" in Poland, 2011, 38–39.

the Jewish actor Jonas Turkow: Norman Ravvin, "Singing at the Café: Vera Gran's Postwar Trials," *Canadian Jewish News*, January 13, 2015, www.cjnews.com/books -and-authors/singing-caf%C3%A9-sztuka -vera-gran%E2%80%99s-postwar-trials.

Everyone is crying: Agata Tuszynska, *Vera Gran: The Accused*, New York: Knopf, 2013, 68, 71.

Wiera was rumored to be part of a group of Jewish people actively collaborating: Dan Kurzman, *The Bravest Battle: The 28 Days of the Warsaw Ghetto Uprising,* Boston: Da Capo Press, 1993, 5.

Who should get the vaccinations?: Sendler, "Youth Associations of the Warsaw Ghetto."

Her family lived in one of the large apartment buildings in the area: Ibid. See also Marian Apfelbaum, *Two Flags: Return to the Warsaw Ghetto,* Jerusalem: Gefen Publishing House, 2007, 49.

Józef would tell her about the best nightclubs in Warsaw: Aniela Uziembło, "Józef Zysman," *Gazeta Stołeczna,* no. 141, June 20, 2005, 9; Grochowska, "Lista Sendlerowej."

Many members of the ghetto police were former lawyers and even judges: Katarzyna Person, "A Forgotten Voice from the Holocaust," *Warsaw Voice,* March 31, 2011, www.warsawvoice.pl/WVpage/pages/article.php/23365/article.

Along with Adam and Arek, he threw his energies into the Jewish resistance: Yad Vashem, *This Month in Holocaust History,* "Judischer Ordnungsdienst," www.yadvashem.org/yv/en/exhibitions/this_month/resources/jewish_police.asp.

Józef joined an underground socialist press: Anna Poray, 2004, "Waclaw and Irena Szyszkowski," *Polish Righteous,* www

.savingjews.org/righteous/sv.htm. See also August Grabski and Piotr Grudka, "Polish Socialists in the Warsaw Ghetto," Emanuel Ringelblum Jewish Historical Institute, Warsaw, www.jhi.pl/en/publications/52.

Józef's secret cell met for weekly organizational meetings: Grabski and Grudka, "Polish Socialists in the Warsaw Ghetto"; see also "A Forgotten Voice from the Holocaust" and Sendler, "Youth Associations of the Warsaw Ghetto."

Chapter 5: Calling Dr. Korczak

But the fact was, Jan didn't mind saying: Jan Engelgard, "To Dobraczyński był bohaterem tamtego czasu," *Konserwatyzm,* June 19, 2013, http://www.konserwatyzm.pl/artykul/10342/to-dobraczynski-byl-bohaterem-tamtego-czasu. Review of Ewa Kurek, *Dzieci żydowskie w klasztorach. Udział żeńskich zgromadzeń zakonnych w akcji ratowania dzieci żydowskich w Polsce w latach 1939–1945* [Jewish Children in the Monasteries: The Role of Female Religious Congregations in the Rescue of Jewish Children in Poland from 1939–1945], Zakrzewo: Replika, 2012.

After the first office purges, Jan was promoted to director: Mirosława Pałaszewska, personal correspondence. I owe a significant debt of gratitude to Ms. Pałaszewska for making her entire personal archive of material available for this project. Many of the items are newspaper clippings and private archival materials from the families, most in Polish, which would otherwise have been nearly impossible to reconstruct.

It occurred to Irena that the chemistry was obvious: Ibid.

The frontline task of locating and caring for Warsaw's children: Marek Haltof, *Polish Film and the Holocaust: Politics and Memory,* New York: Berghahn Books, 2012, 149; Nahum Bogner, "The Convent Children: The Rescue of Jewish Children in Polish Convents During the Holocaust," Yad Vashem, www.yadvashem.org/yv/en/righteous/pdf/resources/nachum_bogner.pdf. See also Cynthia Haven, "Life in Wartime Warsaw . . . Not Quite What You Thought," (interview with Hana Rechowicz), May 21, 2011, http://bookhaven.stanford.edu/2011/05/life-in-wartime-warsaw-not-quite-what-you-thought.

"For an absurdly low salary you had to be stuck in the office": Mirosława Pałaszewska, personal correspondence.

Whereas they used to send six hundred youngsters a year to the Father Boduen children's home: Klara Jackl, "Father Boduen Children's Home: A Gateway to Life," Museum of the History of Polish Jews, June 11, 2012, www.sprawiedliwi.org .pl/en/cms/your-stories/794/ and personal correspondence.

The two frightened children: Cynthia Haven, "Life in Wartime Warsaw . . . Not Quite What You Thought."

But it was also summary execution for any gentile: Ellen Land-Weber, *To Save a Life: Stories of Holocaust Rescue,* Champaign-Urbana: University of Illinois Press, 2002, 195.

Jan's aging father was a friend of the "old doctor": Jan Dobraczyński, *Tylko w jednym życiu* [Once in a lifetime], Warsaw: Pax, 1977; also Mirosława Pałaszewska, personal correspondence. See also Andras Liv, "1912–1942: Korczak Orphanage Fate in Warsaw: Krochmalna 92 — Chłodna 33 — Sienna 16," January 2, 2012, http://jimbaotoday.blogspot.ca/ 2012/01/korczak-orphanage-in-warsaw_02 .html, excellent selection of historical photographs of the orphanage sites.

"[At] my request," Jan said, "my father telephoned him": Jan Engelgard, "To

Dobraczyński był bohaterem tamtego czasu."

"A few minutes before curfew": Ibid.

Chapter 6: Ghetto Juggernaut

The word floated to mind and hung there stubbornly: Irena Sendler, "O Pomocy Żydom."

The women had made contact with a local priest in the distant city of Lwów: Yad Vashem, "Irena Schultz: Rescue Story," *The Righteous Among the Nations,* db .yadvashem.org/righteous/family.html ?language=en&itemId=4017410; and Anna Poray, 2004, "Waclaw and Irena Szyszkowski," *Polish Righteous,* www .savingjews.org/righteous/sv.htm.

the professor's handmade dolls for the children: Irena Sendler, "Youth Associations of the Warsaw Ghetto"; also "Władysław Witwicki: Rescue Story," database, Yad Vashem.

"Please don't ask me": Irena Sendler, "Youth Associations of the Warsaw Ghetto."

"Above the entrance to the sewer, I said good-bye to Father": *The Last Eyewitnesses: Children of the Holocaust Speak,* eds. Jakub Gutembaum and Agnieszka

Lalała, Vol. 2, Evanston: Northwestern University Press, 2005.

She saw these children every day at Adam's youth circle: Irena Sendler, "Youth Associations of the Warsaw Ghetto."

"You can be calm about the child": Museum of the History of Polish Jews, 2010, "Irena Schultz," *Polscy Sprawiedliwi* (Polish Righteous), www.sprawiedliwi.org.pl/en/family/644/.

"I didn't ask for any details," Władka said: Andrzej Marynowski, personal communication.

"It was enough to know that [Irka] had to take the Jewish children out of the ghetto and put them in a safe place": Ibid.

"My mother took me out," she says. "I don't remember how": Rami Gołąb-Grynberg, personal communication.

He remembers those days with his mother: Andrzej Marynowski, personal communication.

Disaster was coming: How was she going to get a message to Irena?: Irena Sendler, "O Pomocy Żydom."

a thirty-year-old Jewish man named Szlama Ber Winer: "Grojanowski Report," Yad Vashem, www.yadvashem.org/odot_pdf/microsoft%20word%20-%206317.pdf.

In April 1942, the prisoners had been set to work on a new construction project: Yitzhak Arad, *Belzec, Sobibor, Treblinka: The Operation Reinhard Death Camps,* Bloomington: Indiana University Press, 1999. See also Chil Rajchman, *The Last Jew of Treblinka: A Memoir,* New York: Pegasus, 2012.

"said it was to be a bath": Chris Webb, *The Treblinka Death Camp: History, Biographies, Remembrance,* Stuttgart: Ibidem Press, 2014, 14, 21, *passim.*

Tickets would be required of everyone entering the baths: Chil Rajchman, *Treblinka: A Survivor's Memory, 1942–1943,* trans. Solon Beinfeld, London: Maclehose Press, 2009.

"Jews of Warsaw, for your attention!": Yitzhak Arad, "The Nazi Concentration Camps: Jewish Prisoner Uprisings in the Treblinka and Sobibor Extermination Camps," Proceedings of the Fourth Annual Yad Vashem International Conference, Jerusalem, January 1980, Jewish Virtual Library, www.jewishvirtuallibrary .org/jsource/Holocaust/resistyad.html.

In time, an orchestra would play Yiddish

songs: Toby Axelrod, "Treblinka Survivor Attends Berlin Ceremony," Jewish Telegraphic Agency, August 1, 2005, www.jta.org/2005/08/01/life-religion/features/treblinka-survivor-attends-berlin-ceremony. See also Mark Smith, *Treblinka Survivor: The Life and Death of Hershl Sperling,* Mt. Pleasant, SC: The History Press, 2010, 112.

They cost about the same as another increasingly desirable commodity: Axis History Forum, online discussion (thread: Adam Fisher, August 31, 2002, http://forum.axishistory.com/viewtopic.php?t=6901). Measuring historical values is notoriously complex, but, roughly speaking, one USD ($) in the 1940s was roughly equivalent to 5.3 Polish złotych. For a discussion of historical values and calculators, see the excellent academic-run resource Measuring Worth: www.measuringworth.com/uscompare/relativevalue.php.

"protective readiness distribution points": Michał Głowiński, *The Black Seasons,* trans. Marci Shore. Evanston: Northwestern University Press, 2005.

"It became necessary to take the children to the Aryan side": "Fundacja Taubego na rzecz Życia i Kultury Żydowskiej przedstawia Ceremonię Wręczenia Nagrody im.

Ireny Sendlerowej," 2013 program.

Leon worked in the civil transportation office: Jewish Rescuers of the Holocaust, 1933–1945, "Jewish Organizations Involved in Rescue and Relief of Jews," August 25, 2012, http://jewishholocaust rescuers.com/Organizations.html.

The senior priest, Father Marceli Godlewski: Chana Kroll, "Irena Sendler: Rescuer of the Children of Warsaw," Chabad, www.chabad.org/theJewishWoman/article_cdo/aid/939081/jewish/Irena-Sendler.htm; see also Joachim Wieler, "The Long Path to Irena Sendler: Mother of the Holocaust Children," (interview with Irena Sendler), *Social Work and Society* 4, no. 1 (2006), www.socwork.net/sws/article/view/185/591.

As chief nurse of the ghetto hospitals: Joachim Wieler, "The Long Path to Irena Sendler."

a fellow social worker named Róża Zawadzka: Irena Sendler, "Youth Associations of the Warsaw Ghetto"; also Jonas Turkow, *Ala Gólomb Grynberg;* also Marcin Mierzejewski, "Sendler's Children," *Warsaw Voice,* September 25, 2003, www.warsawvoice.pl/WVpage/pages/article.php/3568/article.

"One day she left me with Róża": Personal

correspondence.

Irena called together a meeting of women in his division: According to Jan Dobraczyński, the staff members who came to him were Irena Sendlerowa, Jadwiga Piotrowska, Nonně Jastrzěbie, Halina Kozłowskå, Janina Barczakowå, Halina Szablakówně; Mirosława Pałaszewska, private archives; also Museum of the History of Polish Jews, 2010, "Jan Dobraczyński," *Polscy Sprawiedliwi* (Polish Righteous), www.sprawiedliwi.org.pl/en/family/436,dobraczynski-jan/.

"That whole group": Museum of the History of Polish Jews, 2010, "Jan Dobraczyński," *Polscy Sprawiedliwi* (Polish Righteous), www.sprawiedliwi.org.pl/en/family/436,dobraczynski-jan/.

"[But] I did not look for these children": Ibid.

"Normally," Jaga explained, "the section manager would not sign these papers": Ibid.

From then on, Ala was in contact with Jan Dobraczyński: Nahum Bogner, *At the Mercy of Strangers: The Rescue of Jewish Children with Assumed Identities in Poland*, Jerusalem: Yad Vashem, 2009, 22.

It was increasingly Ala who coordinated advance logistics: Ibid.

For the moment, the infant would stay hidden at the home of Stanisława Bussold: Museum of the History of Polish Jews, 2010, "Stanisława Bussold," *Polscy Sprawiedliwi* (Polish Righteous), www.sprawiedliwi.org.pl/pl/family/331,bussold stanislawa/.

"What we had on those lists": "Fundacja Taubego na rzecz Życia i Kultury Żydowskiej przedstawia Ceremonię Wręczenia Nagrody im. Ireny Sendlerowej," 2013 program.

The doctor was in his early sixties: Betty Jean Lifton, *The King of Children: A Biography of Janusz Korczak,* New York: Schocken, 1989; and Janusz Korczak, *Ghetto Diary,* New Haven: Yale University Press, 2003.

"It is a difficult thing," he wrote, "to be born and to learn to live": Janusz Korczak, *Ghetto Diary,* New Haven: Yale University Press, 2003.

"We are told that all the Jews . . . will be deported to the East": Adam Czerniakow, *Warsaw Diary of Adam Czerniakow: Prelude to Doom,* ed. Raul Hilberg et al., Chicago: Ivan R. Dee, 1999.

"Wednesday, July 22, 1942. So this is the end of the ghetto": Władysław Bartoszweski, *The Warsaw Ghetto.*

Chapter 8: The Good Fairy of the Umschlagplatz

Marek was charged with coordinating the transfers: Michael T. Kaufman, "Marek Edelman, Commander in Warsaw Ghetto Uprising, Dies at 90," *New York Times,* October 3, 2009, www.nytimes.com/2009/10/03/world/europe/03edelman.html.

And they saved an old friend, Jonas Turkow: "Edwin Weiss," Warsaw Ghetto Database, Polish Center for Holocaust Research, http://warszawa.getto.pl/index.php?mod=view_record&rid=09121996103042000001&tid=osoby&lang=en; and "Nachum Remba," Warsaw Ghetto Database, Polish Center for Holocaust Research, http://warszawa.getto.pl/index.php?mod=view_record&rid=05011904155335000002&tid=osoby&lang=en.

Anything to convince the Germans someone could not travel: Eli Valley, *The Great Jewish Cities of Central and Eastern Europe: A Travel Guide,* New York: Jason Aronson Publishers, 1999, 230.

Fussy and frightened children, unable to feign disease: Jonas Turkow, *Ala Gólomb Grynberg.*

She and Remba had diverted an ambulance: Nachum Remba, Warsaw Ghetto Database, Polish Center for Holocaust Research, http://warszawa.getto.pl/index.php?mod=view_record&rid=0501190415533 5000002&tid=osoby&lang=en.

the SS came for the children at Dr. Korczak's orphanage: Agnieszka Witkowska, "Ostatnia droga mieszkańców i pracowników warszawskiego Domu Sierot," *Zagłada Żydów, Studia i Materiały,* vol. 6, 2010, http://korczakowska.pl/wp-content/uploads/2011/12/Agnieszka-Witkowska.-Ostatnia-droga-mieszkancow-i-pracow nikow-warszawskiego-Domu-Sierot.pdf, 22 and *passim*.

That day she happened to come early, well before noon: Ibid.

When Irena heard the news that the children were all destined for deportation: David Cesarani and Sarah Kavanaugh, *Holocaust: Jewish Confrontations with Persecution and Mass Murder,* vol. 4 of *The Holocaust: Critical Concepts in Historical Study,* London: Routledge, 2004, 56.

"The children were to have been taken away alone": Jürgen Oelkers, "Korczak's *Memoirs:* An Educational Interpretation," Universität Zürich, Institut für Erziehungswissenschaft, Lehrstühle und Forschungs stellen [published lecture], 95–96. See also Władysław Szpilman, *The Pianist: The*

Extraordinary True Story of One Man's Survival in Warsaw, 1939–1945, trans. A. Bell, with extracts from the diary of Wilm Hosenfeld, New York: Picador, 1999.

"You do not leave a sick child in the night": Diane Ackerman, The Zookeeper's Wife.

The children set off from the orphanage singing: Jürgen Oelkers, "Korczak's Memoirs."

With children, the march across the ghetto, from south to north: Agnieszka Witkowska, "Ostatnia droga mieszkańców."

It was a swelteringly hot day already: Ibid.

witnessed the doctor's three-mile walk: I. M. Sidroni, "Rabbi Zalman Hasid," trans. Alex Weingarten, The Community of Sierpc: Memorial Book, Efraim Talmi, ed., Tel Aviv, 1959, www.jewishgen.org/Yizkor/Sierpc/sie377.html.

But that morning his back was straight: Vladka Meed, On Both Sides of the Wall: Memoirs from the Warsaw Ghetto, trans. Steven Meed, Jerusalem: Ghetto Fighters' House, 1972, review by Rivka Chaya Schiller, Women in Judaism 9, no. 1 (2012), http://wjudaism.library.utoronto.ca/index.php/wjudaism/article 125/view/19161/15895.

What is the possible guilt of these children?:

Janusz Korczak, *The Child's Right to Respect,* Strasbourg: Council of Europe Publishing, 2009, www.coe.int/t/commissioner/source/prems/PublicationKorczak_en.pdf.

Dr. Witwicki, her old psychology professor at the University of Warsaw: Ibid.

"Clutching the dolls in their little hands": Irena Sendler, "Youth Associations of the Warsaw Ghetto."

That they were going to the freight yard and to their execution: "Irena Sendler Tells the Story of Janusz Korczak," Gariwo/Gardens of the Righteous World-Wide Committee, (documentary/video interview with Irena Sendler), http://en.gariwo.net/pagina.php?id=9114.

There under the hot sun, after the chaos and bruising gauntlet, the children and the doctor waited: Marek Edelman, "The Ghetto Fights," in *The Warsaw Ghetto: The 45th Anniversary of the Uprising,* Interpress Publishers, 1987, 17–39; archived at www.writing.upenn.edu/~afilreis/Holocaust/warsaw-uprising.html.

I cannot leave the children, not even for a moment: Stanislaw Adler, *In the Warsaw Ghetto.*

"I will never forget that sight," said Nachum: "Janusz Korczak," Adam Mickiewicz Institute, Warasw, www.diapozytyw.pl/ en/site/ludzie/; "Janusz Korczak: A Polish Hero at the Jewish Museum," *Culture 24,* December 7, 2006, www.culture24.org.uk/ history-and-heritage/art41997. See also Władysław Bartoszweski, *The Warsaw Ghetto.*

"Remembering that tragic procession of innocent children marching to their death": "Irena Sendler Tells the Story of Janusz Korczak," Gariwo.

"Of all my most dramatic war-time experiences, including my 'residence' and torture in the Pawiak": Janusz Korczak, "A Child's Right to Respect."

"She was also waging a quiet and intense battle inside herself": Irena Sendler, "Youth Associations of the Warsaw Ghetto."

Dozens of refugees were hiding in the empty animal cages: Ludwik Hirszfeld, *The Story of One Life,* (memoir), trans. Marta A. Balińska, Rochester: University of Rochester Press, 2014, Kindle location 8897.

"I give my child in your care, raise my child as if it was yours": "Ala Gołąb [Golomb] Grynberg," Warsaw Ghetto Database, Polish Center for Holocaust Research, http:// warszawa.getto.pl/index.php?mod=view _record&rid=07051998094230000004

&tid=osoby&lang=en.

"She struggled between the instinct of a mother and that of a nurse": Ludwik Hirszfeld, *The Story of One Life,* location 8897.

When Adam's aunt Dora was shot dead in Warsaw at the end of July: Dekret Bieruta database, www.kodekret.pl/Dekret-Bieruta.pdf.

When word came that his eighteen-year-old cousin, Józefina: United States Holocaust Memorial Museum, "Såd Grodzki w Warszawie, Akta Zg.1946 (Sygn. 655)," 1946–56, RG Number RG-15.270M, Accession Number 2013.241, Archiwum Państwowe w Warszawie, http://collections.ushmm.org/findingaids/RG-15.270_01_fnd_pl.pdf.

"hardly anyone bothered about the children": Vladka Meed, *On Both Sides of the Wall,* trans. Steven Meed. Washington, DC: Holocaust Memorial Museum, 1999.

"their mother, father, sister, friend": Irena Sendler, "Youth Associations of the Warsaw Ghetto."

"It was a beautiful, warm day": Ibid.

"quiet, soothing, and full of kindness": Ibid.

"Very quickly, we realized that the only way to save the children was to get them out": Ibid.

"They couldn't imagine living without each other": Yisrael Gutman, Ina Friedman, *The Jews of Warsaw, 1939–1943: Ghetto, Underground, Revolt,* Bloomington: Indiana University Press, 1989, 218.

"The trains, already leaving twice a day with 12,000 people each": Władysław Bartoszweski, *The Warsaw Ghetto.* See also Abraham Lewin, *A Cup of Tears: A Diary of the Warsaw Ghetto,* ed. Antony Polonsky, Waukegan, IL: Fontana Press, 1990; see entries for July 1942.

"Never before," survivors remembered later, "had anyone been so inflexible": Marek Edelman, "The Ghetto Fights."

"A communist," said the Gestapo man: *The Last Eyewitnesses,* 111.

"We witnessed terrible scenes": Marilyn Turkovich, "Irena Sendler," September 29, 2009, *Charter for Compassion,* http://voiceseducation.org/category/tag/irena-sendler. Includes extracts from interviews with Irena Sendler and some video content.

What Katarzyna remembers today: Marcin Mierzejewski, "Sendler's Children," *Warsaw Voice,* September 25, 2003, www.warsawvoice.pl/WVpage/pages/article

.php/3568/article; also personal interview source material.

"in a very hot summer (1942)": Marcin Mierzejewski, "Sendler's Children," *Warsaw Voice*, September 25, 2003, www.warsawvoice.pl/WVpage/pages/article.php/3568/article.

These "emergency rooms" — Irena's "protective readiness centers": "The 72nd Anniversary of the Creation of the Council to Aid Jews," Jewish Historical Institute, Warsaw, December 3, 2014, www.jhi.pl/en/blog/2014-12-03-the-72nd-anniversary-of-the-creation-of-the-council-to-aid-jews.

In Jadwiga's apartment: Michalina Taglicht lived with the Piotrowski family, along with her five-year-old daughter Bronia in 1943. Bronia was later hidden in Jadwiga's parents' home, located some sixty-five miles outside of Warsaw in the town of Pionki, and Michelina was hidden in a safe house in Warsaw. Jan and his heavily pregnant wife Zofia Szelubski were also refugees at the home.

The inspector there knew there were Jewish children there: Michał Głowiński, *The Black Seasons.*

When Katarzyna's false papers came: Alexandra Sližová, "Osudy zachráněných dětí

520

Ireny Sendlerové," master's thesis, 2014, Masarykova University, http://is.muni.cz/th/383074/ff_b/BP-_Alexandra_Slizova.pdf.

We must not acquiesce in the spiritual destruction of our children: Nahum Bogner, "The Convent Children," 7.

the Jewish envoy was almost certainly Dr. Adolf Berman: "Adolf Abraham Berman," Yad Vashem, www.yadvashem.org/odot_pdf/Microsoft%20Word%20-%205996.pdf.

"Those are tough terms," the doctor snapped: Nahum Bogner, "The Convent Children," 7.

Once or twice Henia was driven to wild risks: Alexandra Sližová, "Osudy zachráněných dětí Ireny Sendlerové."

Chapter 10: Agents of the Resistance

"Be quiet," the strange man said to them: IPN TV, "Relacja Piotra Zettingera o Ucieczce z Warszawskiego Getta," (video interview of Piotr Zettinger), www.youtube.com/watch?v=tY3WxXUiYzo.

"To this day, I can see the look in his kind and wise eyes": Sendler, "Youth Associations of the Warsaw Ghetto."

Piotr went home to Irena's apartment: Anna

Poray, 2004, "Wacław and Irena Szysz-kowski," *Polish Righteous,* www.savingjews .org/righteous/sv.htm.

"They treated me," Piotr says, "like their own child": "The Woman Who Smuggled Children from the Ghetto," *Jewniverse,* February 15, 2013, http://thejewniverse .com/2013/the-woman-who-smuggled -children-from-the-ghetto.

Piotr disappeared into one of the Catholic orphanages in her network: "Poles Saving Jews: Irena Sendlerowa, Zofia Kossak, Sister Matylda Getter," Mint of Poland, https://www.nbp.pl/en/banknoty/kolek cjonerskie/2009/2009_13___polacy _ratujacy_zydow_en.pdf.

"I hid my fear," she said, "in my pocket": News clippings, undated, "Jaga Pi-otrowska" and "Stowarzszenie Dzieci Ho-locaustu w Polsce," courtesy Association of "Children of the Holocaust" in Poland and Mirosława Pałaszewska. See also "50 Razy Kara Śmierci: Z Jadwigą Pi-otrowską," May 11, 1986, ZIH archives, Materialy Zabrane w Latach, 1995–2003, sygn. S/353.

"Where do you want me to drive to?": Anna Mieszkowska, *Irena Sendler,* 82.

"What was happening was as horrible as could be": Janusz Korczak, "A Child's

Right to Respect."

Would Irena agree to act as a signpost for Jan Karski on his trip into the ghetto?: "Address by Irena Sendeler [sic]," Association of "Children of the Holocaust" in Poland, (interviews with Irena Sendler), www.dzieciholocaustu.org.pl/szab58.php?s=en_sendlerowa001_02.php.

Underneath the foundations of the building at number 6, Muranowska Street: E. Thomas Wood and Stanisław M. Jankowski, *Karski: How One Man Tried to Stop the Holocaust,* New York: John Wiley & Sons, Inc., 1994; Stanisław Wygodzki, "Epitaph for Krysia Liebman," *Jewish Quarterly* 16, vol. 1 (1968): 33.

Doctors and nurses had tried to save their own elderly parents: Sharman Apt Russell, *Hunger: An Unnatural History,* New York: Basic Books, 2006.

"To offer one's cyanide to somebody else is a really heroic sacrifice": Marek Edelman, "The Ghetto Fights."

Eighty-five percent of the original total ghetto population of 450,979: Jonas Turkow, *Ala Gólomb Grynberg.*

Another 30,000: "Deportations to and from the Warsaw Ghetto," *Holocaust Encyclopedia,* United States Holocaust Memorial Museum, www.ushmm.org/wlc/en/

article.php?ModuleId=10005413.

But by 1941 the underground had infiltrated the RGO: "Central Welfare Council, Poland," Yad Vashem, www.yadvashem .org/odot_pdf/Microsoft%20Word%20-% 205913.pdf.

She was hiding Jewish children in city orphanages: "K. Dargielowa," Warsaw Ghetto Database, Polish Center for Holocaust Research, http://warszawa.getto.pl/ index.php?mod=view_record&rid=20051 997191448000001&tid=osoby&lang=en.

Some of those children were the youngsters: Jonas Turkow, *Ala Gólomb Grynberg.*

"Our feelings toward Jews have not changed": Joanna B. Michlic, *Poland's Threatening Other: The Image of the Jew from 1880 to the Present,* Lincoln: University of Nebraska, 2008, 170. "Protest" was originally circulated in Warsaw in 1942 in an underground pamphlet, with a print run of 5,000 copies. The anti-Semitic passages were almost immediately deleted that year, when the text was reprinted. On the history of those deletions, see also David Cesarani and Sarah Kavanaugh, *Holocaust: Responses to the Persecution,* 63. Due to those passages, the complete, unexpurgated text is somewhat difficult to obtain; the full material is reprinted in some Holocaust source books, for example, Sebastian Rejak and Elżbieta Frister, eds., *Inferno of Choices: Poles and the Holocaust,* Warsaw: Oficyna Wydawnicza "Rytm," 2012, 34.

By 1944 there would be at least three hundred thousand Home Army members: Teresa Prekerowa, *Żegota: Commision d'aide aux Juifs,* trans. Maria Apfelbaum. Monaco: Éditions du Rocher, 1999, 24.

Aleksander Kamiński and Izabela were close wartime collaborators: Krzysztof Komorowski, *Polityka i walka: Konspiracja zbrojna ruchu narodowego.*

Chapter 11: Żegota

The Germans had cut off the funds to the social welfare office: Marek Halter, *Stories of Deliverance: Speaking with Men and Women Who Rescued Jews from the Holocaust,* Chicago and La Salle, IL: Open Court, 1997, 9–11; qtd. Mark Paul, "Wartime Rescue of Jews," 61–62.

The name on the bell read *Eugenia Wasowska:* "Życie Juliana Grobelnego," October 3, 2007, http://grju93brpo.blog spot.ca/2007/10/ycie-juliana-grobelnego .html; see also Jerzy Korczak, *Oswajanie*

Strachu, Źródło: Tygodnik Powszechny, 2007, extracts at http://www.project inposterum.org/docs/zegota.htm.

A man beckoned Irena to enter: Teresa Prekerowa, *Żegota: Commission d'aide aux Juifs,* Polacy Ratujący Żydów w Latach II Wojny Światowej, IPN (Instytut Pamięci Narodowej), Warsaw, 2005, http://ipn.gov.pl/data/assets/pdf_file/0004/55426/1-21712.pdf.

"In the course of this unusual meeting": Marcin Mierzejewski, "Sendler's Children," *Warsaw Voice,* September 25, 2003, www.warsawvoice.pl/WVpage/pages/article.php/3568/article.

An extra pound of black-market butter: Teresa Prekerowa, *Konspiracyjna Rada Pomocy Żydom w Warszawie, 1942–1945,* Warsaw: PIW, 1982. Some chapters have been translated into English by the Polish-Jewish Heritage Foundation of Canada, www.polish-jewish-heritage.org/eng/teresa_preker_chapters1-2.htm.

"In the fall of 1942, I took control of the Child Welfare Division": Irena Sendler, "Youth Associations of the Warsaw Ghetto."

Some sixty thousand Jewish people were hiding on the Aryan side of the city: Teresa Prekerowa, *Konspiracyjna Rada Pomocy*

Zydom w Warszawie.

In the next ten months — from December 1942 to October 1943: Ibid.

Irena's apartment was always a last resort for the network: Ibid.

"Vast sums passed through my hands": Ibid.

Now the couple's teenage son Kryštof also joined an elite resistance scouting squad: Bohdan Hryniewicz, *My Boyhood War: Warsaw: 1944,* Stroud, UK: The History Press, 2015.

More than twenty Jewish people passed through her apartment: Magdalena Grochowska, "Sendler's List."

Irena herself had introduced him to the hideout in Świder: Irena Sendler, "O Pomocy Żydom," *Lewicowo.*

How dare you disturb the peace of a Polish Christian: Ibid.

With all the subtle charm of youth, Jurek began to stare: Jerzy Korczak, *Oswajanie Strachu,* Warsaw: Wydawnictwo Muza, 2007.

"Forget that you have something in common with the Jewish tribe": Jerzy Korczak, *Oswajanie Strachu.*

So was Roman Bazechesa: "Otwoccy Sprawiedliwi," *Gazeta Otwocka,* July 2012, www.otwock.pl/gazeta/2012/sprawiedliwi .pdf.

So Maria Kukulska's apartment also became a regular meeting place: Ibid.

In the old state mint at number 18, Markowska Street: Guide to Praga, "Building of the Mint," www .warszawskapraga.pl/en/object_route.php ?object_id=332.

More often, when she thought she was being followed: Alanna Gomez, "Jan and Antonia Zabinski: The Zookeepers," Canadian Centre for Bio-Ethical Reform, www.unmaskingchoice.ca/blog/2013/01/ 18/jan-and-antonia-zabinski-zookeepers.

The doors to the couple's white stucco bungalow were always open: Vanessa Gera, "New Exhibition at Warsaw Zoo Honors Polish Couple Who Saved Jews During World War II," *Haaretz*, April 11, 2015, www.haaretz.com/jewish-world/jewish -world-features/1.651285.

Adam was an energetic man who couldn't sit still: Otwoccy Sprawiedliwi," *Gazeta Otwocka*, July 2012, www.otwock.pl/ gazeta/2012/sprawiedliwi.pdf.

Chapter 12: Toward the Precipice

so the quiet tapping that startled Irena: Accounts of this story vary from source to source. Irena Sendler suggests in one

528

interview from the late 1960s that, while she was present for the event, it may have taken place at the home of one of her close conspirators. However, in deemphasizing her role in events, it is more likely that she was simply being both modest and protective of her neighbors during a period in which she herself was subject to considerable persecution. See Irena Sendler, "O Pomocy Żydom."

"For safety's sake, I was the only person who kept and managed the files": Ibid.

"It's clear she doesn't sleep at night": Ibid.

"Jaga took care of me like her own daughter": Halina Złotnicka [Goldsmith], "Czesc Tereska VI," Jewish Calendar, Almanac 1990–1991, file s.138–146; news clipping, courtesy private archives of Mirosława Pałaszewska; personal correspondence.

Irena was needed in the forest outside Otwock: "Życie Juliana Grobelnego."

Many in the ghetto by late autumn were also set on armed resistance: *Journal of Emanuel Ringelblum,* 28.

Now everyone in the ghetto was looking for miraculously clever hiding places: Robert Rozett, "The Little-Known Uprising: Warsaw Ghetto, January," *Jerusalem Post,* January 16, 2013, www.jpost.com/

Opinion/Op-Ed-Contributors/The-little
-known-uprising-Warsaw-Ghetto-January
-1943.

Janka checked Józef as best she could:
"Odznaczenie za bohaterską postawę i
niezwykłą odwagę," Office of the President
of Poland, March 16, 2009, www
.prezydent.pl/archiwum-lecha-kaczyn
skiego/aktualnosci/rok-2009/art,48,61,odz
naczenie-za-bohaterska-postawe-i-nie
zwykla-odwage.html.

Adolf Berman's account books showed that
the same secret courier: "A List (No. VII)
of Welfare Cases According to Caseload
'Cell' Heads," registry number 24092″,
catalog 6210, Ghetto House Fighters'
Archive, database, www.infocenters.co.il/
gfh/multimedia/FilesIdea/%D7%90%
D7%95%D7%A1%20006210.pdf.

"What is this," he retorted indignantly:
Irena Sendler, "O Pomocy Żydom."

"I don't want to be here," she whispered
into his shoulder: Ibid.

"I cannot recall exactly what I happened to
be doing": Qtd. in Michał Głowiński, *The
Black Seasons,* 115.

"My dear, this poster is in the ghetto": *The
Last Eyewitnesses.*

"I know because I passed it one day in the
ghetto with my parents": Ibid.

Stefania was gunned down on the streets of the ghetto: "Zamordowani w różnych rejonach Warzawy," Wieśniowie Pawiaka [Victims of Pawiak in Warsaw], 1939–1944, www.stankiewicze.com/pawiak/warszawa4.htm.

It was early on a beautiful May morning: Courtesy private archives of Mirosława Pałaszewska and courtesy archives of the Association of "Children of the Holocaust" in Poland.

"That morning in our apartment," she explained simply: Courtesy private archives of Mirosława Pałaszewska and courtesy archives of the Association of "Children of the Holocaust" in Poland.

"I did it myself," Jaga remembered: Courtesy private archives of Mirosława Pałaszewska; personal correspondence.

The neighbors and their guests were shot dead at the crossroads: Teresa Prekerowa, *Żegota: Commission d'aide aux Juifs;* Israel Gutman, *The Encyclopedia of the Righteous Among the Nations,* Jerusalem: Yad Vashem, 2007, vol. 5 (Poland), pt. 2, 611–12.

The parents of one Jewish child, Michał Głowiński: Alexandra Sližová, "Osudy zachráněných dětí Ireny Sendlerové."

"I constantly think that I have encountered

a real miracle": Michał Głowiński, *Black Seasons.*

"a harrowing experience for the small heroes": Ibid.

Chapter 13: Ala Rising

The Ferris wheel lifted young courting Polish couples: Imagery here drawn from Czesław Miłosz's poem "Campo dei Fiori."

No one any longer doubted such rumors: "The Warsaw Ghetto Uprising," Yad Vashem, www.yadvashem.org/yv/en/education/newsletter/30/warsaw_ghetto_uprising.asp.

Adolf and Leon carried hand grenades and weapons: Władysław Bartoszewski, *The Warsaw Ghetto.*

they used incendiary bottles to attack the German columns: Marek Edelman, "The Ghetto Fights."

"[We] blew up German tanks and German troops": Ibid.

carried hand grenades hidden "in their bloomers up to the last moment": "The Warsaw Ghetto: Stroop's Report on the Battles in the Warsaw Ghetto Revolt (May 16, 1943)," Jewish Virtual Library, www.jewishvirtuallibrary.org/jsource/

Holocaust/sswarsaw.html.

"we threw our grenades and saw German blood": Transcripts of the Eichmann trial, Nizkor Project, www.nizkor.org/hweb/people/e/eichmann-adolf/transcripts/Sessions/Session-025-04.html.

"the first real entertainment the Germans had provided": David Danow, *The Spirit of Carnival: Magical Realism and the Grotesque,* Lexington: University of Kentucky Press, 2005.

As apartment buildings exploded, eager bets were laid: Ibid.

"Give me some addresses where we can take people who make it to the Aryan side": Teresa Prekerowa, *Żegota: Commission d'aide aux Juifs.*

Can Żegota transmit the addresses to the Jewish combat organization?: Ibid.

Irena waited at sewer manholes: Anna Mieszkowska, *Prawdziwa Historia Ireny Sendlerowej,* 127.

Ala was working directly with him and with the others in the Jewish resistance: Jonas Turkow, *Ala Gólomb Grynberg.*

On May 8, 1943, close to the end: Some sources alternatively list this date as May 9.

"There was no air, only black, choking smoke and heavy, burning heat": Marek

Edelman, "The Ghetto Fights."

"The flames cling to our clothes": Ibid.

"Brother, Please Help!": Ibid.

"half-walked, half-crawled for twenty hours": "Marek Edelman: Last Surviving Leader of the 1943 Warsaw Ghetto Uprising Against the Nazis," *Independent,* October 7, 2009, www.independent.co.uk/news/obituaries/marek-edelman-last-surviving-leader-of-the-1943-warsaw-ghetto-uprising-against-the-nazis-1798644.html.

"Jews, bandits, and subhumans were destroyed": Marian Apfelbaum, *Two Flags: Return to the Warsaw Ghetto,* New York: Gefen Publishing, 2007, 317.

The governor-general proudly reported: Ibid.

The Hotel Polski was a seedy four-story building at number 29, Długa Street: For a more complete account of the Hotel Polski affair, see Abraham Shulman, *The Case of Hotel Polski: An Account of One of the Most Enigmatic Episodes of World War II,* New York: Holocaust Library, 1982.

Rumor had it, too, that the hotel was being set up as a kind of neutral staging ground: "Adam Żurawin," Warsaw Ghetto Database, Polish Center for Holocaust Research, http://warszawa.getto.pl/index.php?mod=view_record&rid=270320032

04554000076&tid=osoby&lang=en.

Irena was convinced that Wiera was a Gestapo informer: Andrew Nagorski, " 'Vera Gran: The Accused' by Agata Tuszynska," (review), *Washington Post,* March 22, 2013, www.washingtonpost .com/opinion/vera-gran-the-accused-by -agata-tuszynskatranslated-from-the -french-of-isabelle-jannes-kalinowski-by -charles-ruas/2013/03/22/6dce6116-75f2 -11e2-8f84-3e4b513b1a13_story.html.

"Jewess, before the war, a cabaret dancer": Vera Gran claimed after the war that she had not been a collaborator, and the topic has been the subject of some controversy, as discussed in Andrew Nagorski's review, among others. In her recollections late in life, Vera Gran also accused the "pianist" Władysław Szpilman himself of having been a collaborator. This is generally understood by scholars as a diversionary tactic and possibly as a reflection of Vera Gran's advanced age and decades of animosity. The publication of the biography prompted Szpilman's son to protest the libel of his father. In 1983, Irena Sendler also made a denunciation of Vera Gran in written testimony to Professor Dr. Horn Maurycy, director of the Jewish Historical Institute in Warsaw (file A.051/

535

488/80): www.veragran.com/sendler1pdf.pdf and www.veragran.com/sendler2pdf.pdf. Jonas Turkow, saved by Ala Gołąb-Grynberg and the author of the only biography of her, also made a denunciation after the war of Vera Gran for known collaborationist activities.

"Wiera Gran, a cabaret actress . . . worked for the Gestapo alongside Leon Skosowski": "New Book Full of 'Lies and Libel' Says Son of Władysław Szpilman," *Polskie Radio,* broadcast and transcript, November 5, 2011, www2.polskieradio.pl/eo/dokument.aspx?iid=142897.

"A wonderful man died a martyr's death": Irena Sendler, "Youth Associations of the Warsaw Ghetto."

There the prisoners were set to work fabricating German military uniforms: Lawrence N. Powell, *Troubled Memory: Anne Levy, the Holocaust, and David Duke's Louisiana,* Charlotte: University of North Carolina Press, 2002, 249; Deborah Charniewitch-Lubel, "Kolno Girls in Auschwitz," in *Kolno Memorial Book,* eds. Aizik Remba and Benjamin Halevy, Tel Aviv: Kolner Organization and Sifirat Poalim, 1971, www.jewishgen.org/Yizkor/kolno/kole056.html.

Chaja Estera Stein was the first of Irena's

own two foster daughters: Jadwiga Rytlowa, "Chaja Estera Stein (Teresa
Tucholska-Körner): 'The First Child of
Irena Sendler,' " Museum of the History
of Polish Jews, September 14, 2010, www
.sprawiedliwi.org.pl/en/cms/your-stories/
360,chaja-estera-stein-teresa-tucholska-k
-rner-the-first-child-of-irena-sendler-/.
Zofia and Stanisław had four children of
their own: Irena Sendler, "O Pomocy
Żydom."

Chapter 14: Aleja Szucha

Regina Mikelberg, along with her sister:
Ibid. See also Museum of the History of
Polish Jews, 2010, "The Stolarski Family,"
Polscy Sprawiedliwi (Polish Righteous),
www.sprawiedliwi.org.pl/en/family/123,
the-stolarski-family/.
This is a list of our children; hide it somewhere:
Museum of the History of Polish Jews,
2010, "Irena Sendler," *Polscy Sprawiedliwi*
(Polish Righteous), www.sprawiedliwi.org
.pl/pl/cms/biografia-83/.
Irena at last convinced the agents that Janka
was an innocent out-of-town visitor: Irena
Sendler, "O Pomocy Żydom."
That was what people on the streets of
Warsaw called the squat gray compound:

Wanda D. Lerek, *Hold on to Life, Dear: Memoirs of a Holocaust Survivor,* n.p.: W. D. Lereck, 1996.

Soon cries of terror came from the hallway: Holocaust Education & Archive Research Team, "Gestapo Headquarters: Szucha Avenue and Pawiak Prison — Warsaw," 2007, www.holocaustresearchproject.org/nazioccupation/poland/pawaiak.html; although a nonacademic site, the resource includes a strong collection of historical photos of Pawiak and an excellent summary.

"One could hear curt questions, the murmur of low answers": Ibid.

On the first day of their arrest, prisoners were severely beaten: Anna Czuperska-Śliwicka, *Cztery Lata Ostrego Dyżuru: Wspomnienia z Pawiaka, 1930–1944,* Warsaw: Czytelnik, 1965; see also Pawiak Museum, Warsaw, exhibition materials, 2013.

Those destined for the concentration camps of Ravensbrück and Auschwitz: Regina Domańska, Pawiak, *Więzienie Gestapo: Kronika 1939–1944,* Warsaw: Książka i Wiedza, 1978; see also Anna Czuperska-Śliwicka, *Cztery Lata Ostrego Dyżuru* and Pawiak Museum, Warsaw, exhibition materials, 2013.

In her cell that first night, Irena and her

neighbor Basia Dietrich: "Barbara Dietrych-Wachowska," online biography, http://pl.cyclopaedia.net/wiki/Barbara _Dietrych-Wachowska. Some sources say that Helena Pĕchcin and Barbara Dietrych-Wachowska were arrested as early as August. Other sources say that the two women were arrested only days before Irena. But those who knew Irena Sendler personally report that the three women were arrested the same day in the roundup that resulted as the breach of the laundry post office. Whatever the case, what is certain is that Irena Sendler and Basia Dietrich shared a cell at Pawiak at this time. Thanks also for this research to the late Yoram Gross, personal communication.

By the spring of 1943, when the Insurgent Special Forces were combined with Home Army operations: Mirosław Roguszewski, *Powstańcze Oddziały Specjalne "Jerzyki" w latach 1939–1945*, Bydgoszcz: n.p., 1994.

The window of the cramped office into which she was led looked out over the ruins: Anna Czuperska-Śliwicka, *Cztery Lata Ostrego Dyżuru*.

"We are doing everything we can to get you out of that hell": Irene Tomaszewski and Tecia Werbowski, *Code Name: Żegota*.

Before long, the bones of Irena's legs and feet were broken: "Gestapo Torture of Jews in Warsaw Prisons Reported, List of Guilty Nazis," October 19, 1942, Jewish Telegraphic Agency, www.jta.org/1942/10/19/archive/gestapo-torture-of-jews-in-warsaw-prisons-reported-list-of-guilty-nazis-published.

"One could have an impression that this was an ambulance": Pawiak Museum, exhibition materials, 2013.

"They weren't just worried about me": Irene Tomaszewski and Tecia Werbowski, *Code Name: Żegota*, 58.

"She's at Szucha, and perhaps already in Pawiak": Jerzy Korczak, *Oswajanie Strachu*.

So was the indefatigable Ala Gołąb-Grynberg: Jonas Turkow, *Ala Gólomb Grynberg*.

Then nearly fifteen thousand slave laborers lay down together: "Aktion Erntefest (Operation "Harvest Festival")," *Holocaust Encyclopedia*, United States Holocaust Memorial Museum, www.ushmm.org/wlc/en/article.php?ModuleId=10005222.

Helena was, Irena always said, "full of initiatives": Teresa Prekerowa, *Żegota: Commission d'aide aux Juifs*.

On November 25, Jadwiga was checking in on some Jewish refugees: Władysław Bartoszewski and Zofia Lewinówna, *Ten jest z ojczyzny mojej: Polacy z pomocå Żydom, 1939–1945,* Warszawa: Świat Książki, 2007, 370.

Basia and Zbigniew were executed that day: "Irenê Sendlerowå i Barbarê Ditrich: niezwykłe såsiadki z ul. Ludwiki wspomina Barbara Jankowska-Tobijasiewicz," Urząd Dzielnicy Wola, January 28, 2010, file 46/347, www.wola.waw.pl/page/341,internetowe-wydanie-kuriera-wolskiego—-wszystkie-numery.html?date=2010-01-00&artykul_id=394; contains testimony of Barbara Jankowska-Tobijasiewicz, who lived in the apartment building of Irena Sendler and Basia Dietrich as a child.

Jadwiga was executed in the ruins of the ghetto: Marcin Mierzejewski, "Sendler's Children," *Warsaw Voice,* September 25, 2003, www.warsawvoice.pl/WVpage/pages/article.php/3568/article. See also Yad Vashem, "Deneko Family: Rescue Story," *The Righteous Among the Nations,* http://db.yadvashem.org/righteous/family.html?language=en&itemId=4014550.

"One day, I heard my name": Teresa Prekerowa, *Żegota: Commission d'aide aux Juifs.*

"You are free. Save yourself fast": Ibid.

"You lousy thug, get lost," he snarled, and he pounded his fist into her mouth: Irena Sendler, autobiographical notes, ZIH archives, Materialy Zabrane w Latach, 1995–2003, sygn. S/353, file IS-04-85-R.

"I could not go on": Ibid.

"I was so naïve," Irena said afterward: Irena Sendler, "O Pomocy Żydom."

"We died inside from fear," Irena said simply: Ibid.

"I do not know how long it took — minutes seemed like an eternity — until we heard the sound of running shoes, moving away": Ibid.

"They were looking for you again": Ibid.

in Home Army files on her there was a description of her: Government Delegation for Poland, archival files, signature 202 / II-43, Department of the Interior, rpt. Krzysztofa Komorowskiego, *Polityka i Walka: Konspiracja Zbrojna Ruchu Narodowego, 1939–1945,* Warsawa: Oficyna Wydawnicza "Rytm," 2000; see Zołnierze Przeklieci Nacjonalizmzabija, December 20, 2013, https://zolnierzeprzekleci .wordpress.com/listy-nienawisci.

She stayed for a time with her uncle near

Nowy Sącz: Museum of the History of Polish Jews, 2010, "Irena Sendler," *Polscy Sprawiedliwi* (Polish Righteous), www .sprawiedliwi.org.pl/en/cms/biography-83/.

she spent some time back in Praga: Diane Ackerman, *The Zookeeper's Wife,* 196.

Maria Palester, with her weekly bridge games: Halina Grubowska, personal correspondence/interview.

Maria's fourteen-year-old daughter, Małgorzata Palester: Janina Goldhar, personal correspondence.

"Żegota sent me letters so that I would be assured that they were doing everything possible to get me out": "Fundacja Taubego na rzecz Życia i Kultury Żydowskiej przedstawia Ceremonię Wręczenia Nagrody im. Ireny Sendlerowej," program 2013.

"They only knew from my letters that the Germans did not find the index": Ibid. See also Anna Mieszkowska, *Prawdziwa Historia Ireny Sendlerowej.*

Zofia and Stanisław's house: Joanna Papuzińska-Beksiak, Muzeum Powstania Warszawskiego, oral history archives, January 13, 2012, http://ahm.1944.pl/Joanna _Papuzinska-Beksiak/1. The details here are drawn largely from this oral history interview.

Irena swung into action and moved Estera: Museum of the History of Polish Jews, 2010, "Chaja Estera Stein," *Polscy Sprawiedliwi* (Polish Righteous), www .sprawiedliwi.org.pl/en/cms/your-stories/ 360,chaja-estera-stein-teresa-tucholska-k -rner-the-first-child-of-irena-sendler-/.

Julian and Halina Grobelny owned a small country house: Yad Vashem, "Grobelny Family: Rescue Story," *The Righteous Among the Nations,* db.yadvashem.org/ righteous/family.html?language=en& itemId=4034600.

Dr. Majkowski smuggled extra food and supplies into the prison: "Życie Juliana Grobelnego," RelatioNet, October 3, 2007, http://grju93brpo.blogspot.ca/2007/ 10/ycie-juliana-grobelnego.html.

Żegota — for another immense bribe — arranged for Julian's escape: Teresa Prekerowa, *Żegota: Commission d'aide aux Juifs.*

the apartment of Stefan Wichliński: Anna Mieszkowska, *Prawdziwa Historia Ireny Sendlerowej.*

"I had to steal my dying mother from our home": "Irena Sendlerowa," Association of "Children of the Holocaust" in Poland.

"Which is the dead woman's daughter?": Ibid.

"It was a desperate SOS": Ibid.

the women dug up the lists buried in Jaga's garden: "Irena Sendlerowa," Association of "Children of the Holocaust" in Poland.

Chapter 16: Warsaw Fighting

Janka Grabowska's husband, Józef: Museum of the History of Polish Jews, 2010, "The Stolarski Family," *Polscy Sprawiedliwi* (Polish Righteous), www.sprawiedliwi.org.pl/en/family/123,the-stolarski-family/.

Ultimately, the Soviets also refused to allow the other Allies: Alexandra Richie, *Warsaw 1944: Hitler, Himmler, and the Warsaw Uprising,* New York: Farrar, Strauss and Giroux, New York, 2013, review by Irene Tomaszewski, *Cosmopolitan Review* 6, no. 1 (2014), http://cosmopolitanreview.com/warsaw-1944.

In the words of one general, Władysław Anders: Ibid.

Luftwaffe planes, marked on their underbellies with ominous black crosses: Zygmunt Skarbek-Kruszewski, *Bellum Vobiscum: War Memoirs,* ed. Jurek Zygmunt Skarbek, n.p: Skarbek Consulting Pty Ltd, 2001.

"almost all Warsaw is a sea of flames": Diary of Hans Frank, National Archives of the United States, Washington, DC, publication T992, microfilm, www.archives.gov/

research/captured-german-records/micro film/t992.pdf.

"They shot at us when we passed": Central Commission for Investigation of German Crimes in Poland, *German Crimes in Poland,* New York: Howard Fertig, 1982.

Dr. Maria Skokowska, and a young Jewish woman named Jadzia Pesa Rozenholc: Museum of the History of Polish Jews, 2010, "Irena Sendler," *Polscy Sprawiedliwi* (Polish Righteous), www.sprawiedliwi.org .pl/en/cms/biography-83/.

The next day they went to work setting up an emergency field hospital: Museum of the History of Polish Jews, 2010, "Maria Palester," *Polscy Sprawiedliwi* (Polish Righteous), www.sprawiedliwi.org.pl/en/ family/434,palester-maria/.

Kryštof Palester disappeared to rejoin his old "Parasol" battalion: Memoirs of Andrzej Rafal Ulankiewicz, " 'Warski II': Battalion 'Parasol' (Umbrella)," qtd. Warsaw Uprising 1944, www.warsawuprising.com/ witness/parasol.htm. One of those young women was Maria Stypułkowska, code name "Kama." She had joined the Home Army at seventeen as a messenger, and was already a legendary crack assassin and saboteur. The execution of Franz Kutschera, the German SS and Reich's police chief in Warsaw, who was killed on February 1, 1944, was Maria's handiwork. Maria survived the war to tell her stories; see, for example, her video testimony, "Maria 'Kama' Stypułkowska-Chojecka Popiera Komorowskiego — a Ty?," recorded by Bronisław Komorowski, May 27, 2010, www.youtube.com/watch?v=LOQaeuv9b6Y.

"She was a totally different person," Irena remembered: Irena Sendler, "Youth Associations of the Warsaw Ghetto."

Drunken SS officers made forays into basement shelters: Zygmunt Skarbek-Kruszewski, *Bellum Vobiscum.*

A German soldier ran his bayonet through Irena's leg: Anna Mieszkowska, *Prawdziwa Historia Ireny Sendlerowej.*

Jaga Piotrowska rushed into burning buildings during the destruction of her street: Archives of Mirosława Pałaszewska and personal correspondence.

The razing of Warsaw included the destruction of Jaga's own house: Archives of Mirosława Pałaszewska.

Thirty refugees were hiding in the makeshift medical clinic with Irena and Adam and the Palester family: Museum of the History of Polish Jews, 2010, "Irena Sendler," *Polscy Sprawiedliwi* (Polish Righteous),

www.sprawiedliwi.org.pl/en/cms/biography
-83/.

It oozed pus: Anna Mieszkowska, *Prawdziwa
Historia Ireny Sendlerowej.*

"She treated me like a daughter," Anna said
of Irena later: Magdelena Grochowska,
"Lista Sendlerowej."

"Even after the final liquidation [of the
ghetto], we clung to fairy tales about
underground bunkers": Ada Pagis, "A
Rare Gem," *Haaretz,* May 9, 2008, www
.haaretz.com/a-rare-gem-1.245497; review
of *Ir betoch ir* [City Within a City], diary
of Batia Temkin-Berman, trans. Uri Orlev,
Jerusalem: Yad Vashem, 2008.

According to Yad Vashem, only five thousand
children out of that million survived the
war: *The Last Eyewitnesses: Children of the
Holocaust Speak.* Ed. Wiktoria Śliwówska,
trans. Julian and Fay Bussgang. Evanston:
Northwestern University Press, 1999.

"She never talked about those things again,"
Irena said later: Irena Sendler, "Youth Associations of the Warsaw Ghetto."

Chapter 17: How the Stories Ended

The human heart is not symmetrical or
neat, either: Arash Kheradvar and Gianni
Pedrizzetti, *Vortex Formation in the Cardio-*

vascular System, New York: Springer, 2012.

Irena never forgot Józef's words when he gave her Piotr: Irena Sendler, "Youth Associations of the Warsaw Ghetto."

"My birth certificate is a small silver spoon engraved with my name and birth date": "Elżbieta Ficowska," testimony, Association of "Children of the Holocaust" in Poland, www.dzieciholocaustu.org.pl/szab58.php?s=en_myionas_11.php.

"If the aunt had not seen the address on a package": Michał Głowiński, *The Black Seasons.*

"[But] I am still unable to write about my stay in the Warsaw ghetto": Ibid.

Ala's small child, Rami Gołąb-Grynberg, reunited after the war with her uncle: personal correspondence.

In 1945, Warsaw was bleak and treeless: A. M. Rosenthal, "The Trees of Warsaw," *New York Times,* www.nytimes.com/1983/08/07/magazine/the-trees-of-warsaw.html.

Irena's wartime journals and account books, like so much else in the city, were lost: "Fundacja Taubego na rzecz Życia i Kultury Żydowskiej przedstawia Ceremonię Wręczenia Nagrody im. Ireny Sendlerowej," 2013 program. Also archives of Mirosława Pałaszewska and personal correspondence.

Irena gave the list to Dr. Adolf Berman: Ibid. See also obituary, "Irena Sendler, Saviour of Children in the Warsaw Ghetto, Died on May 12th, Aged 98," *Economist,* May 24, 2008, www.economist.com/node/11402658.

"Let me stress most emphatically that we who were rescuing children are not some kind of heroes": "Irena Sendlerowa," Association of "Children of the Holocaust" in Poland.

Jaga Piotrowska and Jan Dobraczyński also made their own lists of the Jewish children: Archives of Mirosława Pałaszewska and personal correspondence; also Michał Głowiński, *The Black Seasons,* 87.

"When Poland was liberated in 1945, a Jewish community was established": Archives of Mirosława Pałaszewska; also Michał Głowiński, *The Black Seasons,* 86.

"During the conversation," Jaga said, "we were told": Ibid.

When Mietek returned to Poland from a prisoner-of-war camp in Germany, Irena was already five months pregnant: Iwona Rojek, "To była matka całego świata — córka Ireny Sendler opowiedziała nam o swojej mamie," *Echo Dnia Śilȇtokrzyskie,* December 9, 2012, www.echodnia.eu/

swietokrzyskie/wiadomosci/kielce/art/
8561374,to-byla-matka-calego-swiata
-corka-ireny-sendler-opowiedzi ala-nam-o
-swojej-mamie,id,t.html.

his Jewish mother, Leokadia, was furious:
Anna Mieszkowska, *Prawdziwa Historia
Ireny Sendlerowej*.

"the brightest star in the black sky of the
occupation": Michał Głowiński, *The Black
Seasons*.

Coda: The Disappearing Story of Irena Sendler, 1946-2008

"There are times when she avoids me,"
Irena wrote of that long postwar friendship: Irena Sendler, "Youth Associations
of the Warsaw Ghetto."

"In my dreams," Irena said, "I still hear the
cries": Joseph Bottum, "Good People, Evil
Times: The Women of Żegota," *First
Things*, April 17, 2009, www.firstthings
.com/blogs/firstthoughts/2009/04/good
-people-evil-times-the-women-of-Zegota.

When Adam Celnikier died of heart trouble
in 1961: Anna Mieszkowska, *Prawdziwa
Historia Ireny Sendlerowej*, 20.

Yad Vashem, the Holocaust memorial organization in Israel, awarded Irena Sendler:

Alexandra Sližová, "Osudy zachráněných dětí Ireny Sendlerové."

So, too, in time were Jaga Piotrowska, Maria Kukulska: "Fundacja Taubego na rzecz Życia i Kultury Żydowskiej przedstawia Ceremonię Wręczenia Nagrody im. Ireny Sendlerowej," 2013 program.

"We estimate (today after 40 years it is difficult to determine it exactly) the number of children": Magdelena Grochowska, "Lista Sendlerowej."

"Every time people said that she saved 2,500 Jewish children's lives": Yoram Gross, personal correspondence.

"I want everyone to know that, while I was coordinating our efforts, we were about twenty": Joachim Wieler, "The Long Path to Irena Sendler."

After the war, when Irena made a list of all the people in Warsaw: Magdelena Grochowska, "Lista Sendlerowej."

"If we knew," he told the crowd that day, "the names of all the noble people who risked their lives to save Jews": Hans G. Furth, "One Million Polish Rescuers of Hunted Jews?," *Journal of Genocide Research* 1, no. 2 (1999): 227–32.

"I only have recourse to the memories burned into my mind by the events of those days": Irena Sendler, autobiographical notes, ZIH archives, Materialy Zabrane w Latach, 1995–2003, sygn. S/353, file IS-04-85-R.

In 2003, some of the children she helped to save wrote a joint letter: Aleksandra Zawłocka, "The Children of Ms. Sendler," Polish-Jewish Heritage Foundation of Canada, www.polish-jewish-heritage.org/eng/The_Children_of_Ms_Sendler.htm; also Museum of the History of Polish Jews, 2010, "Irena Sendler," *Polscy Sprawiedliwi* (Polish Righteous), www.sprawiedliwi.org.pl/en/cms/biography-83/.

"Heroes," she said, "do extraordinary things": Scott T. Allison, George R. Goethals, *Heroes: What They Do and Why We Need Them,* Oxford: Oxford University Press, 2010, 24.

"A small body of determined spirits fired by an unquenchable faith in their mission can alter the course of history": Anil Dutta Mishra, *Inspiring Thoughts of Mahatma Gandhi,* Delhi: Concept Publishing, 2008, 36.

Additional sources consulted for this book include: Halina Grubowska, *Ta, Która Ratowała Żydów: rzecz o Irenie Sendlerowej,* Warsaw: Żydowski Instytut Historyczny im. Emanuela Ringelbluma, 2014; Wladyslaw

Bartoszewski, "Powstanie Ligi do Walki z Rasizmem w 1946 r.," *Więź* (1998): 238–45; Tomasz Szarota, "Ostatnia Droga Doktora: Rozmowa z Ireną Sendlerową," *Historia*, vol. 21, May 24, 1997, 94; Janina Sacharewicz, "Irena Sendlerowa: Działanie z Potrzeby Serca," *Słowo Żydowskie*, April 20, 2007; Mary Skinner, *Irena Sendler: In the Name of Their Mothers* (documentary film), 2011; "Bo Ratowała Życie," *Gość Warszawski*, no. 6, February 11, 2007; and Abhijit Thite, *The Other Schindler . . . Irena Sendler: Savior of the Holocaust Children*, trans. Priya Gokhale, Pune, India: Ameya Prakashan, 2010.

BIBLIOGRAPHY

[Anon.] "50 Razy Kara Śmierci: Z Jadwigą Piotrowską," May 11, 1986, ZIH archives, Materialy Zabrane w Latach, 1995–2003, sygn. S/353.

[Anon.] "Ala Gołåb [Golomb] Grynberg," Warsaw Ghetto Database, Polish Center for Holocaust Research, http://warszawa.getto.pl/index.php?mod=view_record&rid=07051998094230000004&tid=oso by&lang=en.

[Anon.] "Bo Ratowała Życie," *Gość Warszawski,* no. 6, February 11, 2007.

[Anon.] "Edwin Weiss," Warsaw Ghetto Database, Polish Center for Holocaust Research, http://warszawa.getto.pl/index.php?mod=view_record&rid=0912199 6103042000001&tid=osoby.

[Anon.] "Grojanowski Report," Yad Vashem, http://www.yadvashem.org/odot_pdf/microsoft%20word%20-%206317.pdf.

[Anon.] "Irena Sendlerowa," Association of

"Children of the Holocaust" in Poland, www.dzieciholocaustu.org.pl/szab58.php ?s=en_sendlerowa.php.

[Anon.] "Jadwiga Maria Józefa Piotrowska," Geni database, http://www.geni.com/people/Jadwiga-Piotrowska/600000001 5472386167.

[Anon.] "Janusz Korczak," Adam Mickiewicz Institute,Warsaw, www.diapozytyw.pl/en/site/ludzie/.

[Anon.] "Marek Edelman: Last Surviving Leader of the 1943 Warsaw Ghetto Uprising Against the Nazis," *Independent,* October 7, 2009, www.independent.co.uk/news/obituaries/marek-edelman-last-surviving-leader-of-the-1943-warsaw-ghetto-uprising-against-the-nazis-1798 644.html.

[Anon.] "Nachum Remba," Warsaw Ghetto Database, Polish Center for Holocaust Research, http://warszawa.getto.pl/index.php?mod=view_record&rid=05011904 155335000002&tid=osoby&lang=en.

[Anon.] "Rediscover Polish Scouting," Polish Scouting and Guiding Association, http://issuu.com/zhp_pl/docs/rediscoverpolishscouting.

[Anon.] "Stanisława Bussold," Museum of the History of Polish Jews, www.sprawiedliwi.org.pl/pl/family/331,bussold

-stanislawa/.

[Anon.] "The Warsaw Ghetto: Stroop's Report on the Battles in the Warsaw Ghetto Revolt (May 16, 1943)," Jewish Virtual Library, https://www.jewishvirtual library.org/jsource/Holocaust/sswarsaw .html.

[Anon.] "The Woman Who Smuggled Children from the Ghetto," *Jewniverse,* February 15, 2013, http://thejewniverse.com/ 2013/the-woman-who-smuggled-children -from-the-ghetto/.

[Anon.] "Zamordowani w różnych rejonach Warzawy," Wiĕźniowie Pawiaka [Victims of Pawiak in Warsaw data], www .stankiewicze.com/pawiak/warszawa4.htm.

[Anon.] "Życie Juliana Grobelnego," October 3, 2007, http://grju93brpo.blogspot.ca/ 2007/10/ycie-juliana-grobelnego.html.

[Anon.] "Fundacja Taubego na rzecz Życia i Kultury Żydowskiej przedstawia Ceremonię Wrĕczenia Nagrody im. Ireny Sendlerowej," October 23, 2013 program, Museum of the History of Polish Jews, http://nagrodairenysendlerowej.pl/dir _upload/download/thumb/9b515fb73c 99cb31408f589b0b27.pdf.

[Anon.] "Terror Against the Intelligentsia and Clergy," United States Holocaust Memorial Museum, www.ushmm.org/

learn/students/learning-materials-and
-resources/poles-victims-of-the-nazi-era/
terror-against-the-intelligentsia-and
-clergy.

[Anon.] Transcripts of the Eichmann trial, Nizkor Project, www.nizkor.org/hweb/ people/e/eichmann-adolf/transcripts/ Sessions/Session-025-04.html.

[Anon.] "Life and Activity of Helena Twóczość Radlińskie," http://sciaga.pl/ tekst/69744-70-zycie_twoczosc_i_dzialal nosc_heleny_radlinskiej.

[Anon.] "Adam Żurawin," Warsaw Ghetto Database, Polish Center for Holocaust Research, http://warszawa.getto.pl/index .php?mod=view_record&rid=270320032 04554000076&tid=osoby&lang=en.

[Anon.] "Adolf Abraham Berman," Yad Vashem, www.yadvashem.org/odot_pdf/ Microsoft%20Word%20-%205996.pdf.

[Anon.] "Barbara Dietrych Wachowska," Cyclopedia.net, http://pl.cyclopaedia.net/ wiki/Barbara_Dietrych-Wachowska.

[Anon.] "Central Welfare Council, Poland," Yad Vashem, www.yadvashem.org/odot _pdf/Microsoft%20Word%20-%205913 .pdf.

[Anon.] "Deportations to and from the Warsaw Ghetto," *Holocaust Encyclopedia,* United States Holocaust Memorial Mu-

seum, www.ushmm.org/wlc/en/article.php
?ModuleId=10005413.

[Anon.] "Directive No. 1 for the Conduct of the War," Avalon Project: Yale Law School, http://www.yale.edu/lawweb/avalon/imt/document/wardir1.htm.

[Anon.] "Gestapo Headquarters: Szucha Avenue and Pawiak Prison — Warsaw," 2007, Holocaust Education & Archive Research Team, www.holocaustresearch project.org/nazioccupation/poland/pawaiak.html.

[Anon.] "Gestapo Torture of Jews in Warsaw Prisons Reported, List of Guilty Nazis," October 19, 1942, Jewish Telegraphic Agency, www.jta.org/1942/10/19/archive/gestapo-torture-of-jews-in-warsaw-prisons-reported-list-of-guilty-nazis-published.

[Anon.] "Irena Sendler Award for Repairing the World," program description, Centrum Edukacji Obywatelskiej, www.ceo.org.pl/pl/sendler/news/program-description.

[Anon.] "Irena Sendler, Saviour of Children in the Warsaw Ghetto, Died on May 12th, Aged 98," *Economist,* May 24, 2008, www.economist.com/node/11402658.

[Anon.] "Judischer Ordnungsdienst," *This Month in Holocaust History,* Yad Vashem, www.yadvashem.org/yv/en/exhibitions/this_month/resources/jewish_police.asp.

[Anon.] "Janusz Korczak: A Polish Hero at the Jewish Museum," *Culture 24,* December 7, 2006, www.culture24.org.uk/history-and-heritage/art41997.

[Anon.] "K. Dargielowa," Warsaw Ghetto Database, Polish Center for Holocaust Research, http://warszawa.getto.pl/index.php?mod=view_record&rid=200519971 91448000001&tid=osoby&lang=en.

[Anon.] "Maria Palester," Museum of the History of Polish Jews, http://www.sprawiedliwi.org.pl/en/family/434,palester -maria/.

[Anon.] "Nachum Remba," Warsaw Ghetto Database, Polish Center for Holocaust Research, http://warszawa.getto.pl/index.php?mod=view_record&rid=05011904 155335000002&tid=osoby&lang=en.

[Anon.] "New Book Full of 'Lies and Libel' Says Son of Władysław Szpilman," *Polskie Radio,* broadcast and transcript, November 5, 2011, www2.polskieradio.pl/eo/dokument.aspx?iid=142897.

[Anon.] "Otwoccy Sprawiedliwi," *Gazeta Otwocka,* July 2012, www.otwock.pl/gazeta/2012/sprawiedliwi.pdf.

[Anon.] "Piotrków: Pamiątkowa tablica ku czci Sendlerowej," *ePiotrkow.pl,* www.epiotrkow.pl/news/Piotrkow-Pamiatkowa -tablica-ku-czci-Sendlerowej-,2801.

[Anon.] "The 72nd Anniversary of the Creation of the Council to Aid Jews," Jewish Historical Institute, Warsaw, December 3, 2014, www.jhi.pl/en/blog/2014-12-03 -the-72nd-anniversary-of-the-creation-of -the-council-to-aid-jews.

[Anon.] "Warsaw," *Holocaust Encyclopedia,* United States Holocaust Memorial Museum, http://www.ushmm.org/wlc/en/ article.php?ModuleId=10005069.

[Anon.] "Aktion Erntefest (Operation "Harvest Festival")," *Holocaust Encyclopedia,* United States Holocaust Memorial Museum, www.ushmm.org/wlc/en/article.php ?ModuleId=10005222.

[Anon.] IPN TV, "Relacja Piotra Zettingera o Ucieczce z Warszawskiego Getta" (video interview with Piotr Zettinger), www .youtube.com/watch?v=tY3WxXUiYzo.

[Anon.] Jewish Historical Institute Association of Warsaw, Virtual Shtetl Project, "Janusz Korczak's Orphanage in Warsaw," trans. Ewelina Gadomska, http://www .sztetl.org.pl/en/article/warszawa/39,heri tage-sites/3518,janusz-korczak-s-orphan age-in-warsaw-92-krochmalna-street-until -1940-/.

[Anon.] State University of New York at Buffalo/Jagiellonian University, "Slow Extermination: Life and Death in the

Warsaw Ghetto," *Info Poland,* http://info-poland.buffalo.edu/web/history/WWII/ghetto/slow.html.

[Frank, Hans.] Diary of Hans Frank, National Archives of the United States, Washington, DC, publication T992, microfilm, www.archives.gov/research/captured-german-records/microfilm/t992.pdf.

[Jankowska-Tobijasiewicz, Barbara.] "Irenė Sendlerowǎ i Barbarė Ditrich: niezwykłe sąsiadki z ul. Ludwiki wspomina Barbara Jankowska-Tobijasiewicz," *Urząd Dzielnicy Wola,* January 28, 2010, file 46/347, www.wola.waw.pl/page/341,internetowe-wydanie-kuriera-wolskiego—wszystkie-numery.html?date=2010-01-00&artykul_id=394.

[Papuzińska-Beksiak, Joanna.] "Interview with Joanna Papuzińska-Beksiak," Muzeum Powstania Warszawskiego, oral history archives, January 13, 2012, http://ahm.1944.pl/Joanna_Papuzinska-Beksiak/1.

[Sendler, Irena.] "Address by Irena Sendeler [*sic*]," Association of "Children of the Holocaust" in Poland, interviews with Irena Sendler, www.dzieciholocaustu.org.pl/szab58.php?s=en_sendlerowa001_02.php.

[Sendler, Irena.] "Irena Sendler Tells the

Story of Janusz Korczak," Gariwo/ Gardens of the Righteous World-Wide Committee, documentary/video interview with Irena Sendler, http://en.gariwo.net/pagina.php?id=9114.

[Sendler, Irena.] "Irena Sendlerowa," Geni database, www.geni.com/people/Irena -Sendlerowa/6000000019948138463.

[Zgrzembska, Janina.] "An Interview with Irena Sendler's Daughter, Janina Zgrzembska," Museum of the History of Polish Jews, www.sprawiedliwi.org.pl/en/cms/news-archive/858,an-interview-with-irena -sendler-s-daughter-janina-zgrzembska/.

Ackerman, Diane. *The Zookeeper's Wife: A War Story,* New York: W. W. Norton, 2008.

Adler, Stanislaw. *In the Warsaw Ghetto: 1940–1943, An Account of a Witness,* trans. Sara Philip. Jerusalem: Yad Vashem, 1982.

Apfelbaum, Marian. *Two Flags: Return to the Warsaw Ghetto.* Jerusalem: Gefen Publishing House, 2007.

Arad, Yitzhak. "The Nazi Concentration Camps: Jewish Prisoner Uprisings in the Treblinka and Sobibor Extermination Camps," Proceedings of the Fourth Annual Yad Vashem International Conference, Jerusalem, January 1980, Jewish Virtual Library, http://www.jewishvirtual

library.org/jsource/Holocaust/resistyad
.html.

Arad, Yitzhak. *Belzec, Sobibor, Treblinka: The Operation Reinhard Death Camps.* Bloomington: Indiana University Press, 1999.

Axelrod, Toby. "Treblinka Survivor Attends Berlin Ceremony," Jewish Telegraphic Agency, August 1, 2005, www.jta.org/2005/08/01/life-religion/features/treblinka -survivor-attends-berlin-ceremony.

Barré, David and Agata Mozolewska. *Elle, elle a sauvé les autres . . .* Paris: Éditions du Cosmogone, 2009.

Bartoszewski, Władysław and Zofia Lewinówna. *Ten jest z ojczyzny mojej: Polacy z pomocą Żydom, 1939–1945.* Warszawa: Świat Książki, 2007.

Bartoszewski, Władysław. "Powstanie Ligi do Walki z Rasizmem w 1946 r.," *Więź* (1998): 238–45.

Bartoszewski, Władysław. *1859 Dni Warszawy,* Kracow: Znak, 1974.

Bartoszewski, Władysław. *The Warsaw Ghetto: A Christian's Testimony,* trans. Stephen J. Cappellari. Boston: Beacon Press, 1987.

Biernacki, Andrzej. *Zatajony artysta. O Wacławie Borowym, 1890–1950.* Lublin:

Norbertinum, 2005.

Bingham, Marjorie Wall. "Women and the Warsaw Ghetto: A Moment to Decide," *World History Connected,* http://worldhistoryconnected.press.illinois.edu/6.2/bingham.html.

Blobaum, Robert, ed. *Antisemitism and Its Opponents in Modern Poland.* Ithaca: Cornell University Press, 2005.

Bogner, Nahum. "The Convent Children: The Rescue of Jewish Children in Polish Convents During the Holocaust," Yad Vashem, www.yadvashem.org/yv/en/righteous/pdf/resources/nachum_bogner.pdf.

Bogner, Nahum. *At the Mercy of Strangers: The Rescue of Jewish Children with Assumed Identities in Poland.* Jerusalem: Yad Vashem, 2009.

Brojek, Paweł. "Piǎta rocznica śmierci Ireny Sendlerowej: Sprawiedliwej wśród Narodów Świata," *Prawy,* May 12, 2013, www.prawy.pl/wiara/3049-piata-rocznica-smierci-ireny-sendlerowej-sprawiedliwej-wsrod-narodow-swiata.

British Broadcasting Corporation, "On This Day: 1939: Germany Invades Poland," http://news.bbc.co.uk/onthisday/hi/dates/stories/september/1/newsid_3506000/3506335.stm.

Budrewicz, Olgierd. *Warszawa w Starej Fotografii.* Olszanica: Wydawnictwo BoSZ, 2012.

Bülow, Louis. "Irena Sendler: An Unsung Heroine," www.auschwitz.dk/sendler.htm.

Cegielski, Tadeusz. "Liberum Conspiro, or the Polish Masonry between the Dictatorship and Totalitarianism, 1926–1989," *Le Communisme et les Elites en Europe Centrale,* March 31, 2004, École Normale Supérieure, colloquium presentation, www1.ens.fr/europecentrale/colloque_elites2004/4Documents/Resumes/Cegielski_resum.htm.

Central Commission for Investigation of German Crimes in Poland, *German Crimes in Poland,* New York: Howard Fertig, 1982.

Cesarani, David and Sarah Kavanaugh. *Holocaust: Jewish Confrontations with Persecution and Mass Murder,* vol. 4 of *The Holocaust: Critical Concepts in Historical Study.* London: Routledge, 2004.

Charniewitch-Lubel, Deborah, "Kolno Girls in Auschwitz," in *Kolno Memorial Book,* ed. Aizik Remba and Benjamin Halevy, Tel Aviv: Kolner Organization and Sifirat Poalim, 1971, www.jewishgen.org/Yizkor/kolno/kole056.html.

Commission of History at the Polish Nurses' Association, "The Nursing School at the Orthodox Jew Hospital at Czyste District in Warsaw," Virtual Museum of Polish Nursing, http://www.wmpp.org.pl/en/nursing-schools/the-nursing-school-at-the-orthodox-jew-hospital-at-czyste-district-in-warsaw.html.

Czerniakow, Adam. *Warsaw Diary of Adam Czerniakow: Prelude to Doom,* ed. Raul Hilberg et al. Chicago: Ivan R. Dee, 1999.

Czuperska-Śliwicka, Anna. *Cztery Lata Ostrego Dyżuru: Wspomnienia z Pawiaka, 1930–1944.* Warsaw: Czytelnik, 1965.

Danow, David. *The Spirit of Carnival: Magical Realism and the Grotesque.* Lexington: University of Kentucky Press, 2005.

Dobraczyński, Jan. *Tylko w jednym życiu.* Warsaw: Pax, 1977.

Domańska, Regina. *Pawiak, Więzienie Gestapo: Kronika, 1939–1944.* Warsaw: Książka I Wiedza, 1978.

Edelman, Marek. "The Ghetto Fights," in *The Warsaw Ghetto: The 45th Anniversary of the Uprising,* Interpress Publishers, 1987, 17–39; archived at www.writing.upenn.edu/~afilreis/Holocaust/warsaw-uprising.html.

Einsatzgruppen Reports. Eds. Yitzhak Arad,

Shmuel Krakowski, Shmuel Spector. Jerusalem: Yad Vashem, 1989.

Engelgard, Jan. "To Dobraczyński był bohaterem tamtego czasu," *Konserwatyzm,* June 19, 2013, http://www.konserwatyzm.pl/artykul/10342/to-dobraczynski-byl-bohaterem-tamtego-czasu, review of Ewa Kurek, *Dzieci żydowskie w klasztorach. Udział żeńskich zgromadzeń zakonnych w akcji ratowania dzieci żydowskich w Polsce w latach, 1939–1945,* Zakrzewo: Replika, 2012.

Ficowska, Elżbieta. "Testimony of Elżbieta Ficowska," Association of "Children of the Holocaust" in Poland, www.dzieciholocaustu.org.pl/szab58.php?s=en_myionas_11.php.

Filipowicz, Bogusław. "Nadzieja spełniona: dzieło Ireny Sendlerowej," *Quarterly Research* 1, no. 1 (2010), www.stowarzyszeniefidesetratio.pl/Presentations0/09Flipipowicz.pdf.

Fox, Frank. "Endangered Species: Jews and Buffaloes," *The Scrolls,* www.zwoje-scrolls.com/zwoje30/text17.htm.

Furth, Hans G. "One Million Polish Rescuers of Hunted Jews?," *Journal of Genocide Research* 1, no. 2 (1999): 227–32.

Głowiński, Michał. *The Black Seasons,* trans. Marci Shore. Evanston: Northwestern University Press, 2005.

Góra, Barbara. "Anna Braude Hellerowa," Warsaw: Association of "Children of the Holocaust" in Poland, 2011, 38–39.

Government Delegation for Poland, Department of the Interior, folder 202/II-43, reprinted in Krzysztof Komorowski, *Polityka i walka: Konspiracja zbrojna ruchu narodowego, 1939–1945,* Warsaw: Oficyna Wydawnicza "Rytm," 2000.

Grabski, August, and Piotr Grudka. "Polish Socialists in the Warsaw Ghetto," Emanuel Ringelblum Jewish Historical Institute, Warsaw, http://www.jhi.pl/en/publications/52.

Grochowska, Magdelena. "Lista Sendlerowej: Reportaž z 2001 Roku," *Gazeta Wyborcza,* May 12, 2008, n.p.

Grodin, Michael A., ed. *Jewish Medical Resistance in the Holocaust.* New York: Berghahn, 2014.

Grubowska, Halina. *Ta, Która Ratowała Żydów: Rzecz o Irenie Sendlerowej.* Warsaw: Żydowski Instytut Historyczny im. Emanuela Ringelbluma, 2014.

Gutembaum, Jakub, and Agnieszka Lałała, eds. *The Last Eyewitnesses: Children of the Holocaust Speak,* vol. 2. Evanston: Northwestern University Press, 2005.

Gutman, Israel. *The Encyclopedia of the Righteous Among the Nations.* Jerusalem: Yad Vashem, 2007, vol. 5 (Poland).

Halter, Marek. *Stories of Deliverance: Speaking with Men and Women Who Rescued Jews from the Holocaust.* Chicago and La Salle, IL: Open Court, 1997.

Haltof, Marek. *Polish Film and the Holocaust: Politics and Memory.* New York: Berghahn Books, 2012.

Hammarberg, Thomas. "2007 Janusz Korczak Lecture: Children Participation," Brussels: Commissioner for Human Rights/Council of Europe, 2007, http://www.rm.coe.int/CoERMPublicCommon SearchServices/DisplayDCTMContent ?documentId=090000168046c47b

Haven, Cynthia. "Life in Wartime Warsaw . . . Not Quite What You Thought," (interview with Hana Rechowicz), May 21, 2011, http://bookhaven.stanford.edu/2011/05/life-in-wartime-warsaw-not-quite-what-you-thought.

Hirszfeld, Ludwik. *The Story of One Life,* trans. Marta A. Balińska. Rochester: University of Rochester Press, 2014.

Hryniewicz, Bohdan. *My Boyhood War: Warsaw: 1944,* Stroud, UK: History Press, 2015.

Hugman, Richard, ed. *Understanding International Social Work: A Critical Analysis.* New York: Palgrave, 2010.

Jackl, Klara. "Father Boduen Children's Home: A Gateway to Life," Museum of the History of Polish Jews, June 11, 2012, www.sprawiedliwi.org.pl/en/cms/your-stories/794/.

Jankowska-Tobijasiewicz, Barbara. "Irenę Sendlerową i Barbarę Ditrich: Niezwykłe sąsiadki z ul: Ludwiki wspomina," *Urząd Dzielnicy Wola,* January 28, 2010, www.wola.waw.pl/page/341,internetowe-wydanie-kuriera-wolskiego—-wszystkie-numery.html?date=2010-01-00&artykul_id=394.

Jockusch, Laura and Tamar Lewinsky. "Paradise Lost? Postwar Memory of Polish Jewish Survival in the Soviet Union," *Holocaust and Genocide Studies* 24, no. 3 (Winter 2010): 373–99.

Kaufman, Michael T. "Marek Edelman, Commander in Warsaw Ghetto Uprising, Dies at 90," *New York Times,* October 3, 2009, www.nytimes.com/2009/10/03/world/europe/03edelman.html.

Komorowski, Bronisław. "Maria 'Kama' Stypułkowska-Chojecka popiera Komorowskiego — a Ty?," recorded by Bronisław Komorowski, May 27, 2010,

https://www.youtube.com/watch?v=LOQ
aeuv9b6Y.

Komorowskiego, Krzysztofa. *Polityka i Walka: Konspiracja Zbrojna Ruchu Narodowego, 1939–1945.* Warsawa: Oficyna Wydawnicza "Rytm," 2000.

Korczak, Janusz. *A Child's Right to Respect.* Strasbourg: Council of Europe Publishing, 2009, http://www.coe.int/t/commis sioner/source/prems/PublicationKorczak _en.pdf.

Korczak, Janusz. *Ghetto Diary.* New Haven: Yale University Press, 2003.

Korczak, Jerzy. *Oswajanie Strachu.* Warsaw: Wydawnictwo Muza, 2007.

Kroll, Chana. "Irena Sendler: Rescuer of the Children of Warsaw," Chabad, www .chabad.org/theJewishWoman/article_cdo/ aid/939081/jewish/Irena-Sendler.htm.

Kurek, Ewa. *Your Life Is Worth Mine: How Polish Nuns Saved Hundreds of Jewish Children in German-Occupied Poland, 1939–1944.* New York: Hippocrene Books, 1997.

Kurzman, Dan. *The Bravest Battle: The 28 Days of the Warsaw Ghetto Uprising.* Boston: Da Capo Press, 1993.

Land-Weber, Ellen. "Conditions for the Jews in Poland," To Save a Life: Stories of Holocaust Rescue, Humboldt State Uni-

versity, www2.humboldt.edu/rescuers/
book/Makuch/conditionsp.html.

Land-Weber, Ellen. *To Save a Life: Stories of Holocaust Rescue.* Champaign-Urbana: University of Illinois Press, 2002.

Lerek, Wanda D. *Hold on to Life, Dear: Memoirs of a Holocaust Survivor.* n.p.: W. D. Lereck, 1996.

Lewin, Abraham. *A Cup of Tears: A Diary of the Warsaw Ghetto,* ed. Antony Polonsky. Waukegan, IL: Fontana Press, 1990.

Lifton, Betty Jean. *The King of Children: A Biography of Janusz Korczak.* New York: Schocken, 1989.

Liv, Andras. "1912–1942: Korczak Orphanage Fate in Warsaw: Krochmalna 92 — Chłodna 33 — Sienna 16," January 2, 2012, http://jimbaotoday.blogspot.ca/2012/01/korczak-orphanage-in-warsaw_02.html.

Marcinkowski, Robert. *Warsaw, Then and Now.* Warsaw: Wydawnictwo Mazowsze, 2011.

Meed, Vladka. *On Both Sides of the Wall: Memoirs from the Warsaw Ghetto,* trans. Steven Meed. Jerusalem: Ghetto Fighters' House, 1972, review by Rivka Chaya Schiller, *Women in Judaism* 9, no. 1 (2012), http://wjudaism.library.utoronto

.ca/index.php/wjudaism/article/view/
19161/15895.

Meed, Vladka. *On Both Sides of the Wall,*
trans. Steven Meed. Washington, DC:
Holocaust Memorial Museum, 1999.

Michlic, Joanna B. *Poland's Threatening
Other: The Image of the Jew from 1880 to
the Present.* Lincoln: University of Nebraska, 2006, 2008.

Mierzejewski, Marcin. "Sendler's Children,"
Warsaw Voice, September 25, 2003, www
.warsawvoice.pl/WVpage/pages/article
.php/3568/article.

Mieszkowska, Anna. *Irena Sendler: Mother
of the Children of the Holocaust,* trans. Witold Zbirohowski-Koscia, Westport, CT:
Praeger, 2010.

Mieszkowska, Anna. *Prawdziwa Historia
Ireny Sendlerowej.* Warsaw: Marginesy,
2014.

Mint of Poland. "Poles Saving Jews: Irena
Sendlerowa, Zofia Kossak, Sister Matylda
Getter," www.mennica.com.pl/en/products
-and-services/mint-products/nbp-coins/
collector-coins/product/zobacz/poles
-saving-jews-irena-sendlerowa-zofia
-kossak-sister-matylda-getter-pln-2.html.

Mórawski, Karol. *Warszawa Dzieje Miasta.*
Warsaw: Wydanictwo Kxiåžka i Wiedza,
1976.

Museum of the History of Polish Jews, 2010, "Irena Sendler," *Polscy Sprawiedliwi* (Polish Righteous), www.sprawiedliwi.org.pl/en/cms/biography-83/.

Nagorski, Andrew. " 'Vera Gran: The Accused' by Agata Tuszynska" (review), *Washington Post,* March 22, 2013, www.washingtonpost.com/opinion/vera-gran-the-accused-by-agata-tuszynskatranslated-from-the-french-of-isabelle-jannes-kalinowski-by-charles-ruas/2013/03/22/6dce6116-75f2-11e2-8f84-3e4b513b1a13_story.html.

Oelkers, Jürgen. "Korczak's *Memoirs:* An Educational Interpretation," Universität Zürich, Institut für Erziehungswissenschaft, Lehrstühle und Forschungsstellen, www.ife.uzh.ch/research/emeriti/oelkers juergen/vortraegeprofoelkers/englishlectures/Oelkers.ER.Korczaks_Tagebuch-def.10.5.12.pdf.

Pagis, Ada. "A Rare Gem," *Haaretz,* May 9, 2008, www.haaretz.com/a-rare-gem-1.245497; review of *Ir Betoch Ir,* diary of Batia Temkin-Berman, trans. Uri Orlev, Jerusalem: Yad Vashem, 2008.

Paul, Mark. "Traditional Jewish Attitudes Toward Poles," January 2015, www.kpk-toronto.org/archives/jewish_attitudes.pdf.

Pawiak Prison Museum, public exhibition

materials.

Person, Katarzyna. "A Forgotten Voice from the Holocaust," *Warsaw Voice,* March 31, 2011, http://www.warsawvoice.pl/WVpage/pages/article.php/23365/article.

Polacy Ratujący Żydów w Latach II Wojny Światowej, IPN (Instytut Pamięci Narodowej), Warsaw, 2005, http://ipn.gov.pl/__data/assets/pdf_file/0004/55426/1-21712.pdf.

Polish Ministry of Information, *The German Invasion of Poland.* London: Hutchinson & Co. Ltd., 1940, http://felsztyn.tripod.com/germaninvasion/id1.html.

Poray, Anna, ed. "The Polish Righteous," 2004, www.savingjews.org.

Powell, Lawrence N. *Troubled Memory: Anne Levy, the Holocaust, and David Duke's Louisiana.* Charlotte: University of North Carolina Press, 2002.

Prekerowa, Teresa. *Żegota: Commision d'aide aux Juifs,* trans. Maria Apfelbaum. Monaco: Éditions du Rocher, 1999.

Rajchman, Chil. *The Last Jew of Treblinka: A Memoir.* New York: Pegasus, 2012.

Rajchman, Chil. *Treblinka: A Survivor's Memory, 1942–1943,* trans. Solon Beinfeld. London: Maclehose Press, 2009.

Rejak, Sebastian and Elżbieta Frister, eds.

Inferno of Choices: Poles and the Holocaust. Warsaw: Oficyna Wydawnicza "Rytm," 2012.

Richie, Alexandra. *Warsaw 1944: Hitler, Himmler, and the Warsaw Uprising.* New York: Farrar, Strauss and Giroux, New York, 2013, review by Irene Tomaszewski, *Cosmopolitan Review* 6, no. 1 (2014), http://cosmopolitanreview.com/warsaw-1944/.

Ringelblum, Emanuel. *Notes from the Warsaw Ghetto.* New York: McGraw-Hill, 1958.

Ringelblum, Emanuel. *The Journal of Emanuel Ringelblum,* trans. Jacob Sloan. New York: Schocken Books, 1974.

Roguszewski, Mirosław. *Powstańcze Oddziały Specjalne "Jerzyki" w latach, 1939–1945.* Bydgoszcz: n.p., 1994.

Rozett, Robert. "The Little-Known Uprising: Warsaw Ghetto, January," *Jerusalem Post,* January 16, 2013, www.jpost.com/Opinion/Op-Ed-Contributors/The-little-known-uprising-Warsaw-Ghetto-January-1943.

Russell, Sharman Apt. *Hunger: An Unnatural History.* New York: Basic Books, 2006.

Rytlowa, Jadwiga. "Chaja Estera Stein (Teresa Tucholska-Körner): 'The First

Child of Irena Sendler,' " Museum of the History of Polish Jews, September 14, 2010, www.sprawiedliwi.org.pl/en/cms/ your-stories/360,chaja-estera-stein-teresa -tucholska-k-rner-the-first-child-of-irena -sendler-/.

Sacharewicz, Janina. "Irena Sendlerowa: Działanie Z Potrzeby Serca," *Słowo Żydowskie*, April 20, 2007.

Seeman, Mary V. "Szymon Rudnicki: Equal, but Not Completely," *Scholars for Peace in the Middle East*, book review, June 7, 2010, http://spme.org/book-reviews/mary -v-seeman-szymon-rudnicki-equal-but-not -completely.

Sendler, Irena, "O Pomocy Żydom," excerpted from Władysław Bartoszewski and Zofia Lewinówna, eds., *Ten jest z ojczyzny mojej. Polacy z pomocå Żydom (This Is My Homeland: Poles Helping Jews), 1939– 1945*, 2d ed., Kraków: Znak, 1969, archived at *Lewicowo,* www.lewicowo.pl/o -pomocy-zydom.

Sendler, Irena. "Testimony of Irena Sendlerowa," Association of "Children of the Holocaust" in Poland, www.dzieci holocaustu.org.pl/szab58.php?s=en _sendlerowa.php.

Sendler, Irena. "The Valor of the Young,"

Dimensions: A Journal of Holocaust Studies 7, no. 2 (1993), 20–25.

Sendler, Irena. "Youth Associations of the Warsaw Ghetto: A Tribute to Jewish Rescuers," ZIH archives (Materialy Zabrane w Latach, 1995–2003, sygn. S/353), trans. Stanisław Barańczak and Michael Barańczak.

Shtokfish, David, ed. and trans. *Jewish Mlawa: Its History, Development, Destruction.* Tel Aviv: Mlawa Societies in Israel and in the Diaspora, 1984, 2 vols., http://www.jewishgen.org/yizkor/mlawa/mla449.html.

Shulman, Abraham. *The Case of Hotel Polski: An Account of One of the Most Enigmatic Episodes of World War II.* New York: Holocaust Library, 1982.

Skarbek-Kruszewski, Zygmunt. *Bellum Vobiscum: War Memoirs,* ed. Jurek Zygmunt Skarbek, n.p: Skarbek Consulting Pty Ltd, 2001, www.skarbek.com.au/bv/warsaw_uprising.htm.

Skinner, Mary. *Irena Sendler: In the Name of Their Mothers* (documentary film), 2011.

Śliwówska. Wiktoria, ed. *The Last Eyewitnesses: Children of the Holocaust Speak,* trans. Julian and Fay Bussgang. Evanston, IL: Northwestern University Press, 1999.

Smith, Mark. *Treblinka Survivor: The Life and Death of Hershl Sperling.* Mt. Pleasant, SC: The History Press, 2010.

Stelmaszuk, Waleria Zofia. "Residential Care in Poland: Past, Present, and Future," *International Journal of Family and Child Welfare,* 2002/3, 101.

Szarota, Tomasz. "Ostatnia Droga Doktora: Rozmowa z Ireną Sendlerową," *Historia* 21, May 24, 1997, 94.

Szpilman, Władysław. *The Pianist: The Extraordinary True Story of One Man's Survival in Warsaw, 1939–1945,* trans. A. Bell, with extracts from the diary of Wilm Hosenfeld. New York: Picador, 1999.

Thite, Abhijit. *The Other Schindler . . . Irena Sendler: Savior of the Holocaust Children,* trans. Priya Gokhale. Pune, India: Ameya Prakashan, 2010.

Tomaszewski, Irene and Tecia Werbowski. *Code Name: Żegota: Rescuing Jews in Occupied Poland, 1942–1945: The Most Dangerous Conspiracy in Wartime Europe.* New York: Praeger, 2010.

Tomaszweski, Irene and Tecia Werbowski. *Żegota, The Council for Aid to Jews in Occupied Poland, 1942–1945.* Montreal: Price-Patterson, 1999.

Turkovich, Marilyn. "Irena Sendler," Sep-

tember 29, 2009, *Charter for Compassion,*
http://voiceseducation.org/category/tag/
irena-sendler.

Turkow, Jonas. *Ala Gólomb Grynberg: La Heroica Enfermera del Ghetto de Varsovia,*
trans. from the Yiddish by Elena Pertzovsky de Bronfman. Buenos Aires: Ejecutivo Sudamericano del Congreso Judío
Mundial, 1970.

Tuszynska, Agata. *Vera Gran: The Accused,*
New York: Knopf, 2013.

Ulankiewicz, Andrzej Rafal. " 'Warski II':
Battalion 'Parasol' (Umbrella)." Memoirs
published online at Warsaw Uprising
1944, www.warsawuprising.com/witness/
parasol.htm.

United States Holocaust Memorial Museum, "Sâd Grodzki w Warszawie, Akta
Zg.1946 (Sygn. 655)," 1946–56, RG
Number RG–15.270M, Accession Number 2013.241, Archiwum Państwowe w
Warszawie, http://collections.ushmm.org/
findingaids/RG-15.270_01_fnd_pl.pdf.

Uziembło, Aniela. "Józef Zysman," *Gazeta
Stołeczna,* no. 141, June 20, 2005.

Valley, Eli. *The Great Jewish Cities of Central
and Eastern Europe: A Travel Guide.* New
York: Jason Aronson Publishers, 1999.

Wanat, Leon. *Za murami Pawiaka.* Warsaw:
Książka i Wiedza, 1985.

Warsaw Ghetto: Oyneg Shabes–Ringelblum Archives: Catalogy and Guide, eds. Robert Moses Shapiro and Tadeusz Epsztein. Bloomington: Indiana University Press, 2009.

Webb, Chris. "Otwock & the Zofiowka Sanatorium: A Refuge from Hell," Holocaust Education & Archive Research Team, www.holocaustresearchproject.org/ghettos/otwock.html.

Webb, Chris. *The Treblinka Death Camp: History, Biographies, Remembrance.* Stuttgart: Ibidem Press, 2014.

Weiner, Miriam. "Otwock," Routes to Roots Foundation, www.rtrfoundation.org/webart/poltownentry.pdf.

Whitlock, Monica. "Warsaw Ghetto: The Story of Its Secret Archive," January 27, 2013, British Broadcasting Corporation, www.bbc.com/news/magazine-21178079.

Wieler, Joachim. "The Long Path to Irena Sendler: Mother of the Holocaust Children," (interview with Irena Sendler), *Social Work and Society* 4, no. 1 (2006), http://www.socwork.net/sws/article/view/185/591.

Witkowska, Agnieszka. "Ostatnia droga mieszkańców i pracowników warszawskiego Domu Sierot," *Zagłada Żydów, Studia i Materiały* 6 (2010), http://

korczakowska.pl/wp-content/uploads/
2011/12/Agnieszka-Witkowska.-Ostatnia
-droga-mieszkancow-i-pracownikow
-warszawskiego-Domu-Sierot.pdf.

Wood, E. Thomas and Stanisław M. Jankowski. *Karski: How One Man Tried to Stop the Holocaust.* New York: John Wiley & Sons, 1994.

Wygodzki, Stanisław. "Epitaph for Krysia Liebman," *Jewish Quarterly* 16, no. 1 (1968): 33.

Zajdman, Renata. "A Tribute to Irena Sendler," bonus material from Hallmark's made-for-television film *The Courageous Heart of Irena Sendler,* www.hallmark.com/online/hall-of-fame/images/TCHISBonus Material.pdf.

Zygmund, Antoni. "Aleksander Rajchman," *Wiadomości Matematyczne* 27 (1987), 219–31, http://www.impan.pl/Great/Rajchman.

ABOUT THE AUTHOR

Tilar J. Mazzeo is the *New York Times* and *San Francisco Chronicle* bestselling author of books that include *The Widow Clicquot*, *The Secret of Chanel No. 5*, and *Hotel on the Place Vendôme*. She also writes on food and wine for the mainstream press, and her work has appeared in venues such as *Food & Wine* and in her *Back-Lane Wineries* guidebook series. Her course on creative nonfiction (Great Courses), featured as in-flight viewing content on Virgin America airlines, is widely distributed and has made her a nationally prominent teacher of writing in nonfiction genres. The Clara C. Piper Associate Professor of English at Colby College, she divides her time among coastal Maine, New York City, and Saanichton, British Columbia, where she lives with her husband and stepchildren.